THIS SPECIAL EDITION OF

RELIGIO MEDICI

by

SIR THOMAS BROWNE, Kt. M.D.

HAS BEEN PRIVATELY PRINTED FOR

THE MEMBERS OF

THE CLASSICS OF MEDICINE LIBRARY

SIR THOMAS BROWNE.

I. RELIGIO MEDICI.

II. LETTER TO A FRIEND.

III. CHRISTIAN MORALS.

RELIGIO MEDICI

together with

A LETTER TO A FRIEND

ON THE DEATH OF HIS INTIMATE FRIEND

and

CHRISTIAN MORALS

By

SIR THOMAS BROWNE Kt. M.D.

EDITED BY HENRY GARDINER M.A.
of Exeter Coll. Oxford

LONDON
WILLIAM PICKERING
1845

CHISWICK, PRINTED BY C. WHITTINGHAM.

Editor's Preface.

T is not eafy to determine with accuracy at what period Sir Thomas Browne compofed his Religio Medici : but the greateft weight of teftimony is in favour of the fuppofition, that it was between the years 1633-35, while he was refiding at Shipden Hall, near Halifax in Yorkfhire, after his return from his travels, and previous to fixing his refidence, as a Phyfician, at Norwich. It was very likely that he would employ a portion of his leifure time, abundant enough no doubt at the commencement of his profeffional career, in thus putting together the impreffions which had been made on his mind by foreign travel, and the refult of thofe impreſſions, as either confirming his faith in God, or enlarging his ſympathies with his fellow creatures. He tells us that the book was not intended for the preſs, but was compoſed for his private exerciſe and ſatisfaction. However, in the year 1642 a work appeared bearing the title, *Religio Medici*, but printed from a broken and imperfect MS. copy, which the Author had allowed to circulate among his friends and which had itſelf ſuffered

from frequent tranſcription.* This book created much ſenſation, and was ſo eagerly ſought for, that two editions were publiſhed in the ſame year, both in very ſmall octavo, one having 190 pp. the other 159 pp. They have no printed title page, but an engraved frontiſpiece, by Marſhall, repreſenting a figure falling from a rock into the ſea, but caught by a hand iſſuing

---

* There are at leaſt five MS. copies of Religio Medici; one in the Bodleian Library (MS. Rawl. Miſcell. 162); another, a fragment dated 1639, in the Britiſh Muſeum (MSS. Lanſdowne 489); and three more are known to be in private collections.

from the clouds. The motto *à coelo salus*, and the words *Religio Medici*, are engraved on the plate, and at the foot: *Printed for Andrew Crooke*, 1642, *Will. Marshall, scu.* A copy of one of these editions falling into the hands of the Earl of Dorset, the work was by him recommended to the notice of Sir Kenelm Digby, then a prisoner in Winchester House, who "returned his judgment upon it, not in a letter, but a book; in which, though mingled with some positions fabulous and uncertain, there are acute remarks, just censures, and profound speculations; yet its principal claim to admiration is, that it was written in twenty-four hours, of which part was spent in procuring Browne's book, and part in reading it." While these animadversions were passing through the press Browne became aware of the fact, and wrote to Digby acknowledging the book to be his, but declaring its unworthiness to engage such notice: at the same time stating his intention, speedily to put forth the true and intended original, by comparing which with the spurious edition, it would clearly appear how far the

Johnson's Life of Browne.

text had been miftaken.   The object of this
letter was doubtlefs to induce Sir Kenelm to
delay the publication of his animadverfions:
in his reply he denies any intention on his own
part of giving them to the public; and amid
much affurance of efteem and regard and high
commendation of the book, apologizes for the
fhort and infufficient way in which he had
treated fo weighty a fubject, but that what liberty he had taken was to be attributed to the
fecurity of a private letter, and to his not knowing

the perfon whom it concerned.   Thefe animadverfions appeared in 1643, in a fmall volume
entitled, *Obfervations upon Religio Medici,
occafionally written by Sir Kenelome * Digby,
Knight*.

Browne fulfilled his promife to Digby, by
publifhing in 1643, " *A true and full coppy of
that which was moft imperfectly and furrepti-*

---

* *Kenelome*. This error feems to corroborate Digby's affertion that the obfervations found their way
to the prefs without his knowledge; a fecond edition
appeared in 1644, *corrected and amended,* and a
third in 1659.

tiouſly printed before under the name of Religio Medici." It is in very ſmall 8vo. with an engraved title, copied from that of the ſurreptitious editions. This work differs very materially from the ſpurious edition, and from all the MSS. and muſt no longer be regarded as written merely " for his own private exerciſe and ſatisfaction ; " but being conſtrained to bring it before the public, the author found it neceſſary to alter ſome, and to expunge other paſſages, which were either unſuited to the taſte of the day, or which no longer accorded with his own ſentiments. It may therefore be conſidered, not only as a confeſſion of the writer's particular belief and opinions, but alſo, in the more general and extended acceptation of its title, as the *Religion of a Phyſician.*

The number of Editions through which the work has paſſed, affords ſome criterion, though not in all caſes a juſt one, of the eſtimation in which it has been held, both at home and abroad.

	Date.	Language.	Printer or Publisher.	Place.	Size.	Authority.
1.	1643.	English.	Andrew Crooke.	London.	8vo.	Bodleian Lib. Ed.
2.	1644.	Latin.	Hackius.	Leyden.	12mo.	Editor.
3.	1645.	English.	Andrew Crooke.	London.	8vo.	Bodl. Ed.
4.	1645.	English.	Slightly altered in the orthography.	London.	8vo.	Ed.
5.	1650.	Latin.	Hackius.	Leyden.	12mo.	Ed.
6.		Latin.	Juxta Exempl. Lug. Batavorum 1644.	Paris.	12mo.	Wilkin.
7.	1652.	Latin.	F. Spoor.	Strasbourg.	8vo.	Ed.
8.	1656.	English.	E. Cotes for Andrew Crook.	London.	8vo.	Bodl. Ed.
9.	1659.	English.	Printed for the good of the Common-wealth.	London.	Folio.	Bodl. (Douce).
10.	1659.	English.	Tho. Milbourn for Andrew Crook.	London.	8vo.	Ed.
11.	1665.	Latin.	Reprint of 7.	Strasbourg.	8vo.	Bodl. Brit. Mus.
12.	1665.	Dutch.		Leyden.	12mo.	Wilkin.
13.	1668.	French.		La Haye.	12mo.	Biogr. Univers.
14.	1669.	English.	Ja. Cotterel for A. C.	London.	8vo.	Ch. ch. Ed.
15.	1672.	English.	Andrew Crooke.	London.	4to.	Ed.
16.	1677.	Latin.	Reprint of 7.	Strasbourg.	8vo.	Wadh. Coll.
17.	1678.	English.	R. Scot, T. Basset.	London.	8vo.	Ed.
18.	1682.	English.	Reprint of 17.	London.	8vo.	Ed.
19.	1683.	Dutch.	2nd. Ed. of 12.	Leyden.	8vo.	Wilkin.
20.	1685.	English.	Robert Scot, Thomas Basset, &c.	London.	Folio.	Ed.

2. This Translation is by John Merryweather, B.D. of Magd. Coll. Camb.

7. Merryweather's Translation with notes by L. N. v Moltke (Memoires de Niceron. xxiii. 356).

8. Called the 4th Ed. with Annotations supposed to be by Thomas Keck.

10. Called the 5th. frontispiece dated 1660.

13. Translated by Nicholas Lefebvre.   14. Called the 6th.

15. Called the 7th.   17. Called the 7th.

18. Called the 8th. This was the last Ed. published during the Author's Life.

20. Called the 8th. Edited by Archbishop Tenison.

	Date.	Language.	Printer or Publisher.	Place.	Size.	Authority.
21.	1732.	French.			2 vols. 12mo.	Watt.
22.	1736.	English.	J. Torbuck.	London.	8vo.	Ed.
23.	1736.	English.	Another ed. without notes.	London.	8vo.	Wilkin.
24.	1746.	German.	Ragozy.	Prenzlau.	8vo.	Europ. Bucher-Lexicon.
25.	1831.	English.	Vincent.	Oxford.	18mo.	
26.	1835.	English.	Pickering.	London.	8vo.	
27.	1838.	English.	Rickerby.	London.	8vo.	
28.	1844.	English.	Longmans.	London.	8vo.	

The *Letter to a Friend* was published after the Author's death, by his son. A portion of it is preserved in MS. in the British Museum (Sloan, 1862). It seems to have been intended as an introduction to the Christian Morals.

	Date.	Language.	Printer or Publisher.	Place.	Size.	Authority.
1.	1690.	English.	Charles Brome.	London.	Folio.	Brit. Muf.
2.	1712.	English.	E. Curll.	London.	8vo.	Ed.
3.	1822.	English.	Blackwood.	Edinburgh.	12mo.	Ed.
4.	1835.	English.	Pickering.	London.	8vo.	Ed.

22. A new Title was attached to the unsold copies of this ed. in 1738.

24. This may be the translation attributed to George Venzky by Jöcher (Allgemeines Gelehrten Lexicon, Leipf. 1750).

26. In the 2d vol. of Mr. Wilkin's ed. of Sir Thomas Browne's Works and Correspondence.

Besides these it is to be supposed that Religio Medici was included in a Dutch Edition of Browne's Works, translated by Johann Gründahl, and published at Amsterdam in 1668; and in a German Edition by Christian Knorr, Baron of Rosenroth (Christian Peganius) at Leipsic in 1680. There is also an Italian Translation said to exist. (Cf. Wilkin, Watt, and Ebert.)

4. In Works ed. Wilkin, vol. 4.

Christian Morals was first published by Archdeacon Jeffery from the original and correct manuscript of the Author.

1.	1716.	English.	Univ. prefs.	Cambridge.	8vo.	Bodl.
2.	1756.	English.	Payne.	London.	8vo.	Ed.
3.	1835.	English.	Pickering.	London.	8vo.	Ed.
4.	1844.	English.	Longmans.	London.	8vo.	Ed.
5.	1845.	English.	Washbourne.	London.	8vo.	Ed.

The present volume contains :

The Eighteenth Edition (in English) of Religio Medici,

The Fifth Edition of a Letter to a Friend,

The Sixth Edition of Christian Morals.
The Editor has endeavoured,

1st. To supply a more correct text than has hitherto been published.

2nd. To add, or direct attention to, some passages in other writers which appear to explain or to illustrate it.

To do this he has carefully collated the text with three of the MSS. and with the most trustworthy of the Editions; and has availed himself of the corrections and annotations of former Editors.   Oxford, October 1845.

---

2. This Ed. has notes, and a life of the Author by Dr. Johnson. Reprint titles were attached to the unsold copies in 1761, 1765.
4. In Works ed. Wilkin vol. iv.

To the Reader.

ERTAINLY that man were greedy of life, who fhould defire to live when all the world were at an end; and he muft needs be very impatient, who would repine at death in the fociety of all things that fuffer under it. Had not almoft every man fuffered by the prefs, or were not the tyranny thereof become univerfal, I had not wanted reafon for complaint: but in times wherein I have lived to behold the higheft perverfion of that excellent invention, the name of his Majefty defamed, the honour of Parliament depraved, the writings of both depravedly, anticipatively, counterfeitly imprinted; complaints may feem ridiculous in private perfons; and men of my condition may be as incapable of affronts, as hopelefs of their reparations. And truly had not the duty I owe unto the importunity of friends, and the allegiance I muſt ever acknowledge unto truth, prevailed with me; the inactivity of my diſpoſition might have made theſe ſufferings continual, and time, that brings other things to light, ſhould have ſatisfied me in the remedy of its oblivion. But becauſe things evidently falſe are not only printed, but many things of truth moſt falſely ſet forth; in this latter I could not but think myſelf engaged: for though we have no power to redreſs the former, yet in the other the reparation being within ourſelves, I have at preſent re-preſented unto the world a full and intended copy of that piece, which was moſt imperfectly and ſurreptitiouſly publiſhed before.

This I confeſs, about ſeven years paſt, with ſome others of affinity thereto, for my private exerciſe and ſatisfaction, I had at leiſurable hours compoſed; which being communicated unto one, it became common unto many, and was by tranſcription ſucceſſively corrupted, until it arrived in a moſt depraved copy at the preſs. He that ſhall peruſe that work, and ſhall take notice of ſundry particularities and perſonal expreſſions therein, will eaſily diſcern the intention was not publick: and

being a private exercife directed to myfelf, what
is delivered therein, was rather a memorial unto
me, than an example or rule unto any other:
and therefore, if there be any fingularity therein
correfpondent unto the private conceptions of
any man, it doth not advantage them; or if
diffentaneous thereunto, it no way overthrows
them. It was penned in fuch a place, and
with fuch difadvantage, that (I proteft) from
the firft fetting of pen unto paper, I had not
the affiftance of any good book, whereby to
promote my invention, or relieve my memory;
and therefore there might be many real lapfes
therein, which others might take notice of, and
more that I fufpected myfelf. It was fet down
many years paft, and was the fenfe of my conceptions at that time, not an immutable law
unto my advancing judgment at all times; and
therefore there might be many things therein
plaufible unto my paffed apprehenfion, which
are not agreeable unto my prefent felf. Therefore are many things delivered rhetorically,
many expreffions therein merely tropical, and
as they beft illuftrate my intention; and therefore alfo there are many things to be taken in
a foft and flexible fenfe, and not to be called
unto the rigid teft of reafon. Laftly, all that is

contained therein, is in fubmiffion unto maturer difcernments ; and as I have declared, fhall no further father them than the beft and learned judgments fhall authorize them : under favour of which confiderations, I have made its fecrecy publick, and committed the truth thereof to every ingenuous Reader.

THOMAS BROWNE.

Religio Medici.

Our Physician a Christian.

FOR my religion, though there be several circumstances that might perfuade the world I have none at all, as the general fcandal of my profeſſion, the natural courfe of my ſtudies, the indifferency of my behaviour and difcourfe in matters of religion, neither violently defending one, nor with that common ardour and contention oppoſing another; yet in defpite hereof I dare, without ufurpation, affume the honourable ftyle of a Chriftian. Not that I merely owe this title to the font, my education, or clime wherein I was born, as being bred up either to confirm thofe principles my parents inftilled into my unwary underftanding, or by a general confent to proceed in the religion of my country; but having, in my riper years and confirmed judgment, feen and examined all,* I find myfelf obliged by the principles of grace, and the law of mine own reafon, to embrace no other name but this: neither doth herein my zeal fo far make me forget the general charity I owe unto humanity, as rather to hate than pity Turks, infidels, and (what is worfe) Jews; rather contenting myfelf to enjoy that happy ftyle, than maligning thofe who refufe fo glorious a title.

Quoufque patiere, bone Jefu!
    Judæi te femel, ego fæpius crucifixi;
Illi in Afia, ego in Britannia,
    Gallia, Germania;
Bone Jefu, miferere mei, et Judæorum!

Our Phyfician a Churchman.

II. But becaufe the name of a Chriftian is become too general to ex-

---

* According to the Apoftolical precept, " Prove all things: hold faft that which is good." 1 Theff. v. 21. K.

prefs our faith, there being a geography
of religion as well as lands, and every
clime being diftinguifhed not only by their
laws and limits, but circumfcribed by their
doctrines and rules of faith; to be particular, I am of that reformed new-caft religion, wherein I diflike nothing but the
name;* of the fame belief our Saviour
taught, the apoftles diffeminated, the fathers authorized, and the martyrs confirmed; but by the finifter ends of princes,
the ambition and avarice of prelates, and
the fatal corruption of times, fo decayed,
impaired, and fallen from its native beauty,

---

* " It is not quite clear what name is here intended.
We fpeak of a proteftant or protefting church, meaning one which protefts againft a certain ufurpation
and certain notions interfering, as it believes, with
its own pofition as a particular church, or fubverting
the idea of the Univerfal Church: but we do not, except in the loofenefs of converfation, fpeak of a proteftant *religion*. The Reformation would be badly
defcribed as new-cafting a Religion: but it belonged
to the character of the 17th century, to fubftitute a
logical conception, like that of Religion, for the idea
of a Spiritual Being, of Man himfelf as a Spirit, and
of the fpiritual bond between the creature and the
Creator."

that it required the careful and charitable hands of thefe times to reftore it to its primitive integrity. Now the accidental occafion whereon, the flender means whereby, the low and abject condition of the perfon by whom fo good a work was fet on foot, which in our adverfaries begets contempt and fcorn, fills me with wonder, and is the very fame objection the infolent Pagans firft caft at Chrift and his difciples.

III. Yet have I not fo fhaken hands * with thofe defperate refolutions, (who had rather venture at large their decayed bottom, than bring her in to be new trimmed in the dock ; who had rather promifcuoufly retain all, than abridge any, and obftinately be what they are, than what they have been,) as to ftand in diameter and fword's point with them : we have reformed from them, not againft

Differences of opinion need not feparate Chriftians.

---

* *Shaken hands.* Browne ufes this phrafe in the fenfe of *turn away from*, or *bid adieu to.* Cf. Sect. xli. p. 106. and alfo in the Garden of Cyrus.

So Harrifon in Holinfhed, vol. i. p. 314, ed.

them; for omitting those improperations, and terms of scurrility betwixt us, which only difference our affections, and not our cause, there is between us one common name and appellation, one faith and necessary body of principles common to us both; and therefore I am not scrupulous to converse and live with them, to enter their churches in defect of ours, and either pray with them, or for them.* I could never perceive any rational consequence from those many texts which prohibit the children of Israel to pollute themselves with the temples of the heathens; we

---

1807. "For it is the custom of the more idle sort, having once served, or but seen the other side of the sea under color of service, to shake hand with labour for ever, thinking it a disgrace for himself to return unto his former trade."

* There is a remarkable similarity between the sentiments of Sir Thomas Browne and those of Hooker in reference to the Church of Rome and the extreme notions of the Puritans. See the Fourth Book of the Eccl. Pol. It is highly probable that Browne had studied Hooker's Works. Hooker died 1600. Browne dates his letter to Sir K. Digby 1642.

being all Chriftians, and not divided by
fuch detefted impieties as might profane
our prayers, or the place wherein we make
them; or that a refolved confcience may
not adore her Creator any where, efpecially in places devoted to his fervice;
where, if their devotions offend him, mine
may pleafe him; if theirs profane it, mine
may hallow it. Holy-water and crucifix
(dangerous to the common people) deceive not my judgment, nor abufe my devotion at all: I am, I confefs, naturally
inclined to that which mifguided zeal
terms fuperftition. My common converfation I do acknowledge auftere, my behaviour full of rigour, fometimes not
without morofity; yet at my devotion I
love to ufe the civility of my knee, my
hat, and hand, with all thofe outward and
fenfible motions which may exprefs or
promote my invifible devotion. I fhould
violate my own arm rather than a church;
nor willingly deface the memory of faint
or martyr. At the fight of a crofs or*

---

* Cf. Hooker's Eccles. Pol. Bk. v. cap. lxv.

crucifix I can difpenfe with my hat, but
fcarce with the thought or memory of my
Saviour. I cannot laugh at, but rather
pity the fruitlefs journeys of pilgrims,
nor contemn the miferable condition of
friars; for though mifplaced in circumftances, there is fomething in it of devotion. I could never hear the Ave Mary
bell* without an elevation; or think it
a fufficient warrant, becaufe they erred
in one circumftance, for me to err in all,
that is, in filence and dumb contempt:
whilft therefore they directed their devotions to her, I offered mine to God, and
rectified the errors of their prayers, by
rightly ordering mine own. At a folemn
proceffion I have wept abundantly, while
my conforts, blind with oppofition and
prejudice, have fallen into an accefs of
fcorn and laughter. There are, queftion-
lefs, both in Greek, Roman, and African

---

* A church bell that tolls every day at fix and
twelve of the clock; at the hearing whereof, every
one in what place foever, either of houfe or ftreet,
betakes himfelf to his prayer, which is commonly
directed to the Virgin.

churches, folemnities and ceremonies, whereof the wifer zeals do make a Chriftian ufe, and ftand condemned by us, not as evil in themfelves, but as allurements and baits of fuperftition to thofe vulgar heads that look afquint on the face of truth, and thofe unftable judgments that cannot confift in the narrow point and centre of virtue without a reel or ftagger to the circumference.*

IV. As there were many reformers, fo likewife there were many reformations; every country proceeding in a particular way and method, according as their national intereft, together with their conftitution and clime inclined them; fome angrily, and with extremity; others calmly, and with mediocrity; not rending, but eafily dividing the community, and leaving an honeft poffibility of a reconci-

---

* This figure is probably borrowed from Ariftotle. Eth. Nic. ii. 9. "Wherefore it is hard to be good: for in each action to find the mean is difficult, as it is not every one that can find the centre of a circle, but he that is fkilled to do fo."

liation; which though peaceable fpirits do defire, and may conceive that revolution of time and the mercies of God may effect, yet that judgment that fhall confider the prefent antipathies between the two extremes, their contrarieties in condition, affection, and opinion, may with the fame hopes expect an union in the poles of heaven.

v. But to difference myfelf nearer, and draw into a leffer circle: there is no church, whofe every part fo fquares unto my confcience; whofe articles, conftitutions, and cuftoms, feem fo confonant unto reafon, and as it were framed to my particular devotion, as this whereof I hold my belief, the Church of England, to whofe faith I am a fworn fubject; and therefore in a double obligation fubfcribe unto her Articles, and endeavour to obferve her Conftitutions: whatfoever is beyond, as points indifferent, I obferve according to the rules of my private reafon, or the humour and fafhion of my devotion; neither believing this, becaufe Luther af-

Of the Church of England.

firmed it, nor difapproving that, becaufe
Calvin hath difavouched it. I condemn
not all things in the council of Trent, nor
approve all in the fynod of Dort. In
brief, where the Scripture is filent, the
Church is my text; where that fpeaks,
'tis but my comment: where there is a
joint filence of both, I borrow not the
rules of my religion from Rome or Ge-
neva, but the dictates of my own reafon.*
It is an unjuft fcandal of our adverfaries,
and a grofs error in ourfelves, to compute the nativity of our religion from
Henry the Eighth, who, though he re-
jected the Pope, refufed not the faith of
Rome, and effected no more than what his
own predeceffors defired and affayed in
ages paft, and was conceived the ftate of
Venice would have attempted in our days.

---

* " For myfelf, I am in religion neither a fantaftic
puritan nor a fuperftitious papift; but fo fettled in
confcience that I have the fure ground of God's
word to warrant all I believe, and the commendable
ordinances of our Englifh Church to approve all I
practife; in which courfe I live a faithful Chriftian
and an obedient fubject; and fo teach my family."
Edward Fairfax, 1621. Vide Appendix A.

It is as uncharitable a point in us to fall upon those popular scurrilities and opprobrious scoffs of the bishop of Rome, to whom as a temporal prince, we owe the duty of good language. I confess there is cause of paffion between us: by his sentence I stand excommunicated, heretic is the best language he affords me; yet can no ear witness, I ever returned him the name of Antichrist, man of sin, or whore of Babylon. It is the method of charity to suffer without reaction: those usual satires and invectives of the pulpit may perchance produce a good effect on the vulgar, whose ears are opener to rhetoric than logic; yet do they in no wise confirm the faith of wifer believers, who know that a good cause needs not to be patron'd by paffion, but can sustain itself upon a temperate dispute.

VI. I could never divide myself from any man upon the difference of an opinion, or be angry with his judgment for not agreeing with me in that, from which within a few days I should

diffent myfelf. I have no genius to difputes in religion, and have often thought
it wifdom to decline them, efpecially upon
a difadvantage, or when the caufe of truth
might fuffer in the weaknefs of my pa-
tronage.* Where we defire to be informed, 'tis good to conteft with men
above ourfelves; but to confirm and eftablifh our opinions, 'tis beft to argue with
judgments below our own, that the frequent fpoils and victories over their reafons, may fettle in ourfelves an efteem
and confirmed opinion of our own. Every
man is not a proper champion for truth,
nor fit to take up the gauntlet in the caufe
of verity: many from the ignorance of
thefe maxims, and an inconfiderate zeal
for truth, have too rafhly charged the
troops of error, and remain as trophies
unto the enemies of truth. A man may
be in as juft poffeffion of truth as of a
city, and yet be forced to furrender; 'tis
therefore far better to enjoy her with
peace, than to hazard her on a battle: if

---

* Cf. Bifhop Butler's Charge to the Clergy of
Durham, 1751, near the beginning.

therefore there rise any doubts in my way, I do forget them, or at least defer them, till my better settled judgment, and more manly reason be able to resolve them; for I perceive every man's own reason is his best Œdipus, and will upon a reasonable truce, find a way to loose those bonds wherewith the subtleties of error have enchained our more flexible and tender judgments. In philosophy, where truth seems double-faced, there is no man more paradoxical than myself: but in divinity I love to keep the road; and, though not in an implicit, yet an humble faith, follow the great wheel of the Church, by which I move, not reserving any proper poles or motion from the epicycle of my own brain;† by these means I leave no gap

Fantasies in divinity dangerous as giving entrance to errors.

---

† " Yes, if the intensities of hope and fear
Attract us still, and passionate exercise
Of lofty thoughts, the way before us lies
Distinct with signs, thro' which in set career,
As thro' a zodiac, moves the ritual year
Of England's Church: stupendous mysteries!
Which whoso travels in her bosom, eyes
As he approaches them, with solemn cheer."
    WORDSWORTH. Ecclesiastical Sonnet.

Whereof
our Physi-
cian confefs-
eth to have
had two or
three.

for herefy, fchifms, or errors, of which at present I hope I fhall not injure truth to say I have no taint or tincture. I muft confefs my greener ftudies have been polluted with two or three, not any begotten in the latter centuries, but old and obfolete, fuch as could never have been revived, but by fuch extravagant and irregular heads as mine; for indeed herefies perifh not with their authors, but like the river Arethufa,* though they lose their currents in one place, they rise up again in another. One general council is not able to extirpate one fingle herefy: it may be cancelled for the prefent; but revolution of time and the like afpects from heaven, will reftore it, when it will flourifh

---

* Arethufa a nymph of Achaia while bathing, on her return from hunting in the Stymphalian wood, was furprifed by the river god Alpheus, in whofe water fhe was difporting herfelf. She fled from him, and after a long chafe was concealed in a cloud by Diana, juft as her ftrength was failing. She thus relates (Ovid. Metam. v. 574,) her transformation into the ftream which bears her name, and with which the waters of Alpheus vainly fought to unite, Diana

till it be condemned again. For as though there was metempſychoſis, and the ſoul of one man paſſed into another, opinions do find after certain revolutions, men and minds like thoſe that firſt begat them. To ſee ourſelves again, we need not look for Plato's year :† every man is not only himſelf; there hath been many Diogenes, and as many Timons, though but few of that name : men are lived over again, the world is now as it was in ages paſt; there was none then, but there hath been ſome one ſince that parallels him, and as it were his revived ſelf.

VII. Now the firſt of mine was that of the Arabians,‡ that the ſouls

1ſt, That the ſoul might, in

---

opening a way for her under ground and bringing her out again in Ortygia, near Syracuſe in Sicily.

† A revolution of certain thouſand years, when all things ſhould return unto their former eſtate, and he be teaching again in his ſchool as when he delivered this opinion.

‡ "It was not only in the point now mentioned, that the doctrine of the Goſpel ſuffered, at this time, from the erroneous fancies of wrong-headed doctors.

some sort, perish, and rise again with the body.

of men perished with their bodies, but should yet be raised again at the last day. Not that I did absolutely conceive a mortality of the soul; but if that were, which faith, not philosophy, hath yet thoroughly disproved, and that both entered the grave together, yet I held the same conceit thereof, that we all do for the body, that it should rise again. Surely it is but the merits of our unworthy natures, if we sleep in darkness until the last alarum. A serious reflex upon my own unworthiness did make me backward from challenging this prerogative of my soul: so I might enjoy my Saviour at the last, I could with patience be nothing almost

2d, That all

unto eternity. The second was that of

For there sprung up now, in Arabia, a certain sort of minute philosophers, the disciples of a master whose obscurity has concealed him from the knowledge of after ages, who denied the immortality of the soul, and believed that it perished with the body: but maintained, at the same time, that it was to be recalled to life with the body, by the power of God. The philosophers, who held this opinion, were called Arabians, from their country. Origen was called

Origen, that God would not perſiſt in his vengeance for ever, but after a definite time of his wrath, he would releaſe the damned ſouls from torture : which error I fell into upon a ſerious contemplation of the great attribute of God, his Mercy ; and did a little cheriſh it in myſelf, be-cauſe I found therein no malice, and a ready weight to ſway me from the other extreme of deſpair, whereunto melancholy and contemplative natures are too eaſily diſpoſed.† A third there is which I did never poſitively maintain or practiſe, but have often wiſhed it had been conſonant to truth, and not offenſive to my religion, and that is the prayer for the dead ; whereunto I was inclined from ſome cha-

men ſhould finally be ſaved.

3d, That we might pray for the dead.

from Egypt, to make head againſt this riſing ſect ; and diſputed againſt them in full council, with ſuch remarkable ſucceſs, that they abandoned their erro-neous ſentiments, and returned to the received doc-trine of the Church." Moſheim, Eccl. Hiſt. vol. i. ch. 5, § 16, p. 307.

† Biſhop Butler ſeems to allude to this and ſimilar errors. Anal. Pt. i. cap. 2, 3.

ritable inducements, whereby I could scarce
contain my prayers for a friend at the
ringing of a bell, or behold his corpse
without an orison for his soul: 'twas a
good way, methought, to be remembered
by posterity, and far more noble than a
history. These opinions I never maintained with pertinacy, or endeavoured to
inveigle any man's belief unto mine, nor
so much as ever revealed or disputed them
with my dearest friends ; by which means
I neither propagated them in others, nor
confirmed them in myself; but suffering
them to flame upon their own substance,
without addition of new fuel, they went
out insensibly of themselves : therefore
these opinions, though condemned by lawful councils, were not heresies in me,* but
bare errors, and single lapses of my un-

But these
he suffered
not to grow
into here-
sies.

---

* For to make an heretic, there must be not only
error in intellectu, but *pertinacia in voluntate.* So
St. Aug. *Qui sententiam suam quamvis falsam atque
perversam nulla pertinaci animositate defendunt, quæ-
runt autem cauta solicitudine veritatem, corrigi parati
cum invenerint, nequaquam sunt inter hæreticos de-
putandi.* Aug. cont. Manich. 24, qu. 3.   K.

derſtanding without a joint depravity of my will. Thoſe have not only depraved underſtandings, but diſeaſed affections, who cannot enjoy a ſingularity without an hereſy, or be the author of an opinion without they be of a ſect alſo: this was the villany of the firſt ſchiſm of Lucifer, who was not content to err alone, but drew into his faction many legions of ſpirits; and upon this experience he tempted only Eve, as well underſtanding the communicable nature of ſin, and that to deceive but one, was tacitly and upon conſequence to delude them both.

VIII. That hereſies ſhould ariſe, we have the prophecy of Chriſt; but that old ones ſhould be aboliſhed, we hold no prediction. That there muſt be hereſies, is true, not only in our church, but alſo in any other: even in doctrines heretical, there will be ſuper-hereſies; and Arians not only divided from their church, but alſo among themſelves: for heads that are diſpoſed unto ſchiſm and complexionably propenſe to innovation, are naturally

Of the manifold nature of ſchiſm, ever multiplying itſelf.

indifpofed for a community; nor will be ever confined unto the order or economy of one body; and therefore when they feparate from others, they knit but loofely among themfelves; nor contented with a general breach or dichotomy with their church, do fubdivide and mince themfelves almoft into atoms. 'Tis true, that men of fingular parts and humours have not been free from fingular opinions and conceits in all ages; retaining fomething not only befide the opinion of their own church or any other, but alfo of any particular author; which notwithftanding a fober judgment may do without offence or herefy; for there is yet, after all the decrees of councils, and the niceties of

* See Aids to Reflection, p. 151.

† On this paffage Tillotfon fays, "I know not what fome men may find in themfelves; but I muft freely acknowledge, that I could never yet attain to that bold and hardy degree of faith, as to believe any thing, for this reafon, becaufe it was impoffible. —So that I am very far from being of his mind, that wanted, not only more difficulties, but even impoffibilities in the Chriftian religion, to exercife his faith

fchools, many things untouched, unima-
gined, wherein the liberty of an honeft
reafon may play and expatiate with fecurity, and far without the circle of an herefy.

IX.* As for thofe wingy myf-
teries in divinity, and airy fubtleties in
religion, which have unhinged the brains
of better heads, they never ftretched the
pia mater of mine: methinks there be not
impoffibilities enough in religion for an
active faith ;† the deepeft myfteries ours
contains, have not only been illuftrated,
but maintained by fyllogifm, and the rule
of reafon. I love to lofe myfelf in a myftery, to purfue my reafon to an *O alti-*

upon." "But by *impoffibilities*, Sir Thomas Browne,
as well as Tertullian, meant *feeming*, not *real* impoffibilities; and what he fays fhould be looked upon
as a *verbum ardens*, a rhetorical flourifh, and a trial
of fkill with Tertullian, in which, however, he had
little chance to come off fuperior. Both of them
were lively and ingenious, but the African had a
warmer complexion than the Briton." Jortin's
Tracts, vol. i. p. 373.

tudo! 'Tis my folitary recreation to pofe my apprehenfion with thofe involved enigmas and riddles of the Trinity, with Incarnation and Refurrection. I can anfwer all the objections of Satan and my rebellious reafon, with that odd refolution I learned of Tertullian, *Certum eft quia impoffibile eft.* I defire to exercife my faith in the difficulteft point; for to credit ordinary and vifible objects, is not faith, but perfuafion.* Some believe the better for feeing Chrift's fepulchre; and when they have feen the Red Sea, doubt not of the miracle. Now contrarily, I blefs myfelf, and am thankful that I lived not in the days of miracles, that I never faw Chrift nor his difciples: I would not have been one of thofe Ifraelites that paffed the Red Sea, nor one of Chrift's patients on whom he wrought his wonders; then had my faith been thruft upon me; nor

Bleffed are they that have not

---

* Compare Hebrews xi. and Keble's Chriftian Year, 9th Sunday after Trinity :—

" Choofe to believe, not fee: fight tempts the heart
From fober walking in true Gofpel ways."

should I enjoy that greater blessing pronounced to all that believe and saw not. 'Tis an easy and necessary belief, to credit what our eye and sense hath examined :† I believe he was dead and buried, and rose again ; and desire to see him in his glory, rather than to contemplate him in his cenotaph or sepulchre. Nor is this much to believe ; as we have reason, we owe this faith unto history : they only had the advantage of a bold and noble faith, who lived before his coming, who upon obscure prophecies and mystical types could raise a belief, and expect apparent impossibilities.§

x. 'Tis true, there is an edge in all firm belief, and with an easy metaphor we may say the sword of faith ;‡ but in these obscurities I rather use it in the adjunct the apostle gives it, a buckler ;

[margin: seen and yet have believed.]

[margin: The armour of a Christian.]

---

† " God forbede but that men should believ
Well more thing than thei han seen with eye."
                                        CHAUCER.
§ See Pearson on the Creed, vol. i. p. 23.
‡ Eph. vi. 16.

under which I conceive a wary combatant
may lie invulnerable. Since I was of underſtanding to know we knew nothing,
my reaſon hath been more pliable to the
will of faith; I am now content to underſtand a myſtery without a rigid definition,
in an eaſy and Platonic deſcription. That
allegorical deſcription* of Hermes pleaſeth
me beyond all the metaphyſical definitions
of divines; where I cannot ſatisfy my
reaſon, I love to humour my fancy: I
had as lieve you tell me that *anima eſt
angelus hominis, eſt corpus Dei*, as ἐντέλεχεια; *Lux eſt umbra Dei*, as *aCtus perſpi-
cui.*† Where there is an obſcurity too

---

* *Sphæra cujus centrum ubique, circumferentia
nullibi.*

† Great variety of opinion there hath been amongſt
the ancient philoſophers touching the definition of
the ſoul. Thales's was, that it is a *nature without
repoſe.* Aſclepiades, that it is *an exercitation of ſenſe:*
Heſiod, that it is *a thing compoſed of earth and
water:* Parmenides holds, *of earth and fire;* Galen,
that it is *heat;* Hippocrates, that it is *a ſpirit diffuſed through the bod*y: some others have held it to
be *light;* Plato ſaith, 'tis *a ſubſtance moving itſelf;*
after cometh Ariſtotle (whom the author here re-

deep for our reason, 'tis good to sit down
with a description, periphrasis, or adum-
bration; for by acquainting our reason
how unable it is to display the visible and
obvious effects of nature, it becomes more
humble and submissive unto the subtleties
of faith; and thus I teach my haggard
and unreclaimed reason to stoop unto the
lure of faith. I believe there was already
a tree whose fruit our unhappy parents
tasted; though in the same chapter, when
God forbids it, 'tis positively said the
plants of the fields were not yet grown,
for God had not caused it to rain upon
the earth.‡ I believe that the serpent,

---

proveth) and goeth a degree farther, and saith it is
ἐντέλεχεια, that is, that which naturally makes the
body to move. But this definition is as rigid as any
of the other; for this tells us not what the essence,
origin, or nature of the soul is, but only marks an
effect of it, and therefore signifieth no more than if
he had said, that it is *angelus hominis*, or an intelligence that moveth man, as he supposed those other
to do the heavens. K. Cf. Cic. Tusc. Disp. I. x.

‡ Sir Thomas makes a difficulty here, for himself,
where none actually exists. In the 2d cap. of Genesis,
the verses 4—7 contain a recapitulation of the prin-

(if we fhall literally underftand it,) from his proper form and figure, made his motion on his belly before the curfe. I find the trial of the pucellage and virginity of women, which God ordained the Jews, is very fallible.* Experience and hiftory inform me, that not only many particular women, but likewife whole nations, have efcaped the curfe of childbirth, which God feems to pronounce upon the whole fex; yet do I believe that all this is true, which indeed my reafon would perfuade me to be falfe; and this I think is no vulgar part of faith, to believe a thing not only above, but contrary to reafon, and againft the arguments of our proper fenfes.

---

cipal events of creation. In the 5th verfe, we are told, that the herbs and plants of the field did not come up of their own accord out of the earth, before God made them, but that God created them before there were any feeds of any fuch thing in the earth, and before there was any rain, or any men to ufe gardening or hufbandry. Next (vv. 7, 8) we have an account of the planting of the garden, and not till then does the command alluded to, occur. Cf. Pfeudodox. Epidem. v. 4.—vii. 1.

XI. In my solitary and re-tired imagination,

———— Neque enim cum lectulus aut me
Porticus excepit, desum mihi——

I remember I am not alone, and there-fore forget not to contemplate him and his attributes who is ever with me, espe-cially those two mighty ones, his wisdom and eternity: with the one I recreate, with the other I confound my under-standing; for who can speak of eternity without a solecism, or think thereof with-out an ecstasy? Time we may compre-hend,† it is but five days older than our-

---

* Cf. Blumenbach Physiol. 539. We must bear in mind that this test was ordained for the *people of the Jews:* and we have no record of its proving fallible among *them.*

† Touching the difference betwixt *eternity* and *time,* there have been great disputes amongst philoso-phers; some affirming it to be no more than *dura-tion perpetual consisting of parts;* and others affirmed that it hath no distinction of tenses, but is, according to Boetius (lib. 5, Consol. pros. 6,) his definition, *interminabilis vitæ tota simul et perfecta possessio.* K. See Appendix B.

felves, and hath the fame horofcope with
the world; but to retire fo far back as to
apprehend a beginning, to give fuch an
infinite ftart forward as to conceive an end
in an effence that we affirm hath neither
the one nor the other, it puts my reafon
to St. Paul's fanctuary: my philofophy
dares not fay the angels can do it; God
hath not made a creature that can comprehend him; it is a privilege of his own
nature: *I am that I am*, was his own definition unto Mofes; and it was a fhort one,
to confound mortality, that durft queftion
God, or afk him what he was. Indeed
he only is; all others have and fhall be;
but in eternity there is no diftinction of
tenfes; and therefore that terrible term
predeftination, which hath troubled fo many
weak heads to conceive, and the wifeft to
explain, is in refpect to God no prefcious
determination of our ftates to come, but
a definitive blaft of his will already fulfilled, and at the inftant that he firft decreed it;* for to his eternity, which is in-

---

* Cf. Butler's Anal. Part i. cap. vi. and the viith
of Davifon's Difcourfes on Prophecy.

divisible, and all together, the last trump is already sounded, the reprobates in the flame, and the blessed in Abraham's bosom. St. Peter speaks modestly, when he saith,† a thousand years to God are but as one day; for to speak like a philosopher, those continued instances of time which flow into a thousand years, make not to him one moment: what to us is to come, to his eternity is present, his whole duration being but one permanent point, without succession, parts, flux, or division.

XII. There is no attribute that adds more difficulty to the mystery of the Trinity, where, though in a relative way of Father and Son, we must deny a priority. I wonder how Aristotle could conceive the world eternal, or how he could make good two eternities: his similitude of a triangle, comprehended in a square, doth somewhat illustrate the trinity of our souls, and that the triple unity of God; for

Of the Trinity.

---

† 2 Pet. iii. 8.

there is in us not three, but a trinity of
fouls, becaufe there is in us, if not three
diftinct fouls, yet differing faculties, that
can and do fubfift apart in different fubjects, and yet in us are fo united as to make
but one foul and fubftance : if one foul
were fo perfect as to inform three diftinct
bodies, that were a petty trinity : conceive
the diftinct number of three, not divided
nor feparated by the intellect, but actually
comprehended in its unity, and that is a
perfect trinity. I have often admired the
myftical way of Pythagoras, and the fecret magic of numbers. " Beware of philofophy," is a precept not to be received
in too large a fenfe : for in this mafs of
nature there is a fet of things that carry in
their front, though not in capital letters,
yet in ftenography and fhort characters,
fomething of divinity, which to wifer reafons ferve as luminaries in the abyfs of
knowledge, and to judicious beliefs as
fcales and roundles to mount the pinna-
cles and highest pieces of divinity. The
fevere fchools fhall never laugh me out of

the philofophy of Hermes, that this vifible world is but a picture of the invisible, wherein as in a portrait things are not truly, but in equivocal shapes, and as they counterfeit some more real substance in that invisible fabric.

XIII. That other attribute wherewith I recreate my devotion, is his Wisdom, in which I am happy; and for the contemplation of this only, do not repent me that I was bred in the way of study: the advantage I have of the vulgar, with the content and happiness I conceive therein, is an ample recompence for all my endeavours, in what part of knowledge soever. Wisdom is his most beauteous attribute; no man can attain unto it, yet Solomon pleased God when he desired it. He is wife, because he knows all things; and he knoweth all things, because he made them all: but his greatest knowledge is in comprehending that he made not, that is, himself. And this is also the greatest knowledge in man: for this I do honour my own profession, and embrace the counsel even of the devil

himſelf: had he read ſuch a lecture in
Paradiſe as he did at Delphos,* we had
better known ourſelves, nor had we ſtood
in fear to know him. I know He is wiſe
in all, wonderful in what we conceive,
but far more in what we comprehend not;
for we behold him but aſquint, upon reflex or ſhadow; our underſtanding is dim-
mer than Moſes' eye; we are ignorant of
the back parts or lower ſide of his divinity; therefore to pry into the maze of
his counſels, is not only folly in man, but
preſumption even in angels: like us, they
are his ſervants, not his ſenators; he holds
no council, but that myſtical one of the
Trinity, wherein though there be three
perſons, there is but one mind that decrees without contradiction: nor needs he
any; his actions are not begot with deliberation, his wiſdom naturally knows what
is beſt; his intellect ſtands ready fraught
with the ſuperlative and pureſt ideas of
gcodneſs; conſultation and election, which
are two motions in us, make but one in

---

* Γνῶθι σεαυτὸν, *Noſce te ipſum.*

him; his actions springing from his power,
at the first touch of his will. These are
contemplations metaphysical: my humble
speculations have another method, and are
content to trace and discover those expres-
sions he hath left in his creatures, and the
obvious effects of nature: there is no danger to profound these mysteries, no *sanc-
tum sanctorum* in philosophy. The world
was made to be inhabited by beasts, but
studied and contemplated by man:* 'tis
the debt of our reason we owe unto God,
and the homage we pay for not being
beasts: without this, the world is still as
though it had not been, or as it was before the sixth day, when as yet there was
not a creature that could conceive or say
there was a world. The wisdom of God
receives small honour from those vulgar
heads that rudely stare about, and with a
gross rusticity admire his works: those
highly magnify him, whose judicious in-

No danger
in attempt-
ing to trace
the hand of
God in his
Works.

---

* In the MS. (in the British Museum) this clause
stands thus: "The world was made not so much to
be inhabited by men, as to be contemplated, studied,
and known, by man."

quiry into his acts, and deliberate research
into his creatures, return the duty of a
devout and learned admiration. Therefore,

> Search while thou wilt, and let thy reason go
> To ransom truth, even to th' abyss below;
> Rally the scattered causes; and that line
> Which nature twists, be able to untwine.
> It is thy Maker's will, for unto none
> But unto reason can he e'er be known.
> The devils do know thee, but those damn'd meteors
> Build not thy glory, but confound thy creatures.
> Teach my endeavours so thy works to read,
> That learning them in thee I may proceed.
> Give thou my reason that instructive flight,
> Whose weary wings may on thy hands still light.
> Teach me to soar aloft, yet ever so,
> When near the sun, to stoop again below.
> Thus shall my humble feathers safely hover,
> And though near earth, more than the heavens dif-
>   cover.
> And then at last, when homeward I shall drive
> Rich with the spoils of nature to my hive,
> There will I sit like that industrious fly,
> Buzzing thy praises, which shall never die,
> Till death abrupts them, and succeeding glory
> Bid me go on in a more lasting story.

And this is almost all wherein an
humble creature may endeavour to re-

quite, and some way to retribute unto his Creator : for if not he that saith, " Lord, Lord, but he that doth the will of his Father," shall be saved; certainly our wills must be our performances, and our intents make out our actions; otherwise our pious labours shall find anxiety in our graves, and our best endeavours not hope, but fear a resurrection.

St. Matt. vii. 21.

XVI. There is but one first cause, and four second causes of all things :* some are without efficient, as God ; others without matter, as angels ; some without form, as the first matter : but every essence created or uncreated hath its final cause, and some positive end both of its

Every created essence hath its proper end.

* One kind of cause is the matter of which any thing is made, as bronze of a statue (material); another is the form and pattern, as the cause of an octave is the ratio of two to one (formal); again, there is the cause which is the origin of the production, as the father of the child (efficient); and again, there is the end, or that for the sake of which any thing is done, as health is the cause of walking (final). Arist. Phys. ii. 3.

essence and operation :* this is the cause
I grope after in the works of nature; on
this hangs the providence of God: to
raise so beauteous a structure, as the world
and the creatures thereof, was but his art;
but their sundry and divided operations,
with their predestinated ends, are from
the treasury of his wisdom. In the causes,
nature, and affections of the eclipses of the
sun and moon, there is most excellent spe-
culation; but to profound farther, and to
contemplate a reason why his providence
hath so disposed and ordered their motions in that vast circle, as to conjoin and
obscure each other, is a sweeter piece of
reason, and a diviner point of philosophy;
therefore sometimes, and in some things,
there appears to me as much divinity in
Galen his books *De usu partium*, as in
Suarez his Metaphysics: had Aristotle
been as curious in the enquiry of this

* Eterne God, that thurgh thy purveance
  Ledest this world by certain governance,
  In idel, as men sain, ye nothing make.
      CHAUCER, Frankeleine's Tale, 11176.

caufe as he was of the other, he had not left behind him an imperfect piece of philofophy, but an abfolute tract of divinity.

xv. *Natura nihil agit fruftra*, is the only indifputable axiom in philofophy; there are no grotefques in nature; not any thing framed to fill up empty cantons, and unneceffary fpaces: in the moft imperfect creatures, and fuch as were not preferved in the ark, but having their feeds and principles in the womb of nature, are every where, where the power of the fun is;* in thefe is the wifdom of his hand difcovered: out of this rank Solomon chofe the object of his admiration; indeed what reafon may not go to fchool to the wifdom of bees, ants, and

Nature doeth nothing in vain.

Prov. vi. 6—8. xxx. 24—28.

---

* Miraculous may feem to him that reades
  So ftrange enfample of conception;
But reafon teacheth that the fruitful feedes
  Of all things living, thro' impreffion
Of the fun-beames in moyft complexion
Doe life conceive, and quick'ned are by kynd.
                              Faerie Queene.

ſpiders? what wiſe hand teacheth them to do what reaſon cannot teach us? Ruder heads ſtand amazed at thoſe prodigious pieces of nature, whales, elephants, dromedaries and camels; theſe, I confeſs, are the coloſſi and majeſtic pieces of her hand: but in theſe narrow engines there is more curious mathematics; and the civility of theſe little citizens, more neatly ſets forth the wiſdom of their Maker. Who admires not Regio-Montanus his fly beyond his eagle,* or wonders not more at the operation of two ſouls in thoſe little bodies, than but one in the trunk of a cedar?† I could never content my contemplation with thoſe general pieces of wonder, the flux and reflux of the ſea, the increaſe of the Nile, the converſion of the needle to the north; and have ſtudied to match and parallel thoſe in the more obvious and neglected pieces of nature, which without further travel I can do in the coſmography of

---

* See Appendix C.
† See Appendix D.

myself: we carry with us the wonders we seek without us: there is all Africa and her prodigies in us; we are that bold and adventurous piece of nature, which he that studies wisely learns in a compendium, what others labour at in a divided piece and endless volume.

XVI. Thus there are two books from whence I collect my divinity; besides that written one of God, another of his servant nature, that universal and public manuscript, that lies expansed unto the eyes of all:* those that never saw him in the one, have discovered him in the other. This was the Scripture and Theology of the heathens: the natural motion of the sun made them more admire him, than its supernatural station did the children of Israel; the ordinary effect of nature wrought more admiration in them, than in the other all his miracles: surely the heathens knew better how to join and

Nature a Bible open to all.

Josh. x. 12, 13.

---

* Cf. Keble's Christian Year. Septuagesima Sunday.

read thefe myftical letters, than we Chriftians, who caft a more carelefs eye on thefe common hieroglyphics, and difdain to fuck divinity from the flowers of nature. Nor do I fo forget God as to adore the name of nature; which I define not, with the fchools, to be the principle of motion and reft, but that ftraight and regular line, that fettled and conftant courfe the wifdom of God hath ordained the actions of his creatures, according to their feveral kinds. To make a revolution every day, is the nature of the fun, becaufe of that neceffary courfe which God hath ordained it, from which it cannot fwerve but by a faculty from that voice which firft did give it motion.*

---

* Cf. Wordfworth's Ode to Duty, vol. v. p. 48.
" Thou doft preferve the ftars from wrong;
And the moft ancient heavens thro' thee, are frefh
     and ftrong."

   Cf. Cowper's Tafk, bk. vi.
" Some fay that in the origin of things,
When all creation ftarted into birth,
The infant elements received a law
From which they fwerve not fince. That under force

Now this courfe of nature God feldom
alters or perverts, but, like an excellent
artift, hath fo contrived his work, that
with the felf fame inftrument, without a
new creation, he may effect his obfcureft
defigns. Thus he fweeteneth the water
with a wood, preferveth the creatures in
the ark, which the blaft of his mouth
might have as eafily created; for God is
like a fkilful geometrician, who when
more eafily, and with one ftroke of his
compafs, he might defcribe or divide a
right line, had yet rather do this in a circle or longer way, according to the con-
ftituted and forelaid principles of his art:
yet this rule of his he doth fometimes
pervert, to acquaint the world with his

Ex. xv. 25.
Ecclus.
xxxviii. 5.

Of that controlling ordinance they move,
And need not his immediate hand who firft
Prefcribed their courfe, to regulate it now.

*   *   *   *   *

The Lord of all, himfelf through all diffuf'd,
Suftains and is the life of all that lives.
Nature is but a name for an effect,
Whofe caufe is God."

Cf. Butler's Anal. pt. i. c. 2.

prerogative, left the arrogancy of our reason should question his power, and conclude he could not. And thus I call the effects of nature the works of God, whose hand and instrument she only is; and therefore to ascribe his actions unto her, is to devolve the honour of the principal agent upon the instrument; which if with reason we may do, then let our hammers rise up and boast they have built our houses, and our pens receive the honour of our writing. I hold there is a general beauty in the works of God, and therefore no deformity in any kind of species whatsoever: I cannot tell by what logic we call a toad, a bear, or an elephant ugly, they being created in those outward shapes and figures which best express those actions of their inward forms. And having passed that general visitation of God, who saw that all that he had made was good, that is, conformable to his will, which abhors deformity, and is the rule of order and beauty; there is no deformity but in monstrosity, wherein notwithstanding there is a kind of beauty,

Ecclus.
xxxix. 33.
34.

Wisd. xv.
18.

Gen. i. 31.

nature fo ingenioufly contriving the irregular parts, that they become fometimes
more remarkable than the principal fabric. To fpeak yet more narrowly, there
was never any thing ugly or mifhapen,
but the chaos; wherein, notwithftanding,
to speak ftrictly, there was no deformity,
becaufe no form, nor was it yet impreg-
nate by the voice of God; now nature
is not at variance with art, nor art with
nature, they being both fervants of his
providence: art is the perfection of nature: were the world now as it was the
fixth day, there were yet a chaos; nature
hath made one world, and art another.
In brief, all things are artificial; for nature is the art of God.

" Nature the art whereby God doth govern the world."

XVII. This is the ordinary
and open way of his providence, which
art and induftry have in a good part difcovered, whofe effects we may foretel
without an oracle: to forefhew thefe, is
not prophecy, but prognoftication. There
is another way, full of meanders and laby-
rinths, whereof the devil and fpirits have

Providence often falfely called For-tune.

no exact Ephemerides, and that is a more
particular and obscure method of his providence, directing the operations of individuals and single essences : this we call fortune, that serpentine and crooked line,
whereby he draws those actions his wisdom
intends, in a more unknown and secret way.
This cryptic and involved method of his
providence have I ever admired ; nor can
I relate the history of my life, the occurrences of my days, the escapes of dan-
gers, and hits of chance, with a *Bezo las
Manos* to fortune, or a bare gramercy to
my good stars.   Abraham might have
thought the ram in the thicket came thi-
ther by accident ; human reason would
have said, that mere chance conveyed
Moses in the ark to the sight of Pharaoh's daughter : what a labyrinth is there
in the story of Joseph, able to convert a
stoic ?   Surely there are in every man's
life certain rubs, doublings, and wrenches,
which pass a while under the effects of
chance, but at the last, well examined,
prove the mere hand of God.   It was
not dumb chance that, to discover the

Gen. xxii.
13.

Ex. ii.

Gen. xxxvii.

fougade or powder-plot, contrived a mif-
carriage in the letter. I like the victory
of 88 the better for that one occurrence,
which our enemies imputed to our difhonour, and the partiality of fortune, to
wit, the tempefts and contrariety of winds.
King Philip did not detract from the nation, when he faid, he fent his armado to
fight with men, and not to combat with
the winds. Where there is a manifeft dif-
proportion between the powers and forces
of two feveral agents, upon a maxim of
reafon we may promife the victory to the
fuperior; but when unexpected accidents
flip in, and unthought of occurrences in-
tervene, thefe muft proceed from a power
that owes no obedience to thofe axioms;
where, as in the writing upon the wall, Dan. v. 5.
we may behold the hand, but fee not the
fpring that moves it. The fuccefs of
that petty province of Holland (of which
the grand Seignior proudly faid, if they
fhould trouble him as they did the Spaniard, he would fend his men with fho-
vels and pickaxes, and throw it into the
fea) I cannot altogether afcribe to the in-

genuity and industry of the people, but the mercy of God, that hath disposed them to such a thriving genius ; and to the will of his providence, that disposeth her favour to each country in their preordinate season. All cannot be happy at once ; for, because the glory of one state depends upon the ruin of another, there is a revolution and vicissitude of their greatness ; and they must obey the swing of that wheel, not moved by intelligences, but by the hand of God, whereby all estates arise to their zenith and vertical points, according to their predestinated periods. For the lives, not only of men, but of commonwealths, and the whole world, run not upon an *helix* that still enlargeth, but on a circle, where arriving to their meridian, they decline in obscurity, and fall under the horizon again.*

---

* This subject is discussed in an Essay by the Rev. A. P. Stanley, to which one of the Chancellor's Prizes was awarded. Oxford, 1840.

Cf. Herod. i. 207.

XVIII. These must not there-
fore be named the effects of fortune but
in a relative way, and as we term the
works of nature : it was the ignorance of
man's reason that begat this very name,
and by a careless term miscalled the providence of God ; for there is no liberty
for causes to operate in a loose and strag-
gling way ; nor any effect whatsoever,
but hath its warrant from some universal
or superior cause. It is not a ridiculous
devotion to say a prayer before a game
at tables ; for even in *sortilegies* and matters of greatest uncertainty, there is a
settled and preordered course of effects.*
It is we that are blind, not fortune : because our eye is too dim to discover the
mystery of her effects, we foolishly paint
her blind, and hoodwink the providence
of the Almighty.† I cannot justify that
contemptible proverb, *That fools only are*

---

* " The lot is cast into the lap : but the whole
disposing thereof is of the Lord." Prov. xvi. 33.

† Cf. Bp. Butler's xv th Sermon.

fortunate, or that insolent paradox, *That a wise man is out of the reach of fortune*, much less those opprobrious epithets of poets, *Whore*, *baud*, and *strumpet*.* It is, I confess, the common fate of men of singular gifts of mind, to be destitute of those of fortune, which doth not any way deject the spirit of wiser judgments, who thoroughly understand the justice of this proceeding; and being enriched with higher donatives, cast a more careless eye on these vulgar parts of felicity. It is a most unjust ambition to desire to engross the mercies of the Almighty, not to be content with the goods of mind, without a possession of those of body or fortune; and it is an error worse than heresy, to adore these complemental and circumstantial pieces of felicity, and undervalue those perfections and essential points of happiness wherein we resemble

---

* So Dryden :

> " But when she dances on the wind,
> And shakes her wings, and will not stay,
> I puff the prostitute away."

our Maker. To wiſer deſires it is ſatiſ-
faction enough to deſerve, though not to
enjoy the favours of fortune: let providence provide for fools; it is not partiality, but equity in God, who deals
with us but as our natural parents: thoſe
that are able of body and mind he leaves
to their deſerts; to thoſe of weaker merits
he imparts a larger portion, and pieces out
the defect of one by the exceſs of the
other. Thus have we no juſt quarrel
with nature for leaving us naked; or to
envy the horns, hoofs, ſkins, and furs of
other creatures, being provided with reaſon, that can ſupply them all.* We need
not labour with ſo many arguments to
confute judicial aſtrology; for if there be
a truth therein, it doth not injure divinity: if to be born under Mercury diſ-
poſeth us to be witty, under Jupiter to be

---

* He were a ſtrange fool that ſhould be angry
becauſe dogs and ſheep need no ſhoes, and yet himſelf is full of care to get ſome: God hath ſupplied
thoſe needs to them by natural proviſions, and to
thee by an artificial: for He hath given thee reaſon
to learn a trade, or ſome means to make or buy them,

wealthy; I do not owe a knee unto these, but unto that merciful hand that hath ordered my indifferent and uncertain nativity unto such benevolous aspects. Those that hold that all things are governed by fortune, had not erred, had they not persisted there. The Romans that erected a temple to Fortune, acknowledged therein, though in a blinder way, somewhat of divinity; for in a wise supputation all things begin and end in the Almighty. There is a nearer way to heaven than Homer's chain; † an easy logic may conjoin heaven and earth in one argument,

---

so that it only differs in the manner of our provision; and which had you rather want, shoes or reason? Taylor's Holy Living, p. 99.

So Anacreon —

φύσις κερατα ταύροις
ὁπλας δ᾽ ἐδωκεν ἱπποις
ποδωκίην λαγωοῖς,
λεουσι χασμ᾽ ὁδόντων,
τοῖς ἰχθυσιν τὸ νηκτον,
τοῖς ὀρνέοις πετασθαι
τοῖς ἀνδρασιν φρονημα.

† Iliad, viii. 18.

and with less than a *forites* resolve all
things into God. For though we christen
effects by their most sensible and nearest
causes, yet is God the true and infallible
cause of all, whose concourse, though it
be general, yet doth it subdivide itself
into the particular actions of every thing,
and is that spirit, by which each singular
essence not only subsists, but performs its
operation.

xix. The bad construction
and perverse comment on these pair of
second causes, or visible hands of God,
have perverted the devotion of many
unto atheism, who forgetting the honest
advisoes of faith, have listened unto the
conspiracy of passion and reason. I have,
therefore, always endeavoured to com-
pose those feuds and angry dissentions between affection, faith, and reason; for
there is in our soul a kind of triumvirate,
or triple government of three competi-
tors, which distract the peace of this our
commonwealth, not less than did that
other the state of Rome.

Danger of confounding the First with Second causes.

As reaſon is a rebel unto faith, ſo paſſion unto reaſon: as the propoſitions of faith ſeem abſurd unto reaſon, ſo the theorems of reaſon unto paſſion, and both unto reaſon;* yet a moderate and peaceable diſcretion may ſo ſtate and order the matter, that they may be all kings, and yet make but one monarchy, every one exerciſing his ſovereignty and prerogative in a due time and place, according to the reſtraint and limit of circumſtance. There are, as in philoſophy, ſo in divinity, ſturdy doubts and boiſterous objections, wherewith the unhappineſs of our knowledge too nearly acquainteth us. More of theſe no man hath known than myſelf, which I confeſs I conquered, not in a martial poſture, but on my knees. For our endeavours are not only to combat with doubts, but always to diſpute with the devil: the villany of that ſpirit takes a hint of infidelity from our ſtudies, and by demonſtrating a naturality in one way, makes us miſtruſt a miracle in another. Thus hav-

---

*· *Reaſon.* So in all the editions: quære, Faith.

ing perused the *Archidoxes*, and read the secret sympathies of things, he would dissuade my belief from the miracle of the brazen serpent, make me conceit that image worked by sympathy, and was but an Egyptian trick to cure their diseases without a miracle. Again, having seen some experiments of *bitumen*, and having read far more of *naphtha*, he whispered to my curiosity the fire of the altar might be natural; and bid me mistrust a miracle in Elias,* when he entrenched the altar round with water; for that inflammable substance yields not easily unto water, but flames in the arms of its antagonist. And thus would he inveigle my belief to think the combustion of Sodom might be natural, and that there was an asphaltic and bituminous nature in that lake before the fire of Gomorrah. I know that manna is now plentifully gathered in Calabria; and Josephus tells me, in his days it was as plentiful in Arabia; the devil therefore made the query, Where was

1 Kings, xviii.

Gen. xix. 24.

---

* Cf. Pseud. Epidem. vii. 15.

Ex. xvi.

then the miracle in the days of Moſes? The Iſraelites ſaw but that in his time, which the natives of thoſe countries behold in ours. Thus the devil played at cheſs with me, and yielding a pawn, thought to gain a queen of me, taking advantage of my honeſt endeavours; and whilſt I laboured to raiſe the ſtructure of my reaſon, he ſtrived to undermine the edifice of my faith.

Atheiſm can hardly exiſt.

xx. Neither had theſe, or any other, ever ſuch advantage of me, as to incline me to any point of infidelity or deſperate poſitions of atheiſm; for I have been theſe many years of opinion there was never any. Thoſe that held religion was the difference of man from beaſts, have ſpoken probably, and proceed upon a principle as inductive as the other. That doctrine of Epicurus, that denied the providence of God, was no atheiſm, but a magnificent and high-ſtrained conceit of his majeſty, which he deemed too ſublime to mind the trivial actions of thoſe inferior creatures. That fatal neceffity of the ftoics is nothing but the immutable law of his will. Thofe that heretofore denied the divinity of the Holy Ghoft, have been condemned but as heretics; and thofe that now deny our Saviour, (though more than heretics,) are not fo much as atheifts; for though they deny two perfons in the Trinity, they hold as we do, there is but one God.

That villain and fecretary of hell, that compofed that mifcreant piece of the three impoftors, though divided from all religions, and was neither Jew, Turk, nor Chriftian, was not a pofitive atheift. I confefs every country hath its Machiavel, every age its Lucian, whereof common heads muft not hear, nor more advanced judgments too rafhly venture on: it is the rhetoric of Satan, and may pervert a loofe or prejudicate belief.

XXI. I confefs I have perufed them all, and can difcover nothing that may ftartle a difcreet belief; yet are their heads carried off with the wind and breath of fuch motives. I remember a Doctor

Inconfiftency of un belief.

in Phyſic of Italy, who could not per-
fectly believe the immortality of the ſoul,
becauſe Galen ſeemed to make a doubt
thereof. With another I was familiarly
acquainted in France, a divine, and a man
of ſingular parts, that on, the ſame point
was ſo plunged and gravelled with three
lines of Seneca, that all our antidotes,
drawn from both Scripture and philoſophy, could not expel the poiſon of his
error. There are a ſet of heads, that
can credit the relations of mariners, yet
queſtion the teſtimonies of St. Paul; and
peremptorily maintain the traditions of
Ælian or Pliny, yet in hiſtories of Scripture raiſe queries and objections, believing
no more than they can parallel in human
authors. I confeſs there are in Scripture,
ſtories that do exceed the fables of poets,
and to a captious reader ſound like Gara-
gantua or Bevis: ſearch all the legends
of times paſt, and the fabulous conceits
of theſe preſent, and it will be hard to
find one that deſerves to carry the buckler
unto Samſon; yet is all this of an eaſy
poſſibility, if we conceive a divine con-

course, or an influence but from the little finger of the Almighty. It is impossible that either in the discourse of man, or in the infallible voice of God, to the weakness of our apprehensions, there should not appear irregularities, contradictions, and antinomies: myself could shew a catalogue of doubts, never yet imagined or questioned, as I know, which are not resolved at the first hearing; not fantastic queries or objections of air, for I cannot hear of atoms in divinity.* I can read the history of the pigeon that was sent out of the ark and returned no more, yet not question how she found out her mate that was left behind: that Lazarus was raised from the dead, yet not demand where in the interim his soul awaited; or raise a law-case, whether his heir might lawfully detain his inheritance bequeathed unto him by his death, and he, though

* " He who believes the Scripture to have proceeded from him who is the Author of Nature, may well expect to find the same sort of difficulties in it, as are found in the Constitution of Nature." Origen, quoted by Butler in Introduct. to Anal.

restored to life, have no plea or title unto his former possessions. Whether Eve was framed out of the left side of Adam, I dispute not, because I stand not yet assured which is the right side of a man, or whether there be any such distinction in nature: that she was edified out of the rib of Adam I believe, yet raise no question who shall arise with that rib at the resurrection:* whether Adam was an hermaphrodite, as the Rabbins contend upon the letter of the text, because it is contrary to reason, that there should be an hermaphrodite, before there was a woman, or a composition of two natures, before there was a second composed. Likewise, whether the world was created in autumn, summer, or spring,† because it was created in them all; for whatsoever sign the sun possesseth, those four seasons are actually existent. It is the nature of this luminary to distinguish the several seasons of the year, all which it makes at one

* Cf. Pseud. Epidem. lib. vii. cap. 2.
† Ibid. lib. vi. cap. 2.

time in the whole earth, and succeffive in any part thereof. There are a bundle of curiofities, not only in philofophy, but in divinity, propofed and difcuffed by men of moft fuppofed abilities, which indeed are not worthy our vacant hours, much lefs our ferious ftudies: pieces only fit to be placed in Pantagruel's library, or bound up with Tartaretus *de modo cacandi.*

XXII. Thefe are niceties that become not thofe that perufe fo ferious a myftery. There are others more generally queftioned and called to the bar, yet methinks of an eafy and poffible truth.

And others which are often raifed, may be eafily folved.

It is ridiculous to put off, or drown the general flood of Noah, in that particular inundation of Deucalion: that there was a deluge once, feems not to me fo great a miracle, as that there is not one always. How all the kinds of creatures, not only in their own bulks, but with a competency of food and fuftenance, might be preferved in one ark, and within the extent of three hundred cubits, to a reafon

that rightly examines it, will appear very
feasible. There is another secret not contained in the scripture, which is more
hard to comprehend, and put the honest
Father to the refuge of a miracle;* and
that is, not only how the distinct pieces
of the world, and divided islands should
be first planted by men, but inhabited by
tigers, panthers, and bears. How America abounded with beasts of prey and
noxious animals, yet contained not in it
that necessary creature, a horse, is very
strange. By what passage those animals,
not only birds, but dangerous and unwel-
come beasts came over; how there be creatures there, which are not found in this
triple continent; all which must needs
be strange unto us, that hold but one
ark, and that the creatures began their
progress from the mountains of Ararat.
They who to salve this would make the

---

* St. Augustine (De Civ. Dei, xvi. 7), says that
this might have been miraculously effected, but he
does not say it could not have been done without a
miracle. See Burnet's Sacred Theory of the Earth,
lib. ii. c. 8.

deluge particular, proceed upon a principle that I can no way grant; not only
upon the negative of Holy Scriptures,
but of mine own reason, whereby I can
make it probable, that the world was as
well peopled in the time of Noah as in
ours; and fifteen hundred years to people the world, as full a time for them, as
four thousand years since have been to
us.* There are other assertions and common tenets drawn from Scripture, and generally believed as Scripture, whereunto
notwithstanding, I would never betray
the liberty of my reason. 'Tis a pos-
tulate to me, that Methusalem was the
longest lived of all the children of Adam;
and no man will be able to prove it, when
from the process of the text I can manifest it may be otherwise.† That Judas
perished by hanging himself, there is no
certainty in Scripture; though in one

Gen. v. 5.
25—27.

S. Matt.
xxvii. 5.

* Cf. Pseud. Epidem. vi. 6.

† His meaning is, that as Adam was created a
man in the prime of life, we may add forty years to
the term of his actual existence. Cf. Sect. xxxix.
Pseud. Epidem. vii. 3.

place it seems to affirm it, and by a doubtful word hath given occasion to translate
it; yet in another place, in a more punctual description, it makes it improbable,
and seems to overthrow it.* That our
fathers, after the flood, erected the tower
of Babel,† to preserve themselves against
a second deluge, is generally opinioned
and believed; yet is there another intention of theirs expressed in scripture: besides, it is improbable from the circum-
stance of the place, that is, a plain in the
land of Shinar: these are no points of
faith, and therefore may admit a free dispute. There are yet others, and those familiarly concluded from the text, wherein
(under favour) I see no consequence. The
church of Rome confidently proves the
opinion of tutelary angels, from that an-
swer when Peter knocked at the door, *it
is not he, but his angel*; that is, might

Acts, i. 18.

Gen. xi. 4.

Acts, xii.
15.

---

* The apparent discrepancy is easily reconciled by
supposing that after he had suspended himself the
rope broke, when he fell down headlong and burst
asunder.

† Pseudodox. Epidem. lib. vii. cap. 6.

some say, his messenger, or somebody from him; for so the original signifies, and is as likely to be the doubtful family's meaning. This exposition I once suggested to a young divine, that answered upon this point; to which I remember the Franciscan opponent replied no more, but, *that it was a new, and no authentic interpretation.*

XXIII. These are but the conclusions and fallible discourses of man upon the word of God, for such I do believe the Holy Scriptures; yet were it of man, I could not choose but say, it was the singularest and superlative piece that hath been extant since the creation. Were I a pagan I should not refrain the lecture of it; and cannot but commend the judgment of Ptolemy,* that thought not his library complete without it. The Alco-

The Bible the best of books.

---

* When Ptolemy Philadelphus, king of Egypt, founded the library at Alexandria, he placed it under the care of Demetrius Phalereus, an Athenian, who persuaded his royal master to add to it the books of the Jewish law. The king wrote to Eleazar, then

ran of the Turks, (I fpeak without prejudice,) is an ill-compofed piece, containing
in it vain and ridiculous errors in philofophy, impoffibilities, fictions, and vanities
beyond laughter; maintained by evident
and open fophifms, the policy of ignorance, depofition of univerfities, and ba-
nifhment of learning: this hath gotten
foot by arms and violence: that without
a blow hath diffeminated itfelf through
the whole earth. It is not unremarkable
what Philo firft obferved, that the law of
Mofes continued two thoufand years without the leaft alteration; whereas, we fee
the laws of other commonweals do alter
with occafions; and even thofe that pretended their original from fome divinity,
to have vanifhed without trace or memory. I believe, befides Zoroafter, there
were divers that writ before Mofes, who,

high prieft, for them; who not only fent him the
books, but with them feventy-two interpreters, fkilled
in both the Hebrew and Greek tongues, to tranflate
them for him into Greek. Their labours produced
the verfion called the Septuagint.

notwithstanding have suffered the common fate of time. Men's works have an age like themselves; and though they outlive their authors, yet have they a stint and period to their duration: this only is a work too hard for the teeth of time, and cannot perish but in the general flames, when all things shall confess their ashes.

XXIV. I have heard some with deep sighs lament the lost lines of Cicero; others with as many groans deplore the combustion of the library of Alexandria;* for my own part, I think there be too many in the world, and could with patience behold the urn and ashes of the Vatican, could I, with a few others, recover the perished leaves of Solomon. I would not omit a copy of Enoch's Pillars had they many nearer authors than Josephus,† or did not relish somewhat of

"Of making many books there is no end," Eccl. xii. 12.

1 Kings iv. 32, 33.

---

* See D'Israeli's Curios. of Lit. p. 17.

† For this, the story is, that Enoch, or his father Seth, having been informed by Adam, that the world was to perish once by water, and a second time by

the fable. Some men have written more than others have spoken; Pineda quotes more authors in one work, than are neceffary in a whole world.* Of thofe three great inventions in Germany, there are two which are not without their incommodities.† It is not a melancholy

---

fire, did caufe two pillars to be erected; the one of ftone againft the water, and another of brick againft the fire; and that upon thofe pillars was engraven all fuch learning as had been delivered to, or invented by mankind; and that thence it came that all knowledge and learning was not loft by means of the flood, by reafon that one of the pillars (though the other perifhed) did remain after the flood: and Jofephus witneffeth, till his time, lib. i. Antiq. Judaic. cap. 3. K. This, though a tale, is truly moralized in our univerfities: Cambridge (of brick) and Oxford (of ftone) wherein learning and religion are preferved, and where the worft college is more fightworthy than the beft Dutch gymnafium. Fuller's Holy State, xliv.

* *Pineda*, in his *Monarchia Ecclefiaftica*, quotes one thoufand and forty authors.

† In all probability he means printing, gunpowder, and the mariner's compafs, or perhaps clocks: but it feems doubtful whether all thefe were not known to the Chinefe before the generally received date of their invention.

utinam of my own, but the defires of better heads, that there were a general fynod; not to unite the incompatible difference of religion, but for the benefit of learning, to reduce it as it lay at firft, in a few and folid authors; and to condemn to the fire thofe fwarms and millions of rhapfodies begotten only to diftract and abufe the weaker judgments of fcholars, and to maintain the trade and myftery of typographers.

XXV. I cannot but wonder with what exceptions the Samaritans could confine their belief to the Pentateuch, or five books of Mofes. I am afhamed at the rabbinical interpretation of the Jews, upon the old Teftament, as much as their defection from the new: and truly it is beyond wonder, how that contemptible and degenerate iffue of Jacob, once fo devoted to ethnic fuperftition, and fo eafily feduced to the idolatry of their neighbours, fhould now in fuch an obftinate and peremptory belief adhere unto their own doctrine, expect impoffibilities, and, in the face and

Obftinacy of the Jews

eye of the Church, perſiſt without the
leaſt hope of converſion : this is a vice in
them, that were a virtue in us ; for obſtinacy in a bad cauſe is but conſtancy in a

and want
of Con-
ſtancy
among
Chriſtians.

good.　And herein I muſt accuſe thoſe
of my own religion, for there is not any
of ſuch a fugitive faith, ſuch an unſtable
belief, as a Chriſtian ; none that do ſo
often transform themſelves, not unto ſeveral ſhapes of Chriſtianity, and of the ſame
ſpecies, but unto more unnatural and contrary forms of Jew and Mahometan ; that
from the name of Saviour, can condeſcend
to the bare term of prophet ; and from
an old belief that he is come, fall to a
new expectation of his coming.　It is the
promiſe of Chriſt to make us all one
flock ; but how and when this union ſhall
be, is as obſcure to me as the laſt day.
Of thoſe four members of religion we
hold a ſlender proportion :* there are, I
confeſs, ſome new additions, yet ſmall to
thoſe which accrue to our adverſaries, and

---

* The population of our globe has been divided
thus :

thofe only drawn from the revolt of Pagans, men but of negative impieties, and
fuch as deny Chrift, but becaufe they
never heard of him : but the religion of
the Jew is expreffly againft the Chriftian,
and the Mahometan againft both ; for
the Turk in the bulk he now ftands, is
beyond all hope of converfion ; if he fall
afunder, there may be conceived hopes,
but not without ftrong improbabilities.
The Jew is obftinate in all fortunes ; the
perfecution of fifteen hundred years hath
but confirmed them in their error : they
have already endured whatfoever may be
inflicted, and have fuffered in a bad caufe,
even to the condemnation of their enemies.   Perfecution is a bad and indirect
way to plant religion : it hath been the
unhappy method of angry devotions, not
only to confirm honeft religion, but wicked

Chriftians	.	.	.	.	.	260,000,000
Jews	.	.	.	.	.	4,000,000
Mahometans		.	.	.	.	96,000,000
Idolaters of all forts			.	.	.	500,000,000
Total population of the world						860,000,000

herefies, and extravagant opinions. It was
the firft ftone and bafis of our faith; none
can more juftly boaft of perfecutions and
glory in the number and valour of martyrs; for, to fpeak properly, thofe are
true and almoft only examples of fortitude: thofe that are fetched from the
field, or drawn from the actions of the
camp, are not oft times fo truly prece-
dents of valour as audacity, and at the
beft attain but to fome baftard piece of
fortitude: if we fhall ftrictly examine the
circumftances and requifites which Ariftotle requires to true and perfect valour,*
we fhall find the name only in his mafter
Alexander, and as little in that Roman
worthy, Julius Cæfar; and if any, in that
eafy and active way, have done fo nobly
as to deferve that name, yet in the paffive
and more terrible piece, thefe have fur-
paffed, and in a more heroical way may
claim the honour of that title. It is not

---

* Thefe are a juft perception of danger, and refolution to fuftain it for the fake of the noblenefs of fo
doing. Ethic Nicom. iii. 10.

in the power of every honeſt faith to proceed thus far, or paſs to heaven through
the flames : every one hath it not in that
full meaſure, nor in ſo audacious and
reſolute a temper, as to endure thoſe terrible teſts and trials ; who, notwithſtanding in a peaceable way do truly adore
their Saviour, and have, no doubt, a faith
acceptable in the eyes of God.

XXVI. Now as all that die in
the war are not termed ſoldiers ; ſo neither
can I properly term all thoſe that ſuffer in
matters of religion, martyrs. The council
of Conſtance condemns John Huſs for an
heretic ; the ſtories of his own party ſtyle
him a martyr. He muſt needs offend the
divinity of both, that ſays he was neither
the one nor the other.* There are many,
(queſtionleſs,) canonized on earth, that
ſhall never be ſaints in heaven ; and have
their names in hiſtories and martyrologies,
who in the eyes of God are not ſo perfect

Not all are
martyrs
who ſuffer
in matters
of religion.

* The Bodleian MS. reads, Is it falſe divinity, if
I ſay he was neither one or the other?

martyrs as was that wife heathen Socrates, that fuffered on a fundamental point of religion, the unity of God. I have often pitied that miferable bifhop that fuffered in the caufe of Antipodes; * yet cannot choofe but accufe him of as much madnefs, for expofing his living on fuch a trifle; as thofe of ignorance and folly, that condemned him. I think my confcience will not give me the lie, if I fay there are not many extant that in a noble way fear the face of death lefs than myfelf; yet from the moral duty I owe to the commandment of God, and the natural refpects that I tender unto the confervation of my effence and being, I would not perifh upon a ceremony, politic points, or indifferency: nor is my belief of that untractable temper, as not to bow at their obftacles, or connive at matters wherein there are not manifeft impieties; the leaven therefore and ferment of all, not only civil

---

* This was Virgilius, Bifhop of Saltzburg. He died Nov. 27, 780. See Curiof. of Literature, i. p. 49, and Whewell's Hiftory of the Inductive Sciences, vol. i. p. 256.

but religious actions, is wisdom; without which, to commit ourselves to the flames is homicide, and, I fear, but to pass through one fire into another.

XXVII. That miracles are ceased, I can neither prove, nor absolutely deny, much less define the time and period of their cessation: that they survived Christ, is manifest upon record of Scripture; that they outlived the apostles also, and were revived at the conversion of nations, many years after, we cannot deny, if we shall not question those writers whose testimonies we do not controvert in points that make for our own opinions; therefore that may have some truth in it that is reported by the Jesuits of their miracles in the Indies. I could wish it were true, or had any other testimony than their own pens: they may easily believe those miracles abroad, who daily conceive a greater at home, the transmutation of those visible elements into the body and blood of our Saviour: for the conversion of water into wine, which he wrought in Cana, or what the devil would have had him done in the wilderneſs, of ſtones into bread, compared to this, will ſcarce deſerve the name of a miracle : though indeed, to ſpeak properly, there is not one miracle greater than another, they being the extraordinary effects of the hand of God, to which all things are of an equal facility ; and to create the world, as eaſy as one ſingle creature ; for this is alſo a miracle, not only to produce effects againſt or above nature, but before nature ; and to create nature, as great a miracle as to contradict or tranſcend her. We do too narrowly define the power of God, reſtraining it to our capacities. I hold that God can do all things ; how he ſhould work contradictions I do not underſtand, yet dare not therefore deny. I cannot ſee why the angel of God ſhould queſtion Eſdras to recal the time paſt, if it were beyond his own power ; or that God ſhould poſe mortality in that which he was not able to perform himſelf. I will not ſay God cannot, but he will not, perform many things,

All equally
eaſy to
God.

2 Eſdr. iv.
5.

which we plainly affirm he cannot: this I am sure is the mannerlieft propofition, wherein, notwithftanding, I hold no paradox. For ftrictly, his power is the fame with his will, and they both with all the reft do make but one God.

XXVIII. Therefore that miracles have been, I do believe; that they may yet be wrought by the living, I do not deny; but have no confidence in thofe which are fathered on the dead; and this hath ever made me fufpect the efficacy of relics, to examine the bones, queftion the habits and appurtenances of faints, and even of Chrift himfelf. I cannot conceive why the crofs that Helena found, and whereon Chrift himfelf died, fhould have power to reftore others unto life: I excufe not Conftantine from a fall off his horfe, or a mifchief from his enemies, upon the wearing thofe nails on his bridle, which our Saviour bore upon the crofs in his hands: I compute among your *piæ fraudes*, nor many degrees before confecrated fwords and rofes, that which Bald-

All relations of miracles not to be received alike.

wyn king of Jerufalem returned the Ge-
novefe for their coft and pains in his war,
to wit, the afhes of John the Baptift.
Thofe that hold the fanctity of their fouls
doth leave behind a tincture and facred
faculty on their bodies, fpeak naturally
of miracles, and do not falve the doubt.
Now one reafon I tender fo little devotion unto relics, is, I think, the flender
and doubtful refpect I have always held
unto antiquities ; for that indeed which I
admire, is far before antiquity, that is,
eternity ; and that is, God himfelf ; who
though he be ftyled the Ancient of Days,
cannot receive the adjunct of antiquity,
who was before the world, and fhall be
after it, yet is not older than it ; for in his
years there is no climacter ; his duration
is eternity, and far more venerable than
antiquity.

Dan. vii.
9-22.

Oracles.

XXIX. But above all things, I
wonder how the curiofity of wifer heads
could pafs that great and indifputable miracle, the ceffation of oracles ;* and in

* Pfeud. Epidem. vii. 12.

what swoon their reasons lay, to content
themselves, and sit down with such a far-
fetched and ridiculous reason as Plutarch
allegeth for it. The Jews, that can believe the supernatural solstice of the sun
in the days of Joshua, have yet the im-
pudence to deny the eclipse, which every
pagan confessed at his death : but for this
it is evident beyond all contradiction, the
devil himself confessed it.* Certainly it is
not a warrantable curiosity, to examine the
verity of Scripture by the concordance of
human history, or seek to confirm the
chronology of Hester or Daniel, by the
authority of Magasthenes or Herodotus ;
I confess, I have had an unhappy curiosity
this way, till I laughed myself out of it
with a piece of Justin,† where he delivers,
that the children of Israel for being scabbed
were banished out of Egypt. And truly
since I have understood the occurrences
of the world, and know in what counterfeiting shapes, and deceitful vizards times

---

* In his oracle to Augustus.
† Justin. Hist. lib. 36. Cf. Tacitus Hist. lib. v.

preſent repreſent on the ſtage things paſt, I do believe them little more than things to come. Some have been of my opinion, and endeavoured to write the hiſtory of their own lives ; wherein Moſes hath out-gone them all, and left not only the ſtory of his life, but as ſome will have it, of his death alſo.

Witchcraft.

xxx. It is a riddle to me, how this ſtory of oracles hath not wormed out of the world that doubtful conceit of ſpirits and witches ; how ſo many learned heads ſhould ſo far forget their metaphy-ſics, and deſtroy the ladder and ſcale of creatures, as to queſtion the exiſtence of ſpirits. For my part, I have ever be-lieved, and do now know, that there are witches : they that doubt of theſe, do not only deny them, but ſpirits ; and are ob-liquely, and upon conſequence a ſort not of infidels, but atheiſts. Thoſe that to confute their incredulity deſire to ſee ap-paritions, ſhall queſtionleſs never behold any, nor have the power to be ſo much as witches ; the devil hath them already in

a herefy as capital as witchcraft; and to
appear to them, were but to convert them.
Of all the delufions wherewith he deceives
mortality, there is not any that puzzleth
me more than the legerdemain of change-
lings.* I do not credit thofe transformations of reafonable creatures into beafts,
—or that the devil hath power to tranf-
peciate a man into a horfe, who tempted
Chrift (as a trial of his divinity) to convert but ftones into bread. I could believe that fpirits ufe with man the act of
carnality, and that in both fexes; I conceive they may affume, fteal, or contrive
a body, wherein there may be action
enough to content decrepit luft, or paffion
to fatisfy more active veneries; yet in

---

* From thence a Faery thee unweeting reft,
There as thou flepft in tender fwadling band,
And her bafe Elfin brood there for thee left :
Such men do Chaungelings call, fo chaung'd by Fae-
    ries theft.

Faery Queene, i. x. 65.

Cf. Midf. Night's Dream, ii. 1.

Luther's Divine Difcourfes, folio, p. 387.

both, without a possibility of generation :*
and therefore that opinion that Antichrist
should be born of the tribe of Dan by
conjunction with the devil, is ridiculous,
and a conceit fitter for a rabbin than a
Christian.　I hold that the devil doth
really possess some men, the spirit of
melancholy others, the spirit of delusion
others ; that as the devil is concealed and
denied by some, so God and good angels
are pretended by others, whereof the late
defection † of the maid of Germany hath
left a pregnant example.

Philosophy
distinguish-
ed from
magic.

XXXI. Again, I believe that
all that use sorceries, incantations, and
spells, are not witches, or, as we term
them, magicians.　I conceive there is a
traditional magic, not learned immediately from the devil, but at second hand
from his scholars, who having once the secret betrayed, are able, and do empirically
practise without his advice, they both pro-

---

* See Taylor's Holy Living, c. 2, S. 3, p. 64.
† *defection*.　MS. W. reads detection.

ceeding upon the principles of nature;
where actives aptly conjoined to difposed
paffives, will under any mafter produce
their effects. Thus, I think at firft a
great part of philofophy was witchcraft,
which being afterward derived to one another, proved but philofophy, and was
indeed no more but the honeft effects of
nature: what invented by us, is philofophy, learned from him, is magic. We
do furely owe the difcovery of many fe-
crets to the difcovery of good and bad
angels. I could never pafs that fentence
of Paracelfus, without an afterifk, or an-
notation: *afcendens aftrum multa revelat
quærentibus magnalia naturæ, i. e. opera
Dei. I do think that many myfteries
afcribed to our own inventions have been
the courteous revelations of fpirits; for
thofe noble effences in heaven bear a
friendly regard unto their fellow natures
on earth; and therefore believe that thofe
many prodigies and ominous prognoftics,

*The fug-
geftions of
angels.*

---

* Thereby is meant our good angel appointed us
from our nativity.

which forerun the ruins of ſtates, princes, and private perſons, are the charitable premonitions of good angels, which more careleſs enquiries term but the effects of chance and nature.*

The Spirit of God diffuſed throughout the world.

XXXII. Now beſides theſe particular and divided ſpirits, there may be (for aught I know) an univerſal and common ſpirit to the whole world. It was the opinion of Plato, and it is yet of the Hermetical philoſophers: if there be a common nature that unites and ties the ſcattered and divided individuals into one ſpecies, why may there not be one that unites them all? However, I am ſure there is a common ſpirit that plays within us, yet makes no part of us; and that is, the Spirit of God, the fire and ſcintillation of that noble and mighty eſſence which is the life and radical heat of ſpirits, and thoſe eſſences that know not the virtue of the ſun; a fire quite contrary to the fire of hell: this is that

---

* See Appendix E.

Gen. i. 2.

gentle heat that brooded on the waters, and in ſix days hatched the world; this is that irradiation that diſpels the miſts of hell, the clouds of horror, fear, ſorrow, deſpair; and preſerves the region of the mind in ſerenity: whoſoever feels not the warm gale, and gentle ventilation of this ſpirit, (though I feel his pulſe,) I dare not ſay he lives: for truly without this, to me there is no heat under the tropic; nor any light, though I dwelt in the body of the ſun.

As when the labouring Sun hath wrought his track
Up to the top of lofty Cancer's back;
The icy ocean cracks, the frozen pole
Thaws with the heat of the celeſtial coal;
So when thy abſent beams begin t' impart,
Again a ſolſtice on my frozen heart,
My winter's o'er, my drooping ſpirits ſing,
And every part revives into a Spring.
But if thy quickning beams a while decline,
And with their light bleſs not this orb of mine,
A chilly froſt ſurpriſeth every member,
And in the midſt of June I feel December.
O how this earthly temper doth debaſe
The noble ſoul, in this her humble place.
Whoſe wingy nature ever doth aſpire
To reach that place whence firſt it took its fire.
Theſe flames I feel, which in my heart do dwell,

Are not thy beams, but take their fire from hell:
O quench them all, and let thy Light divine
Be as the Sun to this poor orb of mine;
And to thy facred Spirit convert thofe fires,
Whofe earthly fumes choke my devout afpires.

Of guardian and attendant fpirits.

XXXIII. Therefore for fpirits, I am fo far from denying their exiftence, that I could eafily believe, that not only whole countries, but particular perfons have their tutelary and guardian angels: * it is not a new opinion of the church of Rome, but an old one of Pythagoras and Plato; there is no herefy in it; and if not manifeftly defined in Scripture, yet is it an opinion of a good and wholefome ufe in the courfe and actions of a man's life, and would ferve as an hypothefis to falve many doubts, whereof common philofophy affordeth no folution. Now if you demand my opinion and metaphyficks of their natures, I confefs them very fhallow; moft of them in a negative way, like that of God; or in a comparative,

* Keble's Chriftian Year. Third Sunday after Trinity.

between ourselves and fellow-creatures;
for there is in this universe a stair, or
manifest scale of creatures, rising not dis-
orderly, or in confusion, but with a comely
method and proportion: between creatures of mere existence and things of life,
there is a large disproportion of nature;
between plants and animals or creatures
of sense, a wider difference; between them
and man, a far greater: and if the proportion hold on, between man and angels
there should be yet a greater. We do not
comprehend their natures, who retain the
first definition of Porphyry,* and distinguish them from ourselves by immortality; for before his fall man also was
immortal; yet must we needs affirm that
he had a different essence from the angels:
having therefore no certain knowledge of
their natures, 'tis no bad method of the
schools, whatsoever perfection we find ob-
scurely in ourselves, in a more complete
and absolute way to ascribe unto them. I
believe they have an extemporary know-

---

* Essentiæ rationalis immortalis.

ledge, and upon the firſt motion of their reaſon do what we cannot without ſtudy or deliberation; that they know things by their forms, and define by ſpecifical difference, what we deſcribe by accidents and properties; and therefore probabilities to us may be demonſtrations unto them: that they have knowledge not only of the ſpecifical, but numerical forms of individuals, and underſtand by what reſerved difference each ſingle hypoſtaſis (beſides the relation to its ſpecies) becomes its numerical ſelf: that as the ſoul hath a power to move the body it informs, ſo there's a faculty to move any, though inform none; ours upon reſtraint of time, place, and diſtance; but that inviſible hand that conveyed Habakkuk to the lion's den, or Philip to Azotus, infringeth this rule, and hath a ſecret conveyance, wherewith mortality is not acquainted: if they have that intuitive knowledge, whereby as in reflexion they behold the thoughts of one another, I cannot peremptorily deny but they know a great part of ours. They that to refute the

Bel and the Dragon 36. Acts viii. 40.

invocation of faints, have denied that they have any knowledge of our affairs below, have proceeded too far, and muft pardon my opinion, till I can throughly anfwer that piece of Scripture, *at the converfion of a finner, the angels in heaven rejoice.** I cannot with thofe in that great father fecurely interpret the work of the firft day, *fiat lux*, to the creation of angels; though I confefs, there is not any creature that hath fo near a glimpfe of their nature as light in the fun and elements: we ftyle it a bare accident; but where it fubfifts alone 'tis a fpiritual fubftance, and may be an angel: in brief, conceive light invifible, and that is a fpirit.

St. Luke
xv. 7, 1C.

xxxiv. Thefe are certainly

---

* " Take any moral or religious book, and inftead of underftanding each fentence according to the main purpofe and intention, interpret every phrafe in its literal fenfe as conveying, and defigned to convey, a metaphyfical verity, or hiftorical fact : — what a ftrange medley of doctrines fhould we not educe! And yet this is the way in which we are conftantly in the habit of treating the books of the New Teftament." Coleridge.

Man a Mi-
crocofm,
partaking
of the Na-
ture of all
created
Effences.

the magifterial and mafter-pieces of the
Creator, the flower, or (as we may fay)
the beft part of nothing, actually exifting,
what we are but in hopes and probability :
we are only that amphibious piece between corporal and fpiritual effence, that
middle form that links thofe two together,
and makes good the method of God and
nature, that jumps not from extremes,
but unites the incompatible diftances by
fome middle and participating natures.
That we are the breath and fimilitude of
God, it is indifputable and upon record

Gen. i. 26,
27; ii. 7.

of Holy Scripture ; but to call ourfelves
a microcofm, or little world,* I thought
it only a pleafant trope of rhetoric, till
my near judgment and fecond thoughts
told me there was a real truth therein :
for firft we are a rude mafs, and in the
rank of creatures which only are, and have
a dull kind of being not yet privileged
with life, or preferred to fenfe or reafon ;

---

* It was a faying of the Stoics : Βραχὺν μὲν κόσμον τὸν ἀνθρωπον, μεγαν δε ἀνθρωπον τὸν κόσμον
ε͂ιναι.

next we live the life of plants, the life of animals, the life of men, and at laſt the life of ſpirits, running on in one myſterious nature, thoſe five kind of exiſtences, which comprehend the creatures, not only of the world, but of the univerſe. Thus is man that great and true *amphibium*, whoſe nature is diſpoſed to live not only like other creatures in divers elements, but in divided and diſtinguiſhed worlds : for though there be but one world to ſenſe, there are two to reaſon ; the one viſible, the other inviſible, whereof Moſes ſeems to have left deſcription, and of the other ſo obſcurely, that ſome parts thereof are yet in controverſy. And truly for the firſt chapters of Geneſis, I muſt confeſs a great deal of obſcurity ; though divines have to the power of human reaſon endeavoured to make all go in a literal meaning, yet thoſe allegorical interpretations are alſo probable, and perhaps the myſtical method of Moſes bred up in the hieroglyphical ſchools of the Ægyptians.*

---

* " The ſecond Chapter of Geneſis from v. 4, and

xxxv. Now for the immate-
rial world, methinks we need not wander
so far as the first moveable; for even in
this material fabric the spirits walk as
freely exempt from the affection of time,
place, and motion, as beyond the ex-
tremest circumference: do but extract †
from the corpulency of bodies, or resolve
things beyond their first matter, and you
discover the habitation of angels, which if
I call the ubiquitary and omnipresent essence of God, I hope I shall not offend
divinity: for before the creation of the
world, God was really all things. For
the angels he created no new world, or
determinate mansion, and therefore they
are everywhere where is his essence, and
do live at a distance even in himself: that
God made all things for man, is in some

---

the third Chapter, are to my mind, as evidently sym-
bolical, as the first Chapter is literal. The first Chapter is manifestly by Moses himself; but the second
and third seem to me of far higher antiquity, and
have the air of being translated into words from
graven stones." Coleridge.

† *Abstract*, MS.

sense true, yet not so far as to subordinate the creation of those purer creatures unto ours, though as ministering spirits they do, and are willing to fulfil the will of God in these lower and sublunary affairs of man. God made all things for himself, and it is impossible he should make them for any other end than his own glory; it is all he can receive, and all that is without himself: for honour being an external adjunct, and in the honourer rather than in the person honoured, it was necessary to make a creature, from whom he might receive this homage, and that is in the other world, angels, in this, man; which when we neglect, we forget the very end of our creation, and may justly provoke God, not only to repent that he hath made the world, but that he hath sworn he would not destroy it. That there is but one world, is a conclusion of Faith. Aristotle with all his philosophy hath not been able to prove it, and as weakly that the world was eternal; that dispute much troubled the pen of the ancient philosophers, but Moses decided that

Gen. vi. 6; viii. 21, 22; ix. 9-17.

queſtion, and all is ſalved with the new term of a creation, that is, a production of ſomething out of nothing : and what is that ?* whatſoever is oppoſite to ſomething, or more exactly, that which is truly contrary unto God : for he only is, all others have an exiſtence with dependency, and are ſomething but by a diſtinction ; and herein is divinity conformant unto philoſophy, and generation not only founded on contrarieties, but alſo creation ; God being all things, is contrary unto nothing, out of which were made all things, and ſo nothing became ſomething, and omneity informed† nullity into an eſſence.

Man the
Maſterpiece
of Creation.

Gen. i. 20-
25.

Gen. ii. 7.

XXXVI. The whole creation is a myſtery, and particularly that of man : at the blaſt of his mouth were the reſt of the creatures made, and at his bare word they ſtarted out of nothing : but in the frame of man (as the text deſcribes it) he

---

* See Buckland's Bridgewater Treatiſe, vol. i. p. 22.
† *Informed*, i. e. animated.

played the fenfible operator, and feemed
not fo much to create; as make him : when
he had feparated the materials of other
creatures, there confequently refulted a
form and foul; but having raifed the
walls of man, he has driven to a fecond
and harder creation of a fubftance like
himfelf, an incorruptible and immortal
foul. For thefe two affections we have
the philofophy and opinion of the heathens, the flat affirmative of Plato, and
not a negative from Ariftotle. There is
another fcruple caft in by divinity (concerning its production) much difputed in
the German auditories, and with that indifferency and equality of arguments, as
leave the controverfy undetermined. I
am not of Paracelfus his mind,* that boldly
delivers a receipt to make a man without
conjunction; yet cannot but wonder at
the multitude of heads that do deny traduction, having no other argument to
confirm their belief, than that rhetorical
fentence, and *antimetathefis* of Auguftine,

---

* D'Ifraeli's Curiof. of Lit. 478.

Creando infunditur, infundendo creatur :
either opinion will confist well enough
with religion : yet I fhould rather incline
to this, did not one objection haunt me,
not wrong from fpeculations and fubtilties,
but from common fenfe, and obfervation ;
not picked from the leaves of any author,
but bred amongft the weeds and tares of
mine own brain ; and this is a conclufion
from the equivocal and monftrous productions in the copulation of a man with
a beaft : † for if the foul of man be not
tranfmitted, and transfufed in the feed of
the parents, why are not thofe productions
merely beafts, but have alfo an impreffion
and tincture of reafon in as high a meafure as it can evidence itfelf in thofe im-
proper organs ?   Nor truly can I peremptorily deny that the foul in this her
fublunary eftate, is wholly, and in all acceptions, inorganical, but that for the per-
formance of her ordinary actions, is required not only a fymmetry and proper
difpofition of organs, but a crafis and

---

† Blumenbach rejects fuch ftories as fabulous tales
which do not need contradiction.

temper correspondent to its operations; yet is not this mass of flesh and visible structure the instrument and proper corps of the soul, but rather of sense, and that the hand of reason. In our study of anatomy there is a mass of mysterious philosophy, and such as reduced the very heathens to divinity: yet amongst all these rare discoveries, and curious pieces I find in the fabric of man, I do not so much content myself, as in that I find not,— that is, no organ or instrument for the rational soul; for in the brain, which we term the seat of reason, there is not anything of moment more than I can discover in the crany of a beast: and this is a sensible, and no inconsiderable argument of the inorganity of the soul, at least in that sense we usually so receive it. Thus we are men, and we know not how: there is something in us that can be without us, and will be after us; though it is strange that it hath no history what it was before us, nor cannot tell how it entered in us.*

* See Appendix F.

XXXVII. Now for these walls of flesh, wherein the soul doth seem to be immured before the resurrection, it is nothing but an elemental composition, and a fabric that must fall to ashes. *All flesh is grass*, is not only metaphorically, but literally. true; for all those creatures we behold are but the herbs of the field, digested into flesh in them, or more remotely carnified in ourselves. Nay further, we are what we all abhor, *anthropophagi* and cannibals, devourers not only of men, but of ourselves; and that not in an allegory, but a positive truth: for all this mass of flesh which we behold, came in at our mouths; this frame we look upon, hath been upon our trenchers; in brief, we have devoured ourselves.* I cannot

---

* The Latin annotator is not content to receive this singular passage literally, as the author clearly intended it. He gives the following notes: *Ipsi anthropophagi*. Ut embryones in utero matris; nam mater ex proprio corpore nutrimentum illis præbet: nutriuntur etiam postea ex utero matris egressi lacte fœminino.

Sed et nos ipsos. Nam mæsti et invidi proprium cor comedere dicuntur. Wilkin.

believe the wifdom of Pythagoras did
ever pofitively, and in a literal fenfe, affirm
his metempfychofis, or impoffible tranfmi-
gration of the fouls of men into beafts:
of all metamorphofes, or tranfmigrations,
I believe only one, that is of Lot's wife;
for that of Nebuchadnezzar proceeded
not fo far: in all others I conceive there
is no further verity than is contained in
their implicit fenfe and morality. I believe that the whole frame of a beaft doth
perifh, and is left in the fame ftate after
death as before it was materialled unto
life: that the fouls of men know neither
contrary nor corruption; that they fubfift
beyond the body, and outlive death by
the privilege of their proper natures, and
without a miracle; that the fouls of the
faithful, as they leave earth, take poffeffion of heaven: that thofe apparitions and
ghofts of departed perfons are not the
wandering fouls of men, but the unquiet
walks of devils, prompting and fuggefting
us unto mifchief, blood, and villany; in-
ftilling, and ftealing into our hearts that
the bleffed fpirits are not at reft in their

Gen. xix. 26.
Dan. iv. 33.

graves, but wander folicitous of the affairs of the world: but that thofe phantafms appear often, and do frequent cemeteries, charnel houfes, and churches, it is becaufe thofe are the dormitories of the dead, where the devil, like an infolent champion, beholds with pride the fpoils and trophies of his victory in Adam.

Death

2 Efdr. vii. 48.

XXXVIII. This is that difmal conqueft we all deplore, that makes us fo often cry, *Adam, quid fecifti?* I thank God I have not thofe ftrait ligaments, or narrow obligations to the world, as to dote on life, or be convulfed and tremble at the name of death: not that I am infen-fible of the dread and horror thereof; or by raking into the bowels of the deceafed, continual fight of anatomies, fkeletons, or cadaverous reliques, like vefpilloes, or grave-makers, I am become ftupid, or have forgot the apprehenfion of mortality; but that marfhalling all the horrors, and contemplating the extremities thereof, I

hath no terrors for a Chriftian.

find not any thing therein able to daunt the courage of a man, much lefs a well resolved Christian; and therefore am not angry at the error of our first parents, or unwilling to bear a part of this common fate, and like the best of them to die, that is, to cease to breathe, to take a farewell of the elements, to be a kind of nothing for a moment, to be within one instant of a spirit. When I take a full view and circle of myself without this reasonable moderator, and equal piece of justice, Death, I do conceive myself the miserablest person extant: were there not another life that I hope for, all the vanities of this world should not intreat a moment's breath from me: could the devil work my belief to imagine I could never die, I would not outlive that very thought. I have so abject a conceit of this common way of existence, this retaining to the sun and elements, I cannot think this to be a man, or to live according to the dignity of humanity. In expectation of a better, I can with patience embrace this life, yet in my best meditations do often defy death: I honour any man that contemns it, nor can I highly love any that is afraid of it:

1 Cor. xv. 19.

this makes me naturally love a foldier, and honour thofe tattered and contemptible regiments that will die at the command of a fergeant.   For a Pagan there may be fome motives to be in love with life; but for a Chriftian to be amazed at death, I fee not how he can efcape this dilemma, that he is too fenfible of this life, or hopelefs of the life to come.*

XXXIX. Some divines count Adam thirty years old at his creation, becaufe they fuppofe him created in the perfect age and ftature of man.   And furely we are all out of the computation of our age, and every man is fome months elder

Man has feveral feparate ftates of exiftence.

---

* " Albeit the glafs of my years," fays Sir George Mackenzie, " hath not yet turned five-and-twenty, yet the curiofity I have to know the different limbos of departed fouls, and to view the card of the region of Death, would give me abundance of courage to encounter this King of Terrors, tho' I were a Pagan. But when I confider what joys are prepared for them who fear the Almighty, and what crazinefs attends fuch as fleep in Methufelem's cradle, I pity them who make long life one of the ofteft repeated petitions of their Pater Nofters." Moral Effays, p. 81.

than he bethinks him ; for we live, move, have a being, and are fubject to the actions of the elements, and the malice of difeafes, in that other world, the trueft microcofm, the womb of our mother ; for befides that general and common exiftence we are conceived to hold in our chaos, and whilft we fleep within the bofom of our caufes, we enjoy a being and life in three diftinct worlds, wherein we receive moft manifeft graduations. In that obfcure world, and womb of our mother, our time is fhort, computed by the moon, yet longer than the days of many creatures that behold the fun ; ourfelves being not yet without life, fenfe, and reafon ; though for the manifeftation of its actions, it awaits the opportunity of objects, and feems to live there but in its root and foul of vegetation. Entering afterwards upon the fcene of the world, we rife up and become another creature, performing the reafonable actions of man, and ob- fcurely manifefting that part of divinity in us ; but not in complement and per- fection, till we have once more caft our secondine, that is, this flough of flesh, and are delivered into the last world, that is, that ineffable place of Paul, that proper *ubi* of spirits.* The smattering I have of the philosopher's stone (which is something more than the perfect exaltation of gold) hath taught me a great deal of divinity, and instructed my belief, how that immortal spirit and incorruptible substance of my soul may lie obscure, and sleep a while within this house of flesh. †

2 Cor. xii. 4.

Those strange and mystical transmigrations that I have observed in silkworms, turned my philosophy into divinity. There

---

* " Solitude and Durance will not appear to us in so uncouth and strange a posture if we do but duly consider, how naturally our Maker inures us to it, and is agreeable with it from first to last; for we can't come into being but (per Limbum uterinum) by being strain'd thro' the Lymbeck, or grates of our Mother's womb, after forty weeks solitude and imprisonment, and a great while longer by the law of Nature ('tis as natural for to dye as to be born) must we lye incarcerated close prisoners in the world's womb (the grave) before we come to ourselves and obtain the liberty of the sons of God."   Religio Jurisprudentis.

† Compare Wordsworth's Ode, " Intimations of Immortality," especially stanza v.

is in these works of nature, which seem to puzzle reason, something divine, and hath more in it than the eye of a common spectator doth discover.*

XL. I am naturally bashful; nor hath conversation, age, or travel, been able to effront or enharden me; yet I have one part of modesty which I have seldom discovered in another, that is, (to speak truly,) I am not so much afraid of death, as ashamed thereof: 'tis the very disgrace and ignominy of our natures, that in a moment can so disfigure us, that our nearest friends, wife, and children, stand afraid and start at us. The birds and beasts of the field, that before in a natural fear obeyed us, forgetting all allegiance, begin to prey upon us.† This very conceit hath in a tempest disposed and left me willing to be swallowed up in the abyss of waters, wherein I had perished unseen, unpitied, without wondering eyes, tears of

Death to be ashamed of rather than feared.

---

* See Butler's Analogy, part i. cap. i.
† See Appendix G.

pity, lectures of mortality, and none had said *Quantum mutatus ab illo!* Not that I am ashamed of the anatomy of my parts, or can accuse nature for playing the bungler in any part of me, or my own vicious life for contracting any shameful disease upon me, whereby I might not call myself as wholesome a morsel for the worms as any.

XLI. Some, upon the courage of a fruitful issue, wherein, as in the truest chronicle, they seem to outlive themselves, can with greater patience away with death. This conceit and counterfeit subsisting in our progenies seems to me a mere fallacy, unworthy the desires of a man that can but conceive a thought of the next world ; who, in a nobler ambition, should desire to live in his substance in heaven, rather than his name and shadow in the earth. And therefore at my death I mean to take a total adieu of the world, not caring for a monument, history, or epitaph, not so much as the bare memory of my name to be found anywhere, but in the universal

regifter of God. I am not yet fo cynical
as to approve the teftament of Diogenes ;*
nor do altogether follow that *rodomontado*
of Lucan :

> ———*Cælo tegitur, qui non habet urnam.*
> Pharf. vii. 819.

> He that unburied lies wants not his herfe,
> For unto him a tomb's the univerfe.

but commend in my calmer judgement,
thofe ingenuous intentions that defire to
fleep by the urns of their fathers, and
ftrive to go the neateft way unto corruption. I do not envy the temper of crows
and daws,† nor the numerous and weary
days of our fathers before the flood. If
there be any truth in aftrology I may outlive a jubilee ; as yet I have not feen one
revolution of Saturn, nor hath my pulfe

---

* Who willed his friend not to bury him, but
hang him up with a ftaff in his hand to fright away
the crows.

† As Theophraftus did, who, dying, accufed nature for giving them, to whom it could be of no ufe,
fo long a life, while fhe granted fo fhort a one to man.
Cf. Cic. Tufc. Difp. iii. 69. An extreme longevity
was afcribed to thefe birds. See Pfeud. Epidem. iii. 9.

beat thirty years; and yet, excepting one,*
have seen the afhes of and left under
ground all the Kings of Europe; have
been contemporary to three Emperors,
four Grand Signiors, and as many Popes.†
Methinks I have outlived myfelf, and begin to be weary of the fun: I have fhaken
hands with delight in my warm blood
and canicular days: I perceive I do anticipate the vices of age; the world to me
is but a dream or mock fhow, and we all
therein but pantaloons and antics, to my
feverer contemplations.

Length of
days not to
be prayed
for,

XLII. It is not, I confefs, an
unlawful prayer to defire to furpafs the
days of our Saviour, or wifh to outlive
that age wherein he thought fitteft to die;
yet if (as divinity affirms) there fhall be

---

* *Excepting one;* Chriftiern IV. King of Den-
mark, who died 1647.

† Thefe were Rodolph II. Matthias and Ferdi-
nand II. Emperors of Germany. Achmet I. Muf-
tapha I. Othman II. and Amurath IV. Grand Signiors. Leo XI.? Paul V. Gregory XV. and Urban
VIII. Popes.

no grey hairs in heaven, but all ſhall riſe
in the perfect ſtate of men, we do but
outlive thoſe perfections in this world, to
be recalled unto them by a greater miracle
in the next, and run on here but to be
retrograde hereafter. Were there any
hopes to outlive vice, or a point to be ſuperannuated from ſin, it were worthy our
knees to implore the days of Methuſelah.
But age doth not rectify, but incurvate
our natures, turning bad diſpoſitions into
worſer habits, and (like diſeaſes) brings
on incurable vices; for every day as we
grow weaker in age, we grow ſtronger in
ſin: and the number of our days doth
but make our ſins innumerable. The
ſame vice committed at ſixteen, is not the
ſame, though it agrees in all other circumſtances, as at forty, but ſwells and doubles
from the circumſtance of our ages; wherein, beſides the conſtant and inexcuſable
habit of tranſgreſſing, the maturity of our
judgement cuts off pretence unto excuſe
or pardon:* every ſin the oftener it is

for age
doth but
increaſe
our vices.

---

* Cf. St. Auguſtine, Confeſſ. i. xviii. 30.

committed, the more it acquireth in the
quality of evil; as it fucceeds in time, fo
it proceeds in degrees of badnefs; for as
they proceed they ever multiply, and, like
figures in arithmetic, the laft ftands for
more than all that went before it.* And
though I think that no man can live well
once but he that could live twice, yet for
my own part I would not live over my
hours paft, or begin again the thread of
my days: not upon Cicero's ground, becaufe I have lived them well,† but for fear
I fhould live them worfe. I find my
growing judgement daily inftruct me how
to be better, but my untamed affections
and confirmed vitiofity makes me daily

* "We know that two lines ftarting at a fmall
angle, diverge to greater and greater diftances the
further they are produced: and furely in like manner
a foul living on into eternity may be infinitely changed
for the better or the worfe by very flight influences
exerted on it in the beginning of its courfe, a very
flight deviation at fetting out may be the meafure of
the difference between tending to hell, and tending
to heaven." Newman's Parochial Sermons, vol. iv.
ferm. iii. cf. St. Aug. Confefs. i. vii. 11.
† I fuppofe he alludes to an expreffion in an

do worfe : I find in my confirmed age the
fame fins I difcovered in my youth ; I
committed many then, becaufe I was a
child ; and becaufe I commit them ftill, I
am yet an infant. Therefore I perceive
a man may be twice a child, before the
days of dotage ; and ftand in need of
Æfon's bath* before threefcore.

XLIII. And truly there goes a
great deal of providence to produce a
man's life unto threefcore : there is more
required than an able temper for thofe
years ; though the radical humour contain in it fufficient oil for feventy, yet I
perceive in fome it gives no light paft
thirty : men affign not all the caufes of
long life that write whole books thereof.

A fpecial
providence
preferves
our lives.

Epiftle of Cicero, written in his exile, to his wife and
children, where he hath thefe words to his wife :
Quod reliquum eft, te fuftenta, mea Terentia, ut potes ;
honeftiffime viximus, floruimus. Non vitium noftrum
fed virtus noftra nos afflixit : peccatum eft nullum, nifi
quod non unà animam cum ornamentis amifimus. L.
xiii. Ep. 55. Cf. Cic. De *Senectute*, xxiii.
  * Ovid, Met. vii. 176.

They that found themselves on the radical balsam, or vital sulphur of the parts, determine not why Abel lived not so long as Adam. There is therefore a secret glome or bottom of our days : 'twas His wisdom to determine them, but his perpetual and waking providence that fulfils and accomplisheth them, wherein the spirits, ourselves, and all the creatures of God in a secret and disputed way do execute his will. Let them not therefore complain of immaturity that die about thirty ; they fall but like the whole world, whose solid and well-composed substance must not expect the duration and period of its constitution : when all things are completed in it, its age is accomplished ; and the last and general fever may as naturally destroy it before six thousand, as me before forty. There is therefore some other hand that twines the thread of life than that of nature : we are not only ignorant in antipathies and occult qualities ; our ends are as obscure as our beginnings ; the line of our days is drawn by night, and the various effects therein by a pencil

that is invifible, wherein, though we confefs our ignorance, I am fure we do not
err if we fay it is the hand of God.*

XLIV. I am much taken with
two verfes of Lucan, fince I have been
able not only, as we do at fchool, to con-
ftrue, but underftand:

Victurofque Dei celant, ut vivere durent,
Felix effe mori.   Pharfalia, iv. 519.

We're all deluded, vainly fearching ways
To make us happy by the length of days;
For cunningly to make's protract this breath,
The gods conceal the happinefs of death.

There be many excellent ftrains in that
poet, wherewith his Stoical genius hath
liberally fupplied him; and truly there
are fingular pieces in the philofophy of
Zeno, and doctrine of the Stoics, which I
perceive delivered in a pulpit pafs for
current divinity: yet herein are they in
extremes, that can allow a man to be his
own affaffin, and fo highly extol the end

* Vide Appendix H.

and suicide of Cato;* this is indeed not
to fear death, but yet to be afraid of life.
It is a brave act of valour to contemn
death; but where life is more terrible
than death, it is then the truest valour to
dare to live: and herein religion hath
taught us a noble example; for all the
valiant acts of Curtius, Scævola, or Cod-
rus, do not parallel or match that one of
Job; and sure there is no torture to the
rack of a disease, nor any poniards in
death itself, like those in the way or pro-
logue unto it. *Emori nolo, sed me esse
mortuum nihil æstumo.*† I would not die,
but care not to be dead. Were I of Cæ-

---

* As doth Seneca in several places; but Lactan-
tius saith, he cast away his life, to get the reputation
of a Platonic philosopher, and not for fear of Cæsar;
and 'tis very probable, he was in no great fear of
death, when he slept so securely the night before his
death, as the story reports of him. K.

Of suicide Plato remarks, that it is an injury to the
gods, as depriving them of their servants without
their leave; that it is like leaving your post in battle.
And Aristotle says, that to die in order to escape poverty, love, or something painful, is not a brave, but
rather a cowardly act. Ethics, iii. 11.

† Cic. Tusc. Disp. i. 8.

far's religion, I fhould be of his defires, and wifh rather to go off at one blow, than to be fawed in pieces by the grating torture of a difeafe.* Men that look no farther than their outfides, think health an appurtenance unto life, and quarrel with their conftitutions for being fick; but I that have examined the parts of man, and know upon what tender filaments that fabric hangs, do wonder that we are not always fo; and confidering the thoufand doors that lead to death, do thank my God that we can die but once.† 'Tis not only the mifchief of difeafes, and the villany of poifons, that make an end

---

* Suetonius in vit. J. Cæfar. 87 : "Nam et quondam, cum apud Xenophontem legiffet, Cyrum ultimâ valetudine mandâffe quædam de funere fuo, adfpernatus tam lentum mortis genus, fubitam fibi celeremque optaverat. Et pridie quam occideretur, in fermone nato fuper cœnam, apud M. Lepidum, quifnam effet finis vitæ commodiffimus, repentinum inopinatumque prætulerat."

† "Strange that a harp of a thoufand ftrings
    Should keep in tune fo long."

Pf. cxxxix. 14. "I will praife thee; for I am fearfully and wonderfully made."

I

of us : we vainly accuse the fury of guns, and the new inventions of death ; it is in the power of every hand to deſtroy us, and we are beholding unto every one we meet, he doth not kill us. There is therefore but one comfort left, that though it be in the power of the weakeſt arm to take away life, it is not in the ſtrongeſt to deprive us of death : God would not exempt himſelf from that ; the miſery of immortality in the fleſh He undertook not, that was, in it, immortal. Certainly there is no happineſs within this circle of fleſh, nor is it in the optics of theſe eyes to behold felicity. The firſt day of our jubilee is death ; the devil hath therefore failed of his deſires : we are happier with death than we ſhould have been without it : there is no miſery but in himſelf, where there is no end of miſery ; and ſo indeed, in his own ſenſe, the Stoic is in the right. He forgets that he can die who complains of miſery ; we are in the power of no calamity while death is in our own.*

---

* Death may be ſaid to be in our own power, becauſe no one can deprive us of it. Compare Sect. li.

XLV. Now besides this literal and positive kind of death, there are others whereof divines make mention, and those I think, not merely metaphorical, as mortification, dying unto sin and the world; therefore, I say, every man hath a double horoscope, one of his humanity, his birth; another of his Christianity, his baptism;* and from this do I compute or calculate my nativity, not reckoning those *horæ combustæ* and odd days, or esteeming myself any thing, before I was my Saviour's, and inrolled in the register of Christ: whosoever enjoys not this life, I count him but an apparition, though he wear about him the sensible affections of flesh. In these moral acceptions, the way to be immortal is to die daily; nor can I think I have the true theory of death, when I contemplate a skull, or behold a skeleton, with those vulgar imaginations it casts upon us: I have therefore enlarged that common *memento mori*, into a more Chris-

Death the gate thro' which we pass to immortality.

* " That this child may lead the rest of his life according to this beginning." Office of Baptism.

tian memorandum, *memento quatuor no-*
vissima, those four inevitable points of us
all, Death, Judgement, Heaven, and Hell.
Neither did the contemplations of the
heathens rest in their graves, without a
further thought of Rhadamanth or some
judicial proceeding after death, though in
another way, and upon suggestion of their
natural reasons. I cannot but marvel from
what sibyl or oracle they stole the prophecy of the world's destruction by fire,
or whence Lucan learned to say,

> *Communis mundo superest rogus, ossibus astra*
> *Mixturus——*   Pharsalia, vii. 814.

There yet remains to th' world one common fire,
Wherein our bones with stars shall make one pyre.

I believe the world grows near its end,
yet is neither old nor decayed, nor will
ever perish upon the ruins of its own
principles.* As the work of creation was

---

* The Author of nature has not given laws to the
universe, which, like the institutions of men, carry in
themselves the elements of their own destruction. He
has not permitted in his works any symptom of in-
fancy or old age, or any sign by which we may estimate either their future or their past duration. He

above nature, fo its adverfary, annihilation; without which the world hath not
its end, but its mutation. Now what
force fhould be able to confume it thus
far, without the breath of God, which is
the trueft confuming flame, my philofophy
cannot inform me. Some believe there
went not a minute to the world's creation,
nor fhall there go to its deftruction; thofe
fix days fo punctually defcribed, make
not to them one moment, but rather feem
to manifeft the method and idea of that
great work in the intellect of God, than
the manner how he proceeded in its operation. I cannot dream that there fhould
be at the laft day any fuch judicial proceeding, or calling to the bar, as indeed
the Scripture feems to imply, and the literal commentators do conceive: for un-
fpeakable myfteries in the Scriptures are

Gen. i.

---

may put an end, as he no doubt gave a beginning, to
the prefent fyftem at fome determinate period of time;
but we may reft affured that this great cataftrophe
will not be brought about by the laws now exifting,
and that it is not indicated by anything which we
perceive.—Playfair's Works, vol. iv. p. 55.

often delivered in a vulgar and illuftrative way; and being written unto man, are delivered, not as they truly are, but as they may be underftood; wherein, notwithftanding, the different interpretations according to different capacities may ftand firm with our devotion, nor be any way prejudicial to each fingle edification.

XLVI. Now to determine the day and year of this inevitable time, is not only convincible and ftatute-madnefs, but alfo manifeft impiety. How fhall we interpret Elias's fix thoufand years, or imagine the fecret communicated to a rabbi, which God hath denied unto his angels? It had been an excellent quære to have pofed the devil of Delphos, and muft needs have forced him to fome ftrange amphibology: it hath not only mocked the predictions of fundry aftrologers in ages paft, but the prophecies of many melancholy heads in thefe prefent; who, neither underftanding reafonably things paft or prefent, pretend a knowledge of things to come: heads ordained

St. Matt. xxiv. 36.

only to manifest the incredible effects of
melancholy, and to fulfil old prophecies
rather than be authors of new. *In thofe
days there fhall come wars and rumours
of wars*, to me feems no prophecy, but a
conftant truth in all times verified fince it
was pronounced. *There fhall be figns in
the moon and ftars;* how comes he then
like a thief in the night, when he gives
an item of his coming? That common
fign drawn from the revelation of antichrift, is as obfcure as any: in our common compute he hath been come thefe
many years: for my own part, to fpeak
freely, I am half of opinion that antichrift
is the philofopher's ftone in divinity, for
the difcovery and invention whereof,
though there be prefcribed rules and probable inductions, yet hath hardly any man
attained the perfect difcovery thereof.
That general opinion that the world grows
near its end, hath poffeffed all ages paft
as nearly as ours: I am afraid that the
fouls that now depart, cannot efcape that
lingering expoftulation of the faints under
the altar, *Quoufque, Domine?* How long,

St. Matt.
xxiv. 11—
24.

St. Matt.
xxiv. 6.
St. Mark
xiii. 7.
St. Luke
xxi. 25.

Rev. vi. 9.
10.

O Lord; and groan in the expectation of the great jubilee.

The day of judgment.

XLVII. This is the day that must make good that great attribute of God, his juſtice; that muſt reconcile thoſe unanſwerable doubts that torment the wiſeſt underſtandings; and reduce thoſe ſeeming inequalities and reſpective diſtributions in this world, to an equality and recompenſive juſtice in the next.* This is that one day, that ſhall include and comprehend all that went before it; wherein, as in the laſt ſcene, all the actors muſt enter to complete and make up the cataſtrophe of this great piece. This is the day whoſe memory hath only power to make us honeſt in the dark, and to be virtuous without a witneſs. *Ipſa ſuæ pretium virtus ſibi*—that virtue is her own reward, is but a cold principle, and not able to maintain our variable reſolutions in a conſtant and ſettled way of goodneſs. I have practiſed that honeſt artifice of

---

* This conſideration is applied with great force by Bp. Butler, Serm. iii.

Seneca,† and in my retired and folitary imaginations, to detain me from the foulnefs of vice, have fancied to myfelf the prefence of my dear and worthieft friends, before whom I fhould lofe my head, rather than be vicious : ‡ yet herein I found that there was nought but moral honefty, and this was not to be virtuous for His fake who muft reward us at the laft.   I have tried if I could reach that great refolution of his, to be honeft without a thought of heaven or hell : and indeed I found upon a natural inclination, and in-

† What that artifice was, is to be feen in Senec. l. 1. ep. 11. *Aliquis vir bonus nobis eligendus eft, et femper ante oculos habendus, ut fic tanquam illo fpectante vivamus, et omnia tanquam illo vidente faciamus.* Et paulo poft: *Elige itaque Catonem ; fi bic videtur tibi nimis rigidus, elige remiſſioris animi virum Lelium, etc.* Which though, as the author faith, it be an honeft artifice, yet cannot I but commend the party, and prefer the direction of him (whoever he were) who in the margin of my Seneca, over againft thofe words, wrote thefe : *Deum potius eligamus, qui femper omnibus omnia agentibus non tanquam, fed re ipfa adeft, et videt ; ac etiam ut teftis, vindex, et punitor eft male agentis.* K.

‡ See Appendix I.

bred loyalty unto virtue, that I could serve her without a livery; yet not in that resolved and venerable way, but that the frailty of my nature, upon an easy temptation, might be induced to forget her. The life therefore and spirit of all our actions is the resurrection, and a stable apprehension that our ashes shall enjoy the fruit of our pious endeavours: without this, all religion is a fallacy, and those impieties of Lucian, Euripides, and Julian, are no blasphemies, but subtle verities, and atheists have been the only philosophers.

The resurrection of the dead. 1 Cor. xv. 35.

XLVIII. How shall the dead arise? is no question of my faith; to believe only possibilities, is not faith, but mere philosophy: many things are true in divinity, which are neither inducible by reason nor confirmable by sense; and many things in philosophy confirmable by sense, yet not inducible by reason. Thus it is impossible by any solid or demonstrative reasons to persuade a man to believe the conversion of the needle to

the north; though this be poffible, and
true, and eafily credible, upon a fingle
experiment unto the fenfe. I believe that
our eftranged and divided afhes fhall unite
again; that our feparated duft, after fo
many pilgrimages and transformations into
the parts of minerals, plants, animals,
elements, fhall at the voice of God return
into their primitive fhapes, and join again
to make up their primary and predeftinate
forms. As at the creation there was a
feparation of that confufed mafs into its
fpecies; fo at the deftruction thereof there
fhall be a feparation into its diftinct individuals. As at the creation of the world,
all the diftinct fpecies that we behold lay
involved in one mafs, till the fruitful
voice of God feparated this united multitude into its feveral fpecies; fo at the laft
day, when thefe corrupted reliques fhall
be fcattered in the wildernefs of forms,
and feem to have forgot their proper
habits, God by a powerful voice fhall
command them back into their proper
fhapes, and call them out by their fingle
individuals: then fhall appear the fertility

of Adam, and the magic of that fperm that hath dilated into fo many millions.* I have often beheld as a miracle, that artificial refurrection and revivification of Mercury, how being mortified into a thoufand fhapes, it affumes again its own, and returns into its numerical felf.† Let us fpeak naturally and like philofophers: the forms of alterable bodies in thefe fenfible corruptions perifh not; nor, as we imagine, wholly quit their manfions, but retire and contract themfelves into their fecret and unacceffible parts, where they may beft protect themfelves from the action of their antagonift. A plant or

* What is made to be immortal, nature cannot, nor will the voice of God, deftroy. Thofe bodies that we behold to perifh, were in their created natures immortal, and liable unto death only accidentally, and upon forfeit; and therefore they owe not that natural homage unto death as other bodies do, but may be reftored to immortality with a leffer miracle, and by a bare, and eafy revocation of courfe, return immortal. Edits. 1642.

† Hinc Gregorius Nyffenus putat, fi Deus permittat, corporum noftrorum particulas propter mutuum amorem fpontè iterum coituras: probat id exemplo *argenti vivi*. M.

vegetable confumed to afhes, to a contemplative and fchool-philofopher feems
utterly deftroyed, and the form to have
taken his leave for ever; but to a fenfible
artift the forms are not perifhed, but withdrawn into their incombuftible part, where
they lie fecure from the action of that
devouring element. This is made good
by experience, which can from the afhes
of a plant revive the plant, and from its
cinders recall it into its ftalk and leaves
again.* What the art of man can do in
thefe inferior pieces, what blafphemy is it
to affirm the finger of God cannot do in
thefe more perfect and fenfible ftructures!
This is that myftical philofophy, from
whence no true fcholar becomes an atheift,
but from the vifible effects of nature
grows up a real divine, and beholds not
in a dream, as Ezekiel, but in an ocular
and vifible object, the types of his refurrection.

XLIX. Now the neceffary man-

Heaven, or

* See Appendix K.

Hell, not to be defined.

fions of our reſtored ſelves, are thoſe two contrary and incompatible places we call heaven and hell : to define them, or ſtrictly to determine what and where theſe are, ſurpaſſeth my divinity. That elegant apoſtle which ſeemed to have a glimpſe of heaven, hath left but a negative deſcription thereof : *which neither eye hath ſeen, nor ear hath heard, nor can enter into the heart of man :* he was tranſlated out of himſelf to behold it ; but being returned into himſelf could not expreſs it. St. John's deſcription by emeralds, chryſolites, and precious ſtones, is too weak to expreſs the material heaven we behold. Briefly therefore, where the ſoul hath the full meaſure and complement of happineſs ; where the boundleſs appetite of that ſpirit remains completely ſatisfied, that it can neither deſire addition nor alteration ; that, I think, is truly Heaven : and this can only be in the enjoyment of that eſſence, whoſe infinite goodneſs is able to terminate the deſires of itſelf, and the unſatiable wiſhes of ours : wherever God will thus manifeſt himſelf, there is heaven,

1 Cor. ii. 9. if. lxiv.,4.

Rev. xxi. 19—21.

though within the circle of this fenfible world.* Thus the foul of man may be in heaven any where, even within the limits of his own proper body; and when it ceafeth to live in the body, it may remain in its own foul, that is, its Creator. And thus we may fay that St. Paul, whether in the body or out of the body, was yet in heaven. To place it in the empyreal, or beyond the tenth fphere, is to forget the world's deftruction; for when this fenfible world fhall be deftroyed, all fhall then be here as it is now there, an empyreal heaven, a *quafi* vacuity; when to afk where heaven is, is to demand where the prefence of God is, or where we have the glory of that happy vifion. Mofes that was bred up in all the learning of the Ægyptians, committed a grofs abfurdity in philofophy, when with thefe eyes of flefh he defired to fee God, and petitioned his Maker, that is, Truth itfelf, to a contradiction. Thofe that imagine

2 Cor. xii. 2—4.

Ex. xxxiii. 12—23.

---

* See Keble's Chriftian Year. Sixth Sunday after Epiphany.

St. Luke
xvi. 19—
31.

heaven and hell neighbours, and conceive a vicinity between thofe two extremes, upon confequence of the parable, where Dives difcourfed with Lazarus in Abraham's bofom, do too groffly conceive of thofe glorified creatures, whofe eyes fhall eafily out-fee the fun, and behold without a perfpective the extremeft diftances : for if there fhall be in our glorified eyes, the faculty of fight and reception of objects, I could think the vifible fpecies there to be in as unlimitable a way, as now the intellectual. I grant that two bodies placed beyond the tenth fphere, or in a vacuity, according to Ariftotle's philofophy, could not behold each other, becaufe there wants a body or medium to hand and tranfport the vifible rays of the object unto the fenfe ; but when there fhall be a general defect of either medium to convey, or light to prepare and difpofe that medium, and yet a perfect vifion, we muft fufpend the rules of our philofophy, and make all good by a more abfolute piece of optics.

L. I cannot tell how to fay that fire is the effence of hell: I know not what to make of purgatory, or conceive a flame that can either prey upon, or purify the fubftance of a foul: thofe flames of fulphur mentioned in the Scriptures, I take not to be underftood of this prefent hell, but of that to come, where fire fhall make up the complement of our tortures, and have a body or fubject wherein to manifeft its tyranny. Some who have had the honour to be textuary in divinity, are of opinion it fhall be the fame fpecifical fire with ours. This is hard to conceive; yet can I make good how even that may prey upon our bodies, and yet not confume us: for in this material world there are bodies that perfift invincible in the powerfulleft flames; and though by the action of fire they fall into ignition and liquation, yet will they never fuffer a deftruction. I would gladly know how Mofes with an actual fire calcined or burnt the golden calf unto powder: for that myftical metal of gold, whofe folary

Of Fire as an agent in deftruction.

Exod. xxxii. 20.

and celeftial nature I admire, expofed unto the violence of fire, grows only hot and liquifies, but confumeth* not; fo when the confumable and volatile pieces of our bodies fhall be refined into a more impregnable and fixed temper, like gold, though they fuffer from the actions of flames, they fhall never perifh, but lie immortal in the arms of fire. And furely, if this frame muft fuffer only by the action of this element, there will many bodies efcape; and not only heaven but earth will not be at an end, but rather a beginning. For at prefent it is not earth, but a compofition of fire, water, earth, and air; but at that time, fpoiled of thefe ingredients, it fhall appear in a fubftance more like itfelf, its afhes. Philofophers that opinioned the world's deftruction by fire, did never dream of annihilation, which is beyond the power of fublunary caufes; for the laft and proper action of that element is but vitrification, or a re-

* Mofes is not faid to have *confumed* it, but to have ground it to powder.

duction of a body into glafs; and therefore fome of our chymicks facetioufly
affirm, that at the laft fire all fhall be
cryftallized and reverberated into glafs,
which is the utmoft action of that element.
Nor need we fear this term, annihilation,
or wonder that God will deftroy the works
of his creation; for man fubfifting, who
is, and will then truly appear, a microcofm,
the world cannot be faid to be deftroyed.
For the eyes of God, and perhaps alfo of
our glorified felves, fhall as really behold
and contemplate the world in its epitome
or contracted effence, as now it doth at
large and in its dilated fubftance. In the
feed of a plant to the eyes of God, and to
the underftanding of man, there exifts,
though in an invifible way, the perfect
leaves, flowers, and fruit thereof; for
things that are in *poffe* to the fenfe, are
actually exiftent to the underftanding.
Thus God beholds all things, who con-
templates as fully his works in their epitome, as in their full volume; and beheld
as amply the whole world in that little
compendium of the fixth day, as in the

scattered and dilated pieces of those five before.

LI. **Men commonly set forth** the torments of hell by fire, and the extremity of corporal afflictions, and describe hell in the same method that Mahomet doth heaven. This indeed makes a noise, and drums in popular ears: but if this be the terrible piece thereof, it is not worthy to stand in diameter with heaven, whose happiness consists in that part that is best able to comprehend it, that immortal essence, that translated divinity and colony of God, the soul. Surely though we place hell under earth, the devil's walk and purlieu is about it: men speak too popularly who place it in those flaming mountains, which to grosser apprehensions represent hell. The heart of man is the place the devil dwells in: I feel sometimes a hell within myself:* Lucifer keeps his

---

* So Milton, Paradise Lost, i. 254.

" The mind is its own place, and in itself
Can make a heaven of hell, a hell of heaven."

court in my breaft, Legion is revived in
me. There are as many hells, as Anax-
archus conceited worlds: there was more
than one hell in Magdalene, when there
were feven devils, for every devil is an hell
unto himfelf; he holds enough of torture
in his own *ubi*, and needs not the mifery
of circumference to afflict him: and thus
a diftracted confcience here, is a fhadow
or introduction unto hell hereafter. Who
can but pity the merciful intention of
thofe hands that do deftroy themfelves?
the devil, were it in his power, would do
the like; which being impoffible, his
miferies are endlefs, and he fuffers moft
in that attribute wherein he is impaffible,
his immortality.

LII. I thank God, and with
joy I mention it, I was never afraid of
hell, nor never grew pale at the defcrip-
tion of that place; I have fo fixed my

Contem-
plation of
heaven.

and iv. 18. So alfo, Taffo, c. xii. ft. 77.

" Swift from myfelf I run, myfelf I fear,
Yet ftill my hell within myfelf I bear."

Heb. xii. 2.

2 Efdr. ix.
13.

contemplations on heaven, that I have almoft forgot the idea of hell, and am afraid rather to lofe the joys of the one, than endure the mifery of the other: to be deprived of them is a perfect hell, and needs, methinks, no addition to complete our afflictions. That terrible term hath never detained me from fin, nor do I owe any good action to the name thereof. I fear God, yet am not afraid of him: his mercies make me afhamed of my fins, before his judgements afraid thereof: thefe are the forced and fecondary method of his wifdom, which he ufeth but as the laft remedy, and upon provocation: a courfe rather to deter the wicked, than incite the virtuous to his worfhip. I can hardly think there was ever any fcared into heaven; they go the faireft way to heaven that would ferve God without a hell; other mercenaries, that crouch unto him in fear of hell, though they term themfelves the fervants, are indeed but the flaves of the Almighty.*

* Excellent throughout! The fear of hell may

LIII. And to be true, and speak my soul, when I survey the occurrences of my life, and call into account the finger of God, I can perceive nothing but an abyss and mass of mercies, either in general to mankind, or in particular to myself: and whether out of the prejudice of my affection, or an inverting and partial conceit of his mercies, I know not; but those which others term crosses, afflictions, judgements, misfortunes, to me who inquire farther into them than their visible effects, they both appear, and in event have ever proved, the secret and dissembled favours of his affection. It is a singular piece of wisdom to apprehend truly, and without passion, the works of God, and so well to distinguish his justice from his mercy, as not to miscall

indeed in some desperate cases, like the *moxa*, give the first rouse from a moral lethargy, or like the green venom of copper, by evacuating poison or a dead load from the inner man, prepare it for nobler ministrations and medicines from the realm of light and life, that nourish while they stimulate.   Coleridge.

thofe noble attributes: yet it is likewife an
honeft piece of logic, fo to difpute and
argue the proceedings of God, as to dif-
tinguifh.even his judgements into mercies.
For God is merciful unto all, becaufe
better to the worft than the beft deferve;
and to fay he punifheth none in this world,
though it be a paradox, is no abfurdity.
To one that hath committed murder, if
the judge fhould only ordain a fine, it
were a madnefs to call this a punifhment,
and to repine at the fentence, rather than
admire the clemency of the judge: thus
our offences being mortal, and deferving
not only death, but damnation, if the
goodnefs of God be content to traverfe
and pafs them over with a lofs, misfortune,
or difeafe, what phrenfy were it to term
this a punifhment, rather than an extremity of mercy, and to groan under the rod
of his judgments, rather than admire the
fceptre of his mercies! Therefore to adore,
honour, and admire him, is a debt of
gratitude due from the obligation of our
nature, ftates, and conditions; and with
thefe thoughts, He that knows them beft,

will not deny that I adore him. That I obtain heaven, and the blifs thereof, is accidental, and not the intended work of my devotion; it being a felicity I can neither think to deferve, nor fcarce in modefty to expect. For thefe two ends of us all, either as rewards or punifhments, are mercifully ordained and difpropor-tionably difpofed unto our actions; the one being fo far beyond our deferts, the other fo infinitely below our demerits.

LIV. There is no falvation to thofe that believe not in Chrift, that is, fay fome, fince his nativity, and, as di-vinity affirmeth, before alfo; which makes me much apprehend the end of thofe honeft worthies and philofophers which died before his incarnation. It is hard to place thofe fouls in hell whofe worthy lives do teach us virtue on earth; me-thinks amongft thofe many fubdivifions of hell, there might have been one limbo left for thefe.* What a ftrange vifion

Salvation through Chrift alone.

* See Appendix L.

will it be to fee their poetical fictions
converted into verities, and their imagined
and fancied furies into real devils! How
ftrange to them will found the hiftory of
Adam, when they fhall fuffer for him
they never heard of! when they that
derive their genealogy from the gods,
fhall know they are the unhappy iffue
of finful man! It is an infolent part of
reafon, to controvert the works of God,
or queftion the juftice of his proceedings.
Could humility teach others, as it hath
inftructed me, to contemplate the infinite
and incomprehenfible diftance betwixt the
Creator and the creature; or did we fe-
rioufly perpend that one fimile of St. Paul,
*Shall the veffel fay to the potter, why haft
thou made me thus?* it would prevent
thefe arrogant difputes of reafon; nor
would we argue the definitive fentence of
God, either to heaven or hell. Men that
live according to the right rule and law
of reafon, live but in their own kind, as
beafts do in theirs; who juftly obey the
prefcript of their natures, and therefore
cannot reafonably demand a reward of

Rom. ix.
20.

their actions, as only obeying the natural dictates of their reason.* It will, therefore, and must at last appear, that all salvation is through Christ; which verity, I fear, these great examples of virtue must confirm, and make it good, how the perfecteft actions of earth have no title or claim unto heaven.

LV. Nor truly do I think the lives of these, or of any other, were ever correspondent, or in all points conformable unto their doctrines. It is evident that Aristotle transgressed the rule of his own ethics: the Stoics that condemn passion, and command a man to laugh in Phalaris his bull, could not endure without a groan a fit of the stone or cholic.† The sceptics that affirmed they knew nothing,‡ even in that opinion confute themselves, and thought they knew more than all the

Our practice inconsistent with our theory.

---

* See Preface to Butler's Sermons, pp. xii. xiii.
† Cf. Much Ado about Nothing, v. 1.
‡ —— nihil sciri si quis putat, id quoque nescit an sciri possit; quoniam nihil scire fatetur.
                              Lucret. iv. 471.

world befide. Diogenes I hold to be the
moft vain-glorious man of his time, and
more ambitious in refufing all honours,
than Alexander in rejecting none. Vice
and the devil put a fallacy upon our reafons, and provoking us too haftily to run
from it, entangle and profound us deeper
in it. The duke of Venice, that weds
himfelf unto the fea by a ring of gold, I
will not argue of prodigality, becaufe it is
a folemnity of good ufe and confequence
in the ftate: but the philofopher that
threw his money into the fea to avoid
avarice, was a notorious prodigal.* There
is no road or ready way to virtue: it is

* The Doge performs this ceremony every year,
in token of the fovereignty of the ftate of Venice
over the Adriatic, and to commemorate the celebrated
declaration of Pope Alexander III. "Que la mer
vous foit foumife comme l'épouse l'eft à fon époux,
puifque vous en avez acquis l'empire par la victoire."
Apollonius Thyaneus threw his gold into the fea,
faying thefe words: *Peffundo divitias, ne peffundarer
ab illis*. Polycrates, the tyrant of Samos, caft the
beft jewel he had into the fea, that thereby he might
learn to compofe himfelf againft the viciffitudes of
fortune.

not an eafy point of art to difentangle
ourfelves from this riddle, or web of fin.
To perfect virtue, as to religion, there is
required a *panoplia*, or complete armour;
that whilft we lie at clofe ward againft
one vice, we lie not open to the veny of
another : and indeed wifer difcretions that
have the thread of reafon to conduct them,
offend without a pardon ; whereas, under-
heads may ftumble without difhonour.
There are fo many circumftances to piece
up one good action, that it is a leffon to
be good, and we are forced to be virtuous
by the book.   Again, the practice of men
holds not an equal pace ; yea, and often
runs counter to their theory : we naturally
know what is good, but naturally purfue
what is evil: the rhetoric wherewith I
perfuade another, cannot perfuade myfelf:
there is a depraved appetite in us, that
will with patience hear the learned in-
ftructions of reafon, but yet perform no
farther than agrees to its own irregular
humour.   In brief, we all are monfters,
that is a compofition of man and beaft,
wherein we muft endeavour to be as the

poets fancy that wife man Chiron, that is, to have the region of man above that of beaft, and fenfe to fit but at the feet of reafon. Laftly, I do defire with God, that all, but yet affirm with men, that few fhall know falvation; that the bridge is narrow, the paffage ftrait unto life: yet thofe who do confine the Church of God, either to particular nations, churches, or families, have made it far narrower than our Saviour ever meant it.

1 Tim. ii. 3, 4. 2 Pet. iii. 9.

TheChurch of God not circumfcribed.

LVI. The vulgarity of thofe judgments that wrap the Church of God in Strabo's cloak,* and reftrain it unto Europe, feem to me as bad geographers as Alexander, who thought he had conquered all the world, when he had not

---

* 'Tis *Strabonis tunica* in the tranflation, but *chlamydi* would do better, which is the proper expreffion of the word that Strabo ufeth: it is not Europe, but the known part of the world, that Strabo refembleth to a cloak, and that is it the author here alludeth to; but we have no reafon to think that the refemblance of Strabo is very proper.　K.

　Cf. Hooker.　Eccl. Pol. Bk. iii. cap. i.

subdued the half of any part thereof: for
we cannot deny the Church of God both
in Asia and Africa, if we do not forget
the peregrinations of the apostles, the
deaths of the martyrs, the sessions of
many, and, even in our reformed judgement, lawful councils, held in those parts
in the minority and nonage of ours: nor
must a few differences, more remarkable
in the eyes of man than perhaps in the
judgment of God, excommunicate from
heaven one another; much less those
Christians who are in a manner all martyrs, maintaining their faith in the noble
way of persecution, and serving God in
the fire, whereas we honour him but in
the sunshine.

'Tis true we all hold there is a number
of elect, and many to be saved; yet take
our opinions together, and from the confusion thereof there will be no such thing
as salvation, nor shall any one be saved.
For first, the church of Rome condemneth
us, we likewise them; the sub-reformists
and sectaries sentence the doctrine of our
church as damnable; the atomist, or fa-

A sectarian
spirit hos-
tile to cha-
rity.

milift,* reprobates all thefe; and all thefe,
them again. Thus whilft the mercies of
God do promife us heaven, our conceits
and opinions exclude us from that place.
There muft be therefore, more than one
St. Peter: particular churches and fects
ufurp the gates of heaven, and turn the
key againft each other; and thus we go
to heaven againft each other's wills, conceits, and opinions, and, with as much
uncharity as ignorance, do err, I fear, in
points not only of our own, but one
another's falvation.

LVII. I believe many are faved,
who to man feem reprobated; and many
are reprobated, who, in the opinion and
fentence of man, ftand elected. There
will appear at the laft day, ftrange and
unexpected examples, both of his juftice
and his mercy; and therefore to define
either, is folly in man, and infolency even

"Judge
not that
ye be not
judged."

---

* The *atomifts*, or *familifts*, were religionifts who
fprung up about the year 1575. See Hift. of the
Puritans, i. 273.

in the devils: thofe acute and fubtile
fpirits in all their fagacity, can hardly divine who fhall be faved; which if they
could prognoftic, their labour were at
an end, nor need they compafs the earth
feeking whom they may devour. Thofe
who, upon a rigid application of the law,
fentence Solomon unto damnation, condemn not only him, but themfelves, and
the whole world: for by the letter, and
written word of God, we are without ex-
ception in the ftate of death; but there
is a prerogative of God and an arbitrary
pleafure above the letter of his own law,
by which alone we can pretend unto
falvation, and through which Solomon
might be as eafily faved as thofe who
condemn him.

LVIII. The number of thofe
who pretend unto falvation, and thofe infinite fwarms who think to pafs through
the eye of this needle, have much amazed
me. That name and compellation of
little flock, doth not comfort, but dejeẛt
my devotion; efpecially when I reflect

But few are
faved.

St. Luke
xii. 32.

upon mine own unworthineſs, wherein, according to my humble apprehenſions, I am below them all.　I believe there ſhall never be an anarchy in heaven; but as there are hierarchies amongſt the angels, ſo ſhall there be degrees of priority amongſt the ſaints.　Yet is it (I proteſt) beyond my ambition to aſpire unto the firſt ranks; my deſires only are, and I ſhall be happy therein, to be but the laſt man, and bring up the rear in heaven.

LIX.　Again, I am confident, and fully perſuaded, yet dare not take my oath of my ſalvation.　I am as it were ſure, and do believe without all doubt that there is ſuch a city as Conſtantinople: yet for me to take my oath thereon, were a kind of perjury, becauſe I hold no infallible warrant from my own ſenſe to confirm me in the certainty thereof. And truly, though many pretend an abſolute certainty of their ſalvation, yet when an humble ſoul ſhall contemplate her own unworthineſs, ſhe ſhall meet with many doubts, and ſuddenly find how little we

Our confidence can only be in God's mercy.

ſtand in need of the precept of St. Paul, *work out your ſalvation with fear and trembling.* That which is the cauſe of my election, I hold to be the cauſe of my ſalvation, which was the mercy and *beneplacit* of God, before I was, or the foundation of the world. "Before Abraham was, I am," is the ſaying of Chriſt; yet is it true in ſome ſenſe, if I ſay it of myſelf; for I was not only before myſelf, but Adam, that is, in the idea of God, and the decree of that ſynod held from all eternity: and in this ſenſe, I ſay, the world was before the creation, and at an end before it had a beginning; and thus, was I dead before I was alive: though my grave be England, my dying place was paradiſe: and Eve miſcarried of me, before ſhe conceived of Cain.

Phil. ii. 12.

St. John viii. 58.

LX. Inſolent zeals, that do decry good works and rely only upon faith, take not away merit: for depending upon the efficacy of their faith, they enforce the condition of God, and in a more ſophiſtical way do ſeem to challenge

Faith.

heaven. It was decreed by God, that only thofe that lapt in the water like dogs, fhould have the honour to deftroy the Midianites; yet could none of thofe juftly challenge, or imagine he deferved that honour thereupon. I do not deny, but that true faith, and fuch as God requires, is not only a mark or token, but alfo a means of our falvation; but where to find this, is as obfcure to me, as my laft end. And if our Saviour could object unto his own difciples and favourites, a faith, that, to the quantity of a grain of muftard feed, is able to remove mountains; furely, that which we boaft of, is not any thing, or at the moft, but a remove from nothing. This is the tenor of my belief; wherein, though there be many things fingular, and to the humour of my irregular felf, yet if they fquare not with maturer judgments, I difclaim them, and do no further favour them, than the learned and beft judgments fhall authorize them.

Judges vii. 4—7.

S. Matt. xvii. 20.

The Second Part.

I.

Ow for that other vir-

Charity.

1 Cor. xiii. 2.

tue of charity, without which faith is a mere notion, and of no exiſtence, I have ever en-deavoured to nouriſh the merciful diſpo-ſition and humane inclination I borrowed from my parents, and regulate it to the written and preſcribed laws of charity: and if I hold the true anatomy of myſelf, I am delineated and naturally framed to ſuch a piece of virtue; for I am of a conſtitution ſo general, that it conſorts and ſympathizeth with all things: I have no antipathy, or rather idio-ſyncraſy, in diet, humour, air, any thing. I wonder not at the French for their diſhes of frogs, ſnails, and toadſtools; nor at the Jews for locuſts and graſſhoppers; but being amongſt them, make them my common viands, and I find they agree with my stomach as well as theirs. I could digest a salad gathered in a churchyard, as well as in a garden. I cannot start at the presence of a serpent, scorpion, lizard, or salamander: at the sight of a toad or viper, I find in me no desire to take up a stone to destroy them. I feel not in myself those common antipathies that I can discover in others: those national repugnances do not touch me, nor do I behold with prejudice the French, Italian, Spaniard or Dutch: but where I find their actions in balance with my countrymen's, I honour, love, and embrace them in the same degree. I was born in the eighth climate, but seem for to be framed and constellated unto all: I am no plant that will not prosper out of a garden; all places, all airs, make unto me one country; I am in England, every where, and under any meridian; I have been shipwrecked, yet am not enemy with the sea or winds; I can study, play, or sleep in a tempest. In brief, I am averse from nothing: my conscience would give me

the lie if I fhould abfolutely deteft or
hate any effence but the devil; or fo at
leaft abhor any thing, but that we might
come to compofition. If there be any
among thofe common objects of hatred I
do contemn and laugh at, it is that great
enemy of reafon, virtue, and religion, the
multitude: that numerous piece of monftrofity, which taken afunder, feem men,
and the reafonable creatures of God; but
confufed together, make but one great
beaft, and a monftrofity more prodigious
than Hydra: it is no breach of charity
to call thefe fools; it is the ftyle all holy
writers have afforded them, fet down by
Solomon in canonical Scripture, and a
point of our faith to believe fo. Neither
in the name of multitude do I only include the bafe and minor fort of people;*
there is a rabble even amongft the gentry, a
fort of plebeian heads, whofe fancy moves

---

* " Do not imagine that I confider as *vulgar* thofe
only of the poor and humble claffes; but all who are
ignorant, even be they lords or princes, they muft be
claffed under the denomination *vulgar*."

                                        Cervantes.

with the fame wheel as thefe; men in the
fame level with mechanics, though their
fortunes do fomewhat gild their infirmities,
and their purfes compound for their follies. But as in cafting account, three or
four men together come fhort in account
of one man placed by himfelf below them;
fo neither are a troop of thefe ignorant
Doradoes * of that true efteem and value,
as many a forlorn perfon, whofe condition
doth place him below their feet. Let us
fpeak like politicians: there is a nobility
without heraldry, a natural dignity, whereby one man is ranked with another, another
filed before him, according to the quality
of his defert, and pre-eminence of his
good parts.† Though the corruption of
thefe times and the bias of prefent practice

---

* *Dorado*, Spanifh.   Gilt-head.

† " Nobilitas fola eft atque unica, virtus."
Juvenal.

" Howe'er it be, it feems to me,
'Tis only noble to be good;
Kind hearts are more than coronets,
And fimple faith than Norman blood."
Tennyfon.

wheel another way, thus it was in the firſt
and primitive commonwealths, and is yet
in the integrity and cradle of well-ordered
polities, till corruption getteth ground;
ruder deſires labouring after that which
wiſer conſiderations contemn, every one
having a liberty to amaſs and heap up
riches, and they a licence or faculty to do
or purchaſe any thing.

11. This general and indifferent temper of mine doth more nearly
diſpoſe me to this noble virtue. It is a
happineſs to be born and framed unto
virtue, and to grow up from the ſeeds of
nature, rather than the inoculation and
forced graffs of education: yet if we are
directed only by our particular natures,
and regulate our inclinations by no higher
rule than that of our reaſons, we are but
moraliſts; divinity will ſtill call us heathens. Therefore this great work of charity muſt have other motives, ends, and
impulſions. I give no alms to ſatisfy the
hunger of my brother, but to fulfil and
accompliſh the will and command of my

Charity muſt ſpring from a proper motive.

God: I draw not my purfe for his fake that demands it, but His that enjoined it: I relieve no man upon the rhetoric of his miferies, nor to content mine own commiferating difpofition; for this is ftill but moral charity, and an act that oweth more to paffion than reafon. He that relieves another upon the bare fuggeftion and bowels of pity, doth not this fo much for his fake as for his own; for by compaffion we make others' mifery our own, and fo by relieving them, we relieve ourfelves alfo. It is as erroneous a conceit to redrefs other men's misfortunes upon the common confiderations of merciful natures, that it may be one day our own cafe; for this is a finifter and politic kind of charity, whereby we feem to befpeak the pities of men in the like occafions. And truly I have obferved that thofe profeffed eleemofynaries, though in a crowd or multitude, do yet direct and place their petitions on a few and felected perfons: there is furely a phyfiognomy, which thofe experienced and mafter mendicants obferve, whereby they inftantly difcover a merciful

The nature of created beings fignified in their outward forms.

aspect, and will single out a face wherein they spy the signatures and marks of mercy. For there are mystically in our faces certain characters which carry in them the motto of our souls, wherein he that cannot read A B C may read our natures. I hold moreover that there is a phytognomy, or physiognomy, not only of men, but of plants and vegetables; and in every one of them some outward figures which hang as signs or bushes of their inward forms.* The finger of God hath left an inscription upon all his works, not graphical or composed of letters, but of their several forms, constitutions, parts, and operations, which aptly joined together, do make one word that doth express their natures. By these letters God calls the stars by their names; and by this alphabet Adam assigned to every creature a name peculiar to its nature. Now there are besides these characters in

Ps. cxlvii. 4.

Gen. ii. 19, 20.

---

* Vintners were wont to hang up *bushes*, or garlands of ivy over their doors. Cf. Epilogue to *As you like it*. "If it be true that good wine needs no bush, 'tis true that a good play needs no epilogue."

our faces, certain myftical figures in our hands, which I dare not call mere dafhes, ftrokes *à la volée*, or at random, becaufe delineated by a pencil that never works in vain ; and hereof I take more particular notice, becaufe I carry that in mine own hand which I could never read of nor difcover in another. Ariftotle, I confefs, in his acute and fingular book of phyfiognomy, hath made no mention of chiromancy ;* yet I believe the Egyptians, who were nearer addicted to thofe abftrufe and myftical fciences, had a knowledge therein, to which thofe vagabond and counterfeit Egyptians did after pretend, and perhaps retained a few corrupted principles, which fometimes might verify their prognoftics.

It is the common wonder of all men, how among fo many millions of faces there fhould be none alike. Now contrary, I wonder as much how there fhould be any : he that fhall confider how many thoufand feveral words have been careleffly

---

* Cf. Pfeud. Epid. v. c. 23.

and without study composed out of twenty-
four letters; withal, how many hundred
lines there are to be drawn in the fabric
of one man, shall easily find that this variety is necessary; and it will be very
hard that they shall so concur as to make
one portrait like another. Let a painter
carelessly limn out a million of faces, and
you shall find them all different; yea, let
him have his copy before him, yet after
all his art there will remain a sensible distinction;* for the pattern or example of
every thing is the perfectest in that kind,
whereof we still come short, though we
transcend or go beyond it, because herein
it is wide, and agrees not in all points
unto its copy. Nor doth the similitude
of creatures disparage the variety of nature, nor any way confound the works of
God. For even in things alike there is

---

* M. Wappers, Director of the Academy at Ant-
werp, told me that he has frequently given to ten or
twelve of his pupils as an exercise to copy a subject,
paying particular attention to some portion of the
coloring: and that scarcely ever two of them produced exactly the same tint.

diversity; and those that do seem to accord do manifestly disagree. And thus is man like God; for in the same things that we resemble him, we are utterly different from him. There was never any thing so like another as in all points to concur: there will ever some reserved difference slip in, to prevent the identity, without which two several things would not be alike, but the same, which is impossible.

III. But to return from philosophy to charity: I hold not so narrow a conceit of this virtue, as to conceive that to give alms is only to be charitable, or think a piece of liberality can comprehend the total of charity. Divinity hath wisely divided the act thereof into many branches, and hath taught us in this narrow way many paths unto goodness; as many ways as we may do good, so many ways we may be charitable: there are infirmities not only of body, but of soul, and fortunes, which do require the merciful hand of our abilities. I cannot

The souls of our fellow creatures as much the object of charity as their bodies.

contemn a man for ignorance, but behold
him with as much pity as I do Lazarus.
It is no greater charity to clothe his body,
than apparel the nakedneſs of his ſoul.
It is an honourable object to ſee the reaſons of other men wear our liveries, and
their borrowed underſtandings do homage
to the bounty of ours: it is the cheapeſt
way of beneficence, and like the natural
charity of the ſun, illuminates another
without obſcuring itſelf. To be reſerved
and caitiff in this part of goodneſs, is the
ſordideſt piece of covetouſneſs, and more
contemptible than pecuniary avarice. To
this (as calling myſelf a ſcholar) I am
obliged by the duty of my condition: I
make not therefore my head a grave, but
a treaſury of knowledge: I intend no
monopoly, but a community in learning:
I ſtudy not for my own ſake only, but
for theirs that ſtudy not for themſelves.
I envy no man that knows more than
myſelf, but pity them that know leſs. I
inſtruct no man as an exerciſe of my
knowledge, or with an intent rather to
nouriſh and keep it alive in mine own

The duty
of impart-
ing know-
ledge.

head than beget and propagate it in his: and in the midſt of all my endeavours, there is but one thought that dejects me, that my acquired parts muſt periſh with myſelf, nor can be legacied among my honoured friends. I cannot fall out or contemn a man for an error, or conceive why a difference in opinion ſhould divide an affection;* for controverſies, diſputes, and argumentations, both in philoſophy and in divinity, if they meet with diſcreet and peaceable natures, do not infringe the laws of charity. In all diſputes, ſo much as there is of paſſion, ſo much there is of nothing to the purpoſe; for then reaſon, like a bad hound, ſpends upon a falſe ſcent, and forſakes the queſtion firſt ſtarted. And in this is one reaſon why controverſies are never determined; for though they be amply propoſed, they are ſcarce at all handled; they do ſo ſwell with unneceſſary digreſſions, and the paren-theſis on the party is often as large as the main diſcourſe upon the ſubject. The

Differences of opinion need not divide affection.

* Cf. Bp. Butler, Serm. xii. p. 186.

foundations of religion are already established, and the principles of salvation subscribed unto by all: there remain not many controversies worth a passion; and yet never any disputed without, not only in divinity, but inferior arts. What a βατράχομυομαχία and hot skirmish is betwixt S and T in Lucian?* How do grammarians hack and slash for the genitive case in Jupiter!† How they do break their own pates to salve that of Priscian! *Si foret in terris, rideret Democritus.* Yea, even amongst wiser militants, how many wounds have been given, and credits slain, for the poor victory of an opinion, or beggarly conquest of a distinction! Scholars are men of peace, they bear no arms, but their tongues are sharper than Actius his razor;‡ their pens carry farther, and

---

* In his dialogue, *judicium vocalium*, where there is a large oration made to the vowels, being judges, by Sigma against Tau, complaining that Tau has bereaved him of many words, which should begin with Sigma. K.

† Whether *Jovis* or *Jupitris.*

‡ Accius Nævius, is reported by Livy. Lib. i. cap.

give a louder report than thunder : I had rather ſtand in the ſhock of a baſiliſco,* than in the fury of a mercileſs pen. It is not mere zeal to learning, or devotion to the Muſes, that wiſer princes patron the arts, and carry an indulgent aſpect unto ſcholars ; but a deſire to have their names eternized by the memory of their writings, and a fear of the revengeful pen of ſucceeding ages ; for theſe are the men that, when they have played their parts, and had their *exits*, muſt ſtep out and give the moral of their ſcenes, and deliver unto poſterity an inventory of their virtues and vices. And ſurely there goes a great deal of conſcience to the compiling of an hiſtory : there is no reproach to the ſcandal of a ſtory ; it is ſuch an authentic kind of falſehood that with authority belies our good names to all nations and poſterity.

IV. There is another offence

36, to have cut a whetſtone through with a razor, at the challenge of the King, Tarquinius Priſcus.

   * *Baſiliſco*, a kind of cannon.

unto charity, which no author hath ever
written of, and few take notice of; and
that's the reproach, not of whole pro-
fessions, mysteries, and conditions, but of
whole nations, wherein by opprobrious
epithets we miscall each other, and by an
uncharitable logic, from a disposition in a
few, conclude a habit in all. St. Paul,
that calls the Cretans liars, doth it but
indirectly, and upon quotation of their
own poet.* It is as bloody a thought in
one way, as Nero's was in another;† for

---

* That is, Epimenides; the place is, Tit. i. v. 12,
where St. Paul useth this verse, taken out of Epimenides.

Κρῆτες ἀεὶ ψεῦσται, κακὰ θηρία, γαστέρες ἀργαί.

† I suppose he alludes to that passage in Sueton. 38.
in the life of Nero, where he relates that a certain
person upon a time, spoke in his hearing these words,

Ἐμοῦ θανόντος γαῖα μιχθήτω πυρί,

i. e. When I am dead let earth be mingled with fire.
Whereupon the emperor uttered these words, Ἐμοῦ
ζῶντος, i. e. Yea, whilst I live: there by one word,
he expressed a cruel thought which I think is the
thing he meant. This is more cruel than the wish
of Caligula, that the people of Rome had but one
neck, that he might destroy them all at a blow. K.

by a word we wound a thousand, and at
one blow assassine the honour of a nation. It is as complete a piece of madnefs to miscall and rave against the times,
or think to recall men to reason by a fit
of passion. Democritus, that thought to
laugh the times into goodnefs, seems to
me as deeply hypochondriac as Heraclitus
that bewailed them. It moves not my
spleen to behold the multitude in their
proper humours, that is, in their fits of
folly and madnefs ; as well understanding
that wisdom is not profaned unto the
world, and 'tis the privilege of a few to
be virtuous. They that endeavour to
abolish vice, destroy also virtue ; for con-
traries, though they destroy one another,
are yet the life of one another. Thus
virtue (abolish vice) is an idea. Again,
the community of sin doth not disparage
goodnefs ; for when vice gains upon the
major part, virtue, in whom it remains,
becomes more excellent ; and being lost
in some, multiplies its goodnefs in others
which remain untouched, and persists entire in the general inundation. I can

therefore behold vice without a fatire,
content only with an admonition, or in-
ftructive reprehenfion; for noble natures,
and fuch as are capable of goodnefs, are
railed into vice, that might as eafily be
admonifhed into virtue; and we fhould
be all fo far the orators of goodnefs, as
to protect her from the power of vice,
and maintain the caufe of injured truth.
No man can juftly cenfure or condemn
another, becaufe indeed no man truly
knows another. This I perceive in myfelf; for I am in the dark to all the world,
and my neareft friends behold me but in
a cloud: thofe that know me but fuper-
ficially, think lefs of me than I do of myfelf; thofe of my near acquaintance think
more. God, who truly knows me, knows
that I am nothing; for He only beholds
me and all the world, who looks not on
us through a derived ray, or a trajection
of a fenfible fpecies, but beholds the fubftance without the help of accidents, and
the forms of things as we their operations.
Further, no man can judge another, becaufe no man knows himfelf: for we cen-

Man moft
ignorant in
the know-
ledge of
himfelf.

sure others but as they disagree from that
humour which we fancy laudable in ourselves, and commend others but for that
wherein they seem to quadrate and con-
sent with us. So that in conclusion, all
is but that we all condemn, self-love.*
'Tis the general complaint of these times,
and perhaps of those past, that charity
grows cold; which I perceive most verified in those which most do manifest the
fires and flames of zeal; for it is a virtue
that best agrees with coldest natures, and
such as are complexioned for humility.
But how shall we expect charity towards
others, when we are uncharitable to ourselves? *Charity begins at home*, is the
voice of the world; yet is every man his
greatest enemy, and as it were his own
executioner. *Non occides*, is the commandment of God, yet scarce observed by
any man; for I perceive every man is his
own Atropos, and lends a hand to cut
the thread of his own days. Cain was
not therefore the first murderer, but Adam,

---

* See Bishop Butler's eleventh Sermon.

who brought in death; whereof he beheld the practice and example in his own son Abel, and saw that verified in the experience of another, which faith could not persuade him in the theory of himself.

v. There is, I think, no man that apprehendeth his own miseries less than myself, and no man that so nearly apprehends another's. I could lose an arm without a tear, and with few groans, methinks, be quarter'd into pieces; yet can I weep most seriously at a play, and receive with a true passion the counterfeit griefs of those known and professed impostures. It is a barbarous part of inhumanity to add unto any afflicted party's misery, or endeavour to multiply in any man, a passion, whose single nature is already above his patience: this was the greatest affliction of Job; and those oblique expostulations of his friends, a deeper injury than the downright blows of the devil. It is not the tears of our own eyes only, but of our friends also, that do exhaust the current of our sorrows; which

Of sympathy.

Job. xix.

falling into many ſtreams, runs more
peaceably, and is contented with a narrower channel. It is an act within the
power of charity, to tranſlate a paſſion
out of one breaſt into another, and to divide a ſorrow almoſt out of itſelf; for an
affliction, like a dimenſion, may be ſo divided, as, if not indiviſible, at leaſt to become inſenſible. Now with my friend
I deſire not to ſhare or participate, but
to engroſs his ſorrows, that by making
them mine own, I may more eaſily diſcuſs
them; for in mine own reaſon, and within
myſelf, I can command that, which I cannot intreat without myſelf, and within the
circle of another. I have often thought
thoſe noble pairs and examples of friendſhip not ſo truly hiſtories of what had
been, as fictions of what ſhould be; but
I now perceive nothing in them but poſ-
ſibilities, nor any thing in the heroic examples of Damon and Pythias, Achilles
and Patroclus, which methinks upon ſome
grounds I could not perform within the
narrow compaſs of myſelf. That a man
ſhould lay down his life for his friend,

feems ftrange to vulgar affections, and fuch as confine themfelves within that worldly principle, *Charity begins at home.* For mine own part, I could never remember the relations that I held unto myfelf, nor the refpect that I owe unto my own nature, in the caufe of God, my country, and my friends.* Next to thefe three, I do embrace myfelf. I confefs I do not obferve that order that the fchools ordain our affections, to love our parents, wives, children, and then our friends; for excepting the injunctions of religion, I do not find in myfelf fuch a neceffary and indiffoluble fympathy to all thofe of my blood. I hope I do not break the fifth commandment, if I conceive I may love

---

* Cf. Pope's Effay on Man.

" Self-love but ferves the virtuous mind to wake,
As the fmall pebble ftirs the peaceful lake;
The centre moved, a circle ftraight fucceeds,
Another ftill, and ftill another fpreads;
Friend, parent, neighbour, next it will embrace,
His country next, and next all human race;
Wide and more wide the o'erflowings of the mind
Take every creature in of every kind."

my friend before the neareſt of my blood,
even thoſe to whom I owe the principles
of life: I never yet caſt a true affection
on a woman; but I have loved my friend
as I do virtue, my ſoul, my God. From
hence methinks I do conceive how God
loves man, what happineſs there is in the
love of God. Omitting all other, there
are three moſt myſtical unions; two natures in one perſon; three perſons in one
nature; one ſoul in two bodies. For
though indeed they be really divided, yet
are they ſo united as they ſeem but one,
and make rather a duality than two diftinct ſouls.

The myſ-
tery of true
affection.
VI. There are wonders in true
affection: it is a body of enigmas, myſteries, and riddles; wherein two ſo become one, as they both* become two.
I love my friend before myſelf, and yet
methinks I do not love him enough:
ſome few months hence, my multiplied
affection will make me believe I have not

---

* *Both*, i. e. each.

loved him at all: when I am from him,
I am dead till I be with him; when I am
with him, I am not satisfied, but would
still be nearer him. United souls are not
satisfied with embraces, but desire to be
truly each other; which being impossible,
their desires are infinite, and must proceed without a possibility of satisfaction.
Another misery there is in affection, that
whom we truly love like our ownselves,
we forget their looks, nor can our memory retain the idea of their faces;* and
it is no wonder, for they are ourselves,
and our affection makes their looks our
own. This noble affection falls not on
vulgar and common constitutions, but on
such as are mark'd for virtue: he that
can love his friend with this noble ardour,
will in a competent degree affect all.
Now if we can bring our affections to
look beyond the body, and cast an eye
upon the soul, we have found out the
true object, not only of friendship, but

---

* Cf. Keble's Christian Year, 4th Sunday in Advent.

charity; and the greatest happiness that we can bequeath the soul, is that wherein we all do place our last felicity, salvation; which though it be not in our power to bestow, it is in our charity and pious invocations to desire, if not procure and further. I cannot contentedly frame a prayer for myself in particular, without a catalogue for my friends; nor request a happiness wherein my sociable disposition doth not desire the fellowship of my neighbour. I never hear the toll of a passing bell, though in my mirth, without my prayers and best wishes for the departing spirit: I cannot go to cure the body of my patient, but I forget my profession, and call unto God for his soul:* I cannot see one say his prayers, but instead of imitating him, I fall into a supplication for him, who perhaps is no more to me than a common nature: and if God hath vouchsafed an ear to my supplications, there are surely many happy that never saw me, and enjoy the blessing

* See Appendix M.

of mine unknown devotions. To pray
for enemies, that is, for their salvation, is
no harsh precept, but the practice of our
daily and ordinary devotions. I cannot
believe the story of the Italian : * our
bad wishes and uncharitable desires proceed no further than this life; it is the
devil, and the uncharitable votes of hell,
that desire our misery in the world to
come.

VII. To do no injury, nor
take none, was a principle, which to my
former years, and impatient affections,
seemed to contain enough of morality ;
but my more settled years, and Christian
constitution have fallen upon severer re-
solutions. I can hold there is no such
thing as injury ; that if there be, there is
no such injury as revenge, and no such
revenge as the contempt of an injury ;
that to hate another, is to malign himself;
that the truest way to love another, is to
despise ourselves. I were unjust unto

To forgive
is the sweet-
est revenge.

---

* Cf. Pseud. Epidem. vii. 19.

mine own confcience, if I fhould fay I
am at variance with any thing like myfelf.
I find there are many pieces in this one
fabric of man; this frame is raifed upon
a mafs of antipathies: I am one methinks,
but as the world; wherein notwithftanding, there are a fwarm of diftinct effences,
and in them another world of contrarieties;
we carry private and domeftic enemies
within, public and more hoftile adverfaries
without. The devil, that did but buffet
St. Paul, plays methinks at fharp with
me: let me be nothing, if within the
compafs of myfelf I do not find the
battle of Lepanto, paffion againft reafon,
reafon againft faith, faith againft the devil,
and my confcience againft all. There is
another man within me, that's angry with
me, rebukes, commands, and daftards me.
I have no confcience of marble to refift
the hammer of more heavy offences; nor
yet fo foft and waxen, as to take the impreffion of each fingle peccadillo or fcape
of infirmity: I am of a ftrange belief,
that it is as eafy to be forgiven fome fins,
as to commit fome others. For my ori-

ginal fin, I hold it to be wafhed away in
my baptifm:* for my actual tranfgreffions,
I compute and reckon with God but from
my laft repentance, facrament, or general
abfolution; and therefore am not terrified
with the fins or madnefs of my youth.
I thank the goodnefs of God, I have no
fins that want a name; I am not fingular
in offences, my tranfgreffions are epidem-
ical, and from the common breath of our
corruption. For there are certain tempers
of body, which matched with an humor-
ous depravity of mind, do hatch and produce vitiofities, whofe newnefs and monftrofity of nature admits no name: this
was the temper of that lecher that car-
nalled with a ftatua, and the conftitution
of Nero in his fpintrian recreations. For
the heavens are not only fruitful in new
and unheard-of ftars, the earth in plants

---

* This is moft true as far as the imputation of the
fame is concerned. For where the means of avoiding
its confequences have been afforded, each after tranf-
greffion is actual, by a neglect of thofe means.

Coleridge.

and animals, but men's minds alſo in villany and vices: now the dulneſs of my
reaſon, and the vulgarity of my diſpoſition,
never prompted my invention, nor ſo-
licited my affection unto any of theſe;
yet even thoſe common and quotidian infirmities that ſo neceſſarily attend me,
and do ſeem to be my very nature, have
ſo dejected me, ſo broken the eſtimation
that I ſhould have otherwiſe of myſelf,
that I repute myſelf the moſt abjecteſt
piece of mortality. Divines preſcribe a
fit of ſorrow to repentance: there goes
indignation, anger, ſorrow, hatred, into
mine; paſſions of a contrary nature, which
neither ſeem to ſuit with this action, nor
my proper conſtitution. It is no breach
of charity to ourſelves, to be at variance
with our vices: nor to abhor that part of
us which is an enemy to the ground of
charity, our God; wherein we do but
imitate our great ſelves the world, whoſe
divided antipathies and contrary faces do
yet carry a charitable regard unto the
whole by their particular diſcords, pre-
ſerving the common harmony, and keeping

in fetters those powers, whose rebellions once masters, might be the ruin of all.

VIII. I thank God, amongst those millions of vices I do inherit and hold from Adam, I have escaped one, and that a mortal enemy to charity, the first and father-sin, not only of man but of the devil, pride: a vice whose name is comprehended in a monosyllable, but in its nature not circumscribed with a world: I have escaped it in a condition that can hardly avoid it: those petty acquisitions and reputed perfections that advance and elevate the conceits of other men, add no feathers unto mine. I have seen a grammarian tower and plume himself over a single line in Horace, and shew more pride in the construction of one ode, than the author in the composure of the whole book. For my own part, besides the jargon and *patois* of several provinces, I understand no less than six languages; yet I protest I have no higher conceit of myself, than had our fathers before the confusion of Babel, when there was but one language in the world, and none to boaſt himſelf either linguiſt or critic. I have not only ſeen ſeveral countries, beheld the nature of their climes, the chorography of their provinces, topography of their cities, but underſtood their ſeveral laws, cuſtoms, and policies; yet cannot all this perſuade the dulneſs of my ſpirit unto ſuch an opinion of myſelf, as I behold in nimbler and conceited heads, that never looked a degree beyond their neſts. I know the names, and ſomewhat more, of all the conſtellations in my horizon; yet I have ſeen a prating mariner, that could only name the pointers and the north ſtar, outtalk me, and conceit himſelf a whole ſphere above me. I know moſt of the plants of my country, and of thoſe about me; yet methinks I do not know ſo many as when I did but know a hundred, and had ſcarcely ever ſimpled further than Cheapſide:* for, indeed, heads of capacity,

---

* — "theſe liſping hawthorn buds that come like women in men's apparel, and ſmell like Bucklerſbury in ſimple-time." Merry Wives of Windſor, iii. 3.

and such as are not full with a handful
or easy measure of knowledge, think
they know nothing till they know all;
which being impossible, they fall upon
the opinion of Socrates, and only know
they know not any thing. I cannot
think that Homer pined away upon the
riddle of the fishermen;* or that Aristotle,
who understood the uncertainty of knowledge, and confessed so often the reason of
man too weak for the works of nature,
did ever drown himself upon the flux and
reflux of *Euripus*.† We do but learn to-
day, what our better advanced judgments
will unteach to-morrow; and Aristotle
doth but instruct us, as Plato did him;
that is, to confute himself. I have run
through all sorts, yet find no rest in any:
though our first studies and junior endeavours may style us Peripatetics, Stoics, or
Academics; yet I perceive the wisest heads
prove, at last, almost all Sceptics, and stand
like Janus in the field of knowledge. I

---

* Cf. Plutarch, and Plin. Epist. Lib. ix. Ep. 36.
† Cf. Pseud. Epidem. vii. 14.

have therefore one common and authentic philofophy I learned in the fchools, whereby I difcourfe and fatisfy the reafon of other men; another more referved, and drawn from experience, whereby I content mine own. Solomon, that complained of ignorance in the height of knowledge, hath not only humbled my conceits, but difcouraged my endeavours. There is yet another conceit that hath fometimes made me fhut my books, which tells me it is a vanity to wafte our days in the blind purfuit of knowledge; it is but attending a little longer, and we fhall enjoy that by inftinct and infufion, which we endeavour at here by labour and inquifition: it is better to fit down in a modeft ignorance, and reft contented with the natural bleffing of our own reafons, than buy the uncertain knowledge of this life with fweat and vexation, which death gives every fool gratis, and is an acceffary of our glorification.*

---

* Cf. Bp. Butler's Sermon xv. " Knowledge is not our proper happinefs. Whoever will in the leaft

IX. I was never yet once [married] and commend their refolutions who never marry twice : not that I difallow of fecond marriage ; as neither in all cafes of polygamy, which, confidering fome times, and the unequal number of both fexes, may be alfo neceffary. The whole world was made for man, but the twelfth part of man for woman : man is the whole world, and the breath of God ; woman the rib, and crooked piece of man. I could be content that we might procreate like trees without conjunction,* or that there were any way to perpetuate the world without this trivial and vulgar way of coition : it is the foolifheft act a wife man commits in all his life ; nor is there any thing that will more dejeat his cooled imagination, when he fhall confider what an odd and unworthy piece of folly he hath

---

attend to the thing will fee, that it is the gaining, not the having of it, which is the entertainment of the mind." &c.

* Es wäre doch immer hübscher, wenn man die Kinder von den Bäumen schüttelte. Goethe.

committed. I speak not in prejudice, nor
am averse from that sweet sex, but naturally amorous of all that is beautiful: I
can look a whole day with delight upon
a handsome picture, though it be but of
an horse. It is my temper, and I like it
the better, to affect all harmony; and
sure there is music even in the beauty,
and the silent note which Cupid strikes,
far sweeter than the sound of an instrument:* for there is music wherever there
is harmony, order, or proportion: and
thus far we may maintain *the music of the
spheres*; for those well ordered motions,
and regular paces, though they give no
sound unto the ear, yet to the understand-

---

* So Daniell, (Complaint of Rosamond:)
Ah Beauty! Syren faire, enchanting Good,
Sweet silent Rhetorick of perfuading eyes;
Dumbe eloquence, whose power doth move the blood,
More than the words or wifdom of the wife;
Still Harmony, whose diapafon lies
    Within a brow; the Key which paffions move
    To ravifh fenfe and play a world in love.

" When Love fpeaks, the voice of all the gods
Makes heaven drowfy with the harmony."
Loves Labour Loft. iv. 3.

ing they ſtrike a note moſt full of harmony.* Whatſoever is harmonically compoſed, delights in harmony ; which makes
me much diſtruſt the ſymmetry of thoſe
heads which declaim againſt all church
muſic. For myſelf, not only from my
obedience, but my particular genius, I do
embrace it : for even that vulgar and ta-
vern muſic, which makes one man merry,
another mad, ſtrikes in me a deep fit of
devotion, and a profound contemplation
of the Firſt Compoſer ; there is ſomething
in it of divinity more than the ear diſ-
covers : it is an hieroglyphical and ſha-
dowed leſſon of the whole world, and
creatures of God; ſuch a melody to the
ear, as the whole world, well underſtood,
would afford the underſtanding.† In brief,
it is a ſenſible fit of that harmony which

---

* Cf. Merchant of Ven. v. 1. Milton's Arcades.

† " Is not God's Univerſe a Symbol of the God-
like ; is not Immenſity a Temple ; is not Man's
Hiſtory, and Men's Hiſtory a perpetual Evangel ?
Liſten, and for Organ-muſic thou wilt ever, as of old,
hear the Morning Stars ſing together." Sartor Re-
ſartus, p. 299.

intellectually founds in the ears of God. It unties the ligaments of my frame, takes me to pieces, dilates me out of myself, and by degrees, methinks, resolves me into Heaven.* I will not say with Plato,† the soul is an harmony, but harmonical, and hath its nearest sympathy unto music : thus some, whose temper of body agrees and humours the constitution of their souls, are born poets, though indeed all are naturally inclined unto rhythm.‡ This made

---

* From the MSS.—Cf. Milton's Il Penserofo. 165. —Wordsworth's Tintern Abbey. vol ii. p. 163.

† Phædo. c. xxxvi. 41.

‡ " The old musician, who rather figuratively we may suppose, than with philosophical seriousness, declared the *soul itself to be nothing but harmony*, provoked the sprightly remark of Cicero, *that he drew his philosophy from the Art which he professed ;* but if without departing from his own art, he had merely described the human frame as the noblest and sweetest of musical instruments, endued with a natural disposition to resonance and sympathy, alternately affecting and affected by the soul which pervades it, his description might, perhaps, have been physically just, and certainly ought not to have been hastily ridiculed." Asiatic Researches. vol. iii. p. 56. Cf. Hooker. Eccl. Pol. v. xxxviii. Confessions of an English Opium-Eater, p. 106.

Tacitus, in the very firſt line of his ſtory,
fall upon a verſe ;* and Cicero, the worſt
of poets, but declaiming for a poet, falls
in the very firſt ſentence upon a perfect
hexameter.†   I feel not in me thoſe ſor-
did and unchriſtian deſires of my profeſſion ; I do not ſecretly implore and wiſh
for plagues, rejoice at famines, revolve
ephemerides and almanacks in expectation
of malignant aſpects, fatal conjunctions,
and eclipſes : I rejoice not at unwholeſome
ſprings, nor unſeaſonable winters : my
prayer goes with the huſbandman's ; I deſire every thing in its proper ſeaſon, that
neither men nor the times be out of
temper.   Let me be ſick myſelf, if ſometimes the malady of my patient be not a
diſeaſe unto me ; I deſire rather to cure
his infirmities than my own neceſſities :
where I do him no good, methinks it is
ſcarce honeſt gain ; though I confeſs 'tis
but the worthy ſalary of our well-intended

Our Phyſi-
cian hath
the general
cauſe of
humanity
at heart.

* *Urbem Romam in principio reges habuere.*   An-
nales. i. 1.

† *In qua me non inficior mediocriter eſſe.*   Pro
Archia.

endeavours. I am not only afhamed, but heartily forry, that befides death, there are difeafes incurable : yet not for my own fake, or that they be beyond my art, but for the general caufe and fake of humanity, whofe common caufe I apprehend as mine own. And to fpeak more generally, thofe three noble profeffions which all civil commonwealths do honour, are raifed upon the fall of Adam, and are not exempt from their infirmities ; there are not only difeafes incurable in phyfic, but cafes indiffolvable in laws, vices incorrigible in divinity. If general councils may err, I do not fee why particular courts fhould be infallible : their perfecteft rules are raifed upon the erroneous reafons of man ; and the laws of one, do but condemn the rules of another ; as Ariftotle oft-times the opinions of his predeceffors, becaufe, though agreeable to reafon, yet were they not confonant to his own rules, and the logic of his proper principles. Again, to fpeak nothing of the fin againft the Holy Ghoft, whofe cure not only, but whofe nature is unknown ; I can cure the gout or ftone in

St. Matt. xii. 31. St. Mark iii. 28.

some, sooner than Divinity, pride or avarice in others. I can cure vices by physic
when they remain incurable by divinity;
and they shall obey my pills when they
contemn their precepts. I boast nothing,
but plainly say, we all labour against our
own cure; for death is the cure of all
diseases. There is no *catholicon* or universal remedy I know, but this; which,
though nauseous to queasie stomachs, yet
to prepared appetites is nectar, and a plea-
sant potion of immortality.

x. For my conversation, it is
like the sun's, with all men, and with a
friendly aspect to good and bad. Methinks
there is no man bad, and the worst, best;
that is, while they are kept within the
circle of those qualities wherein they are
good: there is no man's mind of such dis-
cordant and jarring a temper, to which a
tunable disposition may not strike a harmony. *Magnæ virtutes, nec minora vitia:*
it is the posie* of the best natures, and may

Our Physi-
cian think-
eth no man
so bad but
that there
is good in
him,—

---

* *Posie.* The Motto on a ring. Cf. Hamlet, iii.
2. Mer. of Ven. v. 1.

be inverted on the worſt. There are in the moſt depraved and venomous diſpoſitions, certain pieces that remain untouched, which by an *antiperiſtaſis* become more excellent, or by the excellency of their antipathies are able to preſerve themſelves from the contagion of their enemy vices, and perſiſt entire beyond the general corruption. For it is alſo thus in Nature. The greateſt balſams do lie enveloped in the bodies of the moſt powerful corroſives: I ſay, moreover, and I ground upon experience, that poiſons contain within themſelves their own antidote, and that which preſerves them from the venom of themſelves, without which they were not deleterious to others only, but to themſelves alſo. But it is the corruption that I fear within me, not the contagion of commerce without me. 'Tis that unruly regiment within me, that will deſtroy me ; 'tis I that do infect myſelf ; the man without a navel yet lives in me ;* I feel that original canker corrode and devour me ; and there-

and feareth his own corruption more than contagion from others.

---

* *That is*, the old Adam. Cf. Pſeud. Epidem. v. 5.

fore *defenda me Dios de me*, Lord deliver me from myself, is a part of my litany; and the firft voice of my retired imaginations. There is no man alone, becaufe every man is a microcofm, and carries the whole world about him : *Nunquam minus folus quam cum folus*, though it be the apophthegm of a wife man,[*] is yet true in the mouth of a fool ; for indeed, though in a wildernefs, a man is never alone, not only becaufe he is with himfelf and his own thoughts, but becaufe he is with the devil, who ever conforts with our folitude, and is that unruly rebel that mufters up thofe difordered motions which accompany our fequeftered imaginations : and to fpeak more narrowly, there is no fuch thing as folitude, nor any thing that can be faid to be alone and by itfelf, but God, who is his own circle, and can fubfift by himfelf ; all others, befides their diffimilary and heterogenous parts, which in a manner multiply their natures, cannot fubfift without the concourfe of God, and the fociety

---

[*] *Publius Scipio.* Cic. de Off. lib. iii.

of that hand which doth uphold their natures. In brief, there can be nothing
truly alone and by itſelf, which is not truly
one; and ſuch is only God: all others do
tranſcend an unity, and ſo by conſequence
are many.

Man's life a
conſtant
miracle.

XI. Now for my life, it is a
miracle of thirty years, which to relate,
were not a hiſtory, but a piece of poetry,
and would ſound to common ears like a
fable: for the world, I count it not an inn,
but an hoſpital; and a place not to live,
but to die in. The world that I regard
is myſelf; it is the microcoſm of mine
own frame that I caſt mine eye on; for
the other, I uſe it but like my globe, and
turn it round ſometimes for my recreation.
Men that look upon my outſide, peruſing
only my condition and fortunes, do err in
my altitude; for I am above Atlas his
ſhoulders. The earth is a point not only
in reſpect of the heavens above us, but of
that heavenly and celeſtial part within us:
that maſs of fleſh that circumſcribes me,
limits not my mind: that ſurface that tells

the heavens it hath an end, cannot perſuade
me I have any : I take my circle to be
above three hundred and ſixty ; though
the number of the arc do meaſure my
body, it comprehendeth not my mind :
whilſt I ſtudy to find how I am a microcoſm, or little world, I find myſelf ſomething more than the great. There is ſurely
a piece of divinity in us, ſomething that
was before the elements, and owes no
homage unto the ſun. Nature tells me I
am the image of God, as well as Scrip- Gen. i. 27.
ture : he that underſtands not thus much,
hath not his introduction or firſt leſſon,
and is yet to begin the alphabet of man.
Let me not injure the felicity of others,
if I ſay I am as happy as any : *Ruat cœ-
lum, fiat voluntas tua*, ſalveth all ; ſo that
whatſoever happens, it is but what our
daily prayers deſire. In brief, I am content ; and what ſhould Providence add
more ? Surely this is it we call happineſs,
and this do I enjoy ; with this I am happy
in a dream, and as content to enjoy a happineſs in a fancy, as others in a more apparent truth and reality. There is ſurely Of Dreams.

a nearer apprehenfion of any thing that delights us in our dreams, than in our waked fenfes : without this I were unhappy ; for my awaked judgment difcontents me, ever whifpering unto me, that I am from my friend ; but my friendly dreams in the night requite me, and make me think I am within his arms. I thank God for my happy dreams, as I do for my good reft, for there is a fatisfaction in them unto reafonable defires, and fuch as can be content with a fit of happinefs : and furely it is not a melancholy conceit to think we are all afleep in this world, and that the conceits of this life are as mere dreams to thofe of the next ; as the phantafms of the night, to the conceits of the day. There is an equal delufion in both, and the one doth but feem to be the emblem or picture of the other : we are fomewhat more than ourfelves in our fleeps, and the flumber of the body feems to be but the waking of the foul. It is the ligation of fenfe, but the liberty of reafon ; and our waking conceptions do not match the fancies of our fleeps. At my nativity

my afcendant was the watery fign of Scor-
pius; I was born in the planetary hour of
Saturn, and I think I have a piece of that
leaden planet in me.* I am no way face-
tious, nor difpofed for the mirth and galliardize of company; yet in one dream I
can compofe a whole comedy, behold the
action, and apprehend the jefts, and laugh
myfelf awake at the conceits thereof. Were
my memory as faithful as my reafon is
then fruitful, I would never ftudy but in
my dreams; and this time alfo would I
choofe for my devotions: but our groffer
memories have then fo little hold of our
abftracted underftandings, that they forget
the ftory, and can only relate to our awaked
fouls, a confufed and broken tale of that
that hath paffed. Ariftotle, who hath
written a fingular tract of fleep, hath not,
methinks, thoroughly defined it; nor yet
Galen, though he feem to have corrected
it; for thofe noctambuloes and night-
walkers, though in their fleep, do yet enjoy the action of their fenfes: we muft

---

* Cf. Hor. Od. ii. xvii. 17.

therefore fay that there is fomething in us that is not in the jurifdiction of Morpheus; and that thofe abftracted and ecftatic fouls do walk about in their own corps, as fpirits with the bodies they affume, wherein they feem to hear, fee, and feel, though indeed the organs are deftitute of fenfe, and their natures of thofe faculties that fhould inform them. Thus it is obferved, that men fometimes upon the hour of their departure, do fpeak and reafon above themfelves. For then the foul beginning to be freed from the ligaments of the body, begins to reafon like herfelf, and to difcourfe in a ftrain above mortality.*

Of fleep.   XII. We term fleep a death; and yet it is waking that kills us, and deftroys thofe fpirits that are the houfe of life. 'Tis indeed a part of life that beft expreffeth death; for every man truly lives, fo long as he acts his nature, or fome way makes good the faculties of himfelf. Themiftocles, therefore, that flew his fol-

---

* See Appendix N.

dier in his sleep, was a merciful executioner: 'tis a kind of punishment the mildness of no laws hath invented: I wonder the fancy of Lucan and Seneca did not discover it. It is that death by which we may be literally said to die daily; a death which Adam died before his mortality; a death whereby we live a middle and moderating point between life and death: in fine, so like death, I dare not trust it without my prayers, and an half adieu unto the world, and take my farewell in a colloquy with God.

> The night is come; like to the day,
> Depart not thou, great God, away.
> Let not my sins, black as the night,
> Eclipse the lustre of thy light.
> Keep still in my horizon: for to me
> The sun makes not the day, but Thee.
> Thou whose nature cannot sleep,
> On my temples sentry keep:
> Guard me 'gainst those watchful foes,
> Whose eyes are open while mine close.
> Let no dreams my head infest,
> But such as Jacob's temples blest.
> Whilst I do rest, my soul advance;
> Make my sleep a holy trance:
> That I may, my rest being wrought,
> Awake into some holy thought.

And with as active vigour run
My courſe, as doth the nimble ſun.
Sleep is a death, O make me try,
By ſleeping, what it is to die :
And as gently lay my head
On my grave, as now my bed.
Howe'er I reſt, great God, let me
Awake again at laſt with Thee.
And thus aſſur'd, behold I lie
Securely, or to wake or die.
Theſe are my drowſy days ; in vain
I do now wake to ſleep again :
O come that hour, when I ſhall never
Sleep thus again, but wake for ever.*

This is the dormitive I take to bedward ;
I need no other laudanum than this to
make me ſleep ; after which I cloſe mine
eyes in ſecurity, content to take my leave
of the ſun, and ſleep unto the reſurrec-
tion.

Juſtice. XIII. The method I ſhould
uſe in diſtributive juſtice, I often obſerve

---

* Compare this with the beautiful and well-known
' Evening Hymn' of Biſhop Ken : and theſe again
with ſeveral of the Hymni Eccleſiæ, eſpecially that
beginning ' Salvator Mundi, Domine,' with which
Ken and Browne, both Wyckhamiſts, muſt have been
familiar.　See Bowles's Life of Ken.

in commutative, and keep a geometrical proportion in both, whereby becoming equable to others, I become unjuft to my-felf, and fupererogate in that common principle, *Do unto others as thou wouldft be done unto thyfelf.** I was not born unto riches, neither is it, I think, my ftar to be wealthy; or if it were, the freedom of my mind, and franknefs of my difpofition, were able to contradict and crofs my fates: for to me, avarice feems not fo much a vice, as a deplorable piece of madnefs;† to conceive ourfelves urinals, or be per-fuaded that we are dead, is not fo ridicu-lous, nor fo many degrees beyond the power of hellebore,‡ as this. The opi-nions of theory, and pofitions of men, are not fo void of reafon, as their practifed conclufions: fome have held that fnow is

Avarice a ridiculous vice.

---

* See Appendix O.

† "That a man who is Deputy Lieutenant of the whole world, fhould not act like a Prince within his territories, is a thing to be counted more a matter of prodigy than proof." Religio Jurifprudentis.

‡ *Hellebore* was thought to be a fpecific againft madnefs.

black, that the earth moves, that the soul is air, fire, water ; but all this is philosophy, and there is no delirium, if we do but speculate the folly and indisputable dotage of avarice.* To that subterraneous idol, and god of the earth, I do confess I am an atheist ; I cannot persuade myself to honour that the world adores ; whatsoever virtue its prepared substance† may have within my body, it hath no influence nor operation without : I would not entertain a base design, or an action that should call me villain, for the Indies ; and for this only do I love and honour my own soul, and have methinks two arms too few to embrace myself. ‡ Aristotle is too severe, that will not allow us to be truly liberal without wealth, and the bountiful hand of fortune : if this be true, I

---

* i. e. There is nothing worthy of the name delirium when compared with the folly, &c.

† Cf. Pseud. Epidem. ii. 5. iii. 22.

‡ There is an error here. Aristotle distinctly says (Eth. iv. 2.) that true liberality consists not in the magnitude of the gift, but in the disposition of the giver : but he says (Eth. iv. 5.) that a man with slender means cannot be *munificent*.

muſt confeſs I am charitable only in my liberal intentions, and bountiful well-wiſhes. But if the example of the mite be not only an act of wonder, but an example of the nobleſt charity, ſurely poor men may alſo build hoſpitals, and the rich alone have not erected cathedrals. I have a private method which others obſerve not; I take the opportunity of myſelf to do good; I borrow occaſion of charity from my own neceſſities, and ſupply the wants of others, when I am in moſt need myſelf;* for it is an honeſt ſtratagem to take advantage of ourſelves, and ſo to huſband the acts of virtue, that where they were defective in one circumſtance, they may repay their want, and multiply their goodneſs in another.† I have not Peru in my deſires, but a competence and ability to perform thoſe good works, to which the Almighty hath inclined my nature. He is rich, who hath enough to be

St. Luke xxi. 1—4.

and may even build Hoſpitals and Cathedrals.

---

* When I am reduced to the laſt teſter, I love to divide it with the poor. MSS. and Ed. 1642.

† Eſſays of Elia. 1ſt part p. 71.

charitable; and it is hard to be so poor, that a noble mind may not find a way to this piece of goodness. *He that giveth to* Prov. xix. 17. *the poor, lendeth to the Lord:** there is more rhetoric in that one sentence, than in a library of sermons; and indeed if those sentences were understood by the reader, with the same emphasis as they are delivered by the Author, we needed not those volumes of instructions, but might be honest by an epitome. Upon this motive only I cannot behold a beggar without relieving his necessities with my purse, or his soul with my prayers; these scenical and accidental differences between us, cannot make me forget that common and untouched part of us both: there is under these *centoes* and miserable outsides, these

---

* In St. George's Church, Doncaster, is to be seen this epitaph.

How now, who is here?	That I spent, that I had:
I, Robin of Doncastere	That I gave, that I have:
And Margaret my fere.	That I left, that I lost.

A. D. 1579.

Quoth Robertus Byrks, who in this world did reign 3 score yeares and 7, and yet lived not one.

mutilate and femi-bodies, a foul of the same alloy with our own, whose genealogy is God as well as ours, and in as fair a way to salvation as ourselves.* Statists that labour to contrive a commonwealth without poverty, take away the object of charity, not only not understanding the commonwealth of a Christian, but forgetting the prophecy of Christ.

XIV. Now there is another part of charity, which is the basis and pillar of this, and that is the love of God, for whom we love our neighbour; for this I think charity, to love God for himself, and our neighbour for God.‡ All

Job xxxi. 13—15.

St. Matt. xxvi. 11. Cf. Deut. xv. 11.

God alone loved for his own sake; and our neighbour for God's.

---

* So Herbert.

"Man is God's image; but a poor man is
Christ's stamp to boot: both images regard.
God reckons for him, counts the favour His:
Write, So much given to God: thou shalt be heard."

‡ "Flatter not thyself in thy faith to God, if thou wantest charity for thy neighbour: and think not thou hast charity for thy neighbour, if thou wantest faith to God: where they are not both together, they are both wanting; they are both dead if once divided."

Quarles' Enchiridion, Cent. ii. 11. 1650.

that is truly amiable is God, or as it were
a divided piece of him, that retains a reflex or shadow of himself. Nor is it strange
that we should place affection on that
which is invisible: all that we truly love
is thus; what we adore under affection of
our senses, deserves not the honour of so
pure a title. Thus we adore virtue,
though to the eyes of sense she be invisible: thus that part of our noble friends
that we love, is not that part that we embrace, but that insensible part that our
arms cannot embrace. God being all
goodness, can love nothing but himself;
he loves us but for that part which is as
it were himself, and the traduction of his
Holy Spirit.* Let us call to assize the
loves of our parents, the affection of our
wives and children, and they are all dumb
shows and dreams, without reality, truth,
or constancy: for first, there is a strong
bond of affection between us and our parents; yet how easily dissolved! we betake

---

* " Every true Virtue is a part of that Love with
which God loveth himself."   Spinosa.

ourſelves to a woman, forget our mother in a wife, and the womb that bare us, in that that ſhall bear our image : this woman bleſſing us with children, our affection leaves the level it held before, and ſinks from our bed unto our iſſue and picture of poſterity, where affection holds no ſteady manſion. They, growing up in years, deſire our ends ; or applying themſelves to a woman, take a lawful way to love another better than ourſelves. Thus I perceive a man may be buried alive, and behold his grave in his own iſſue.

xv. I conclude therefore and ſay, there is no happineſs under (or, as Copernicus will have it, above) the ſun, nor any crambe in that repeated verity and burthen of all the wiſdom of Solomon, All is vanity and vexation of ſpirit ; there is no felicity in that the world adores. Ariſtotle, whilſt he labours to refute the ideas of Plato, falls upon one himſelf : for his *ſummum bonum* is a chimera, and there is no ſuch thing as his felicity. That wherein God himſelf is happy, the holy

Our Phyſician concludeth and declareth his belief that there is no happineſs but in God.

angels are happy, in whofe defect the devils are unhappy; that dare I call happinefs: whatfoever conduceth unto this,
may with an eafy metaphor, deferve that
name; whatfoever elfe the world terms
happinefs, is to me a ftory out of Pliny,
an apparition, or neat delufion, wherein
there is no more of happinefs, than the
name. Blefs me in this life with but peace
of my confcience, command of my affections, the love of Thyfelf and my deareft
friends, and I fhall be happy enough to
pity Cæfar. Thefe are, O Lord, the
humble defires of my moft reafonable ambition, and all I dare call happinefs on
earth; wherein I fet no rule or limit to thy
hand or providence: difpofe of me
according to the wifdom of thy
pleafure: thy will be done,
though in my own
undoing.

A Letter to a Friend

Upon occasion of the Death

of his intimate

Friend.

Letter to a Friend.

Ive me leave to wonder that news of this nature ſhould have ſuch heavy wings that you ſhould hear ſo little concerning your deareſt Friend, and that I muſt make that unwilling repetition to tell you, *ad portam rigidos calces extendit*, that he is dead and buried, and by this time no puny among the mighty nations of the dead ; for though he left this world not very many days paſt, yet every hour you know largely addeth unto that dark ſociety ; and conſidering the inceſſant mortality of mankind, you cannot conceive there dieth in the whole earth ſo few as a thouſand an hour.

Although at this diſtance you had no early account or particular of his death, yet your affection may ceafe to wonder that you had not fome fecret fenfe or intimation thereof by dreams, thoughtful whifperings, mercurifms, airy nuncio's, or fympathetical infinuations, which many feem to have had at the death of their deareft friends: for fince we find in that famous ftory,* that fpirits themfelves were fain to tell their fellows at a diftance that the great *Antonio* was dead, we have a fufficient excufe for our ignorance in fuch particulars, and muft reft content with the common road, and *Appian* way of knowledge by information. Though the uncertainty of the end of this world hath confounded all human predictions, yet they who fhall live to fee the fun and moon darkened, and the ftars to fall from heaven, will hardly be deceived in the advent of the laft day; and therefore ftrange it is, that the common fallacy of confumptive perfons, who feel not themfelves

St. Matt.
xxiv. 29.

---

* In *Plutarch* his *Defect of Oracles*, wherein he relates that a voice was heard crying to mariners at fea, *Great Pan is dead.*

dying, and therefore ſtill hope to live,
ſhould alſo reach their friends in perfect
health and judgment: that you ſhould be
ſo little acquainted with Plautus his ſick
complexion, or that almoſt an Hippocra-
tical face ſhould not alarum you to higher
fears, or rather deſpair, of his continuation
in ſuch an emaciated ſtate, wherein medical predictions fail not, as ſometimes in
acute diſeaſes, and wherein 'tis as dangerous to be ſentenced by a Phyſician as a
Judge.

Upon my firſt viſit I was bold to tell
them who had not let fall all hopes of his
recovery, that in my ſad opinion he was
not like to behold a graſſhopper, much
leſs to pluck another fig; and in no long
time after, ſeemed to diſcover that odd
mortal ſymptom in him not mentioned
by Hippocrates, that is, to loſe his own
face, and look like ſome of his near relations: for he maintained not his proper
countenance, but looked like his uncle,
the lines of whoſe face lay deep and inviſible in his healthful viſage before: for as
from our beginning we run through va-

riety of looks, before we come to confiftent and fettled faces, fo before our end, by fick and languifhing alterations, we put on new vifages, and in our retreat to earth, may fall upon fuch looks, which from community of feminal originals, were before latent in us.

He was fruitlefsly put in hope of advantage by change of air, and imbibing the pure aerial nitre of thefe parts; and therefore, being fo far fpent, he quickly found Sardinia in Tivoli,* and the moft healthful air of little effect, where Death had fet her broad arrow; † for he lived not unto the middle of May, and confirmed the obfervation of Hippocrates of that mortal time of the year, when the leaves of the fig-tree refemble a daw's claw. He is happily feated who lives in places whofe air, earth,

---

* The unwholefome atmofphere of *Sardinia* was as proverbial as the falubrity of *Tivoli*.

" Nullo fata loco poffis excludere: cum mors Venerit, in medio Tibure Sardinia eft."

　　　　Mart. iv. lx. 5. Cf. Tac. Annal. ii. 85.

† In the Queen's forefts the mark of a broad arrow is fet upon fuch trees as are to be cut down.

and water, promote not the infirmities of
his weaker parts, or is early removed into
regions that correct them. He that is ta-
bidly inclined were unwife to pafs his days
in Portugal : cholical perfons will find little
comfort in Auftria or Vienna : he that is
weak-legged muft not be in love with
Rome, nor an infirm head with Venice or
Paris. Death hath not only particular
ftars in heaven, but malevolent places on
earth, which fingle out our infirmities and
ftrike at our weaker parts ; in which concern, paffager and migrant birds have the
great advantages, who are naturally con-
ftituted for diftant habitations, whom no
feas nor places limit, but in their appointed
feafons will vifit us from Greenland and
Mount Atlas, and as fome think, even
from the Antipodes.

Though we could not have his life, yet
we miffed not our defires in his foft departure, which was fcarce an expiration ;
and his end not unlike his beginning,
when the *falient point* fcarce affords a fenfible motion, and his departure fo like unto fleep, that he fcarce needed the civil

ceremony of clofing his eyes; contrary
unto the common way, wherein death
draws up, fleep lets fall the eyelids. With
what ftrife and pains we come into the
world we know not, but 'tis commonly
no eafy matter to get out of it: yet if it
could be made out, that fuch who have
eafy nativities have commonly hard deaths,
and contrarily; his departure was fo eafy,
that we might juftly fufpect his birth was
of another nature, and that fome *Juno* fat
crofs-legged at his nativity. Befides his
foft death, the incurable ftate of his difeafe might fomewhat extenuate your for-
row, who know that monfters but feldom
happen, miracles more rarely, in Phyfick.
Angelus Victorius gives a ferious account
of a confumptive, hectical, phthyfical woman, who was fuddenly cured by the in-
terceffion of Ignatius. We read not of
any in Scripture who in this cafe applied
unto our Saviour, though fome may be
contained in that large expreffion, that
He went about Galilee healing all manner
of ficknefs, and all manner of difeafes.
Amulets, fpells, figils, and incantations,

Garden of
Cyrus, cap.
v.

Vide Con-
fultationes.

St. Matt.
iv. 23.

practised in other diseases, are seldom pretended in this; and we find no sigil in the
Archidoxis of Paracelsus to cure an extreme consumption or marasmus, which,
if other diseases fail, will put a period unto
long livers, and at last makes dust of all.
And therefore the stoics could not but
think that the fiery principle would wear
out all the rest, and at last make an end
of the world; which notwithstanding, without such a lingering period, the Creator
may effect at his pleasure, and to make
an end of all things on earth, and our
planetical system of the world, He need
but put out the sun.

*Religio
Medici, xlv.*

I was not so curious to entitle the stars
unto any concern of his death, yet could
not but take notice that he died when the
moon was in motion from the meridian:
at which time, an old Italian long ago
would persuade me, that the greatest part
of men died: but herein I confess I could
never satisfy my curiosity, although from
the time of tides in places upon or near
the sea, there may be considerable deduc-
tions, and Pliny hath an odd and remark-

able paffage concerning the death of men
and animals upon the recefs or ebb of the
fea.*   However, certain it is, he died in
the dead and deep part of the night, when
Nox might be moft apprehenfibly faid to
be the daughter of *Chaos*, the mother of
Sleep and *Death*, according to old genealogy ; and fo went out of this world about
that hour when our bleffed Saviour entered
it, and about what time many conceive he
will return again unto it.   Cardan hath a
peculiar and no hard obfervation from a
man's hand, to know whether he was born
in the day or night, which I confefs holdeth
in my own ; and Scaliger to that purpofe hath another from the tip of the ear.
Moft men are begotten in the night, animals in the day ; but whether more perfons have been born in the night or the
day, were a curiofity undecidable, though
more have perifhed by violent deaths in
the day, yet in natural diffolutions both
times may hold an indifferency, at leaft

Hefiod,
Theog. 756.

---

* Cf. Plin. Hift. Nat. ii. 98. Mead *de Imperio
Solis atque Lunæ*.   Shakf. Henry Vth. ii. 3.

but contingent inequality. The whole course of time runs out in the nativity and death of things; which whether they happen by succession or coincidence, are best computed by the natural, not artificial, day.

That Charles the Vth was crown'd upon the day of his nativity, it being in his own power so to order it, makes no singular animadversion; but that he should also take King Francis prisoner upon that day, was an unexpected coincidence, which made the same remarkable. Antipater, who had an anniversary feast every year upon his birth-day, needed no astrological revolution to know what day he should die on. When the fixed stars have made a revolution unto the points from whence they first set out, some of the ancients thought the world would have an end, which was a kind of dying upon the day of its nativity. Now the disease prevailing and swiftly advancing about the time of his nativity, some were of opinion that he would leave the world on the day he entered into it: but this being a lingering disease, and creeping softly on, nothing critical was found or expected, and he died not before fifteen days after. Nothing is more common with infants than to die on the day of their nativity, to behold the worldly hours, and but the fractions thereof; and even to perish before their nativity in the hidden world of the womb, and before their good angel is conceived to undertake them. But in persons who outlive many years, and when there are no less than three hundred and sixty-five days to determine their lives every year—that the first day should make the last, that the tail of the snake should return into its mouth precisely at that time, and they should wind up upon the day of their nativity,—is indeed a remarkable coincidence, which, though astrology hath taken witty pains to salve, yet hath it been very wary in making predictions of it.* In this consumptive condition, and remarkable extenuation, he came to be almost half

---

* This remarkable coincidence happened in our Author's case: he himself died on the 76th anniversary of his birthday.

himfelf, and left a great part behind him
which he carried not to the grave.   And
though that ftory of Duke John Erneftus   Turkifh
Hiftory, p.
1483.
Mansfield be not fo eafily fwallowed that
at his death his heart was not found to be
fo big as a nut; yet if the bones of a good
fkeleton weigh little more than twenty
pounds, his inwards and flefh remaining
could make no bouffage, but a light bit for
the grave.   I never more lively beheld the
ftarved characters of Dante in any living
face ;* an *arufpex* might have read a lecture upon him without exenteration, his
flefh being fo confumed, that he might,
in a manner have difcerned his bowels
without opening of him : fo that to be
carried, *fextâ cervice*, to the grave, was

---

  * Dante defcribing a very emaciated countenance
fays :

" Who reads the name
Of man upon his forehead, there the M
Had trac'd moft plainly."

Purg. c. xxiii. 28.
alluding to the conceit that the letters O M O may
be traced in the human face. Cf. Hydriotaphia. cap.
3.

De arte me-
dica infan-
tium.

but a civil unneceffity ; and the comple-
ments of the coffin might out-weigh the
fubject of it.   Omnibonus Ferrarius, in
mortal dyfenteries of children, looks for
a fpot behind the ear ; in confumptive
difeafes fome eye the complexion of moles ;
Cardan eagerly views the nails, fome the
lines of the hand, the *thenar* or mufcle of
the thumb ; fome are fo curious as to obferve the depth of the throat-pit, how the
proportion varieth of the fmall of the legs
unto the calf, or the compafs of the neck
unto the circumference of the head : but
all thefe, with many more, were fo drowned
in a mortal vifage, and laft face of Hippocrates, that a weak phyfiognomift might
fay at firft eye, this was a face of earth,

Aul. Gell.
iii. 36.

and that *Morta* had fet her hard feal upon
his temples, eafily perceiving what *caricatura* draughts Death makes upon pined
faces, and unto what an unknown degree
a man may live backward.

    Though the beard be only made a dif-
tinction of fex, and fign of mafculine heat

Phyfiologia
barbæ hu-
manæ.

by Ulmus, yet the precocity and early
growth thereof in him, was not to be liked

in reference unto long life. Lewis, that virtuous but unfortunate King of Hungary, who loſt his life at the battle of Mohacz, was ſaid to be born without a ſkin, to have bearded at fifteen, and to have ſhewn ſome gray hairs about twenty; from whence the diviners conjectured, that he would be ſpoiled of his kingdom and have but a ſhort life: but hairs make fallible predictions, and many temples early gray have out-lived the Pſalmiſt's period. Hairs which have moſt amuſed me have not been in the face or head, but on the back, and not in men but children, as I long ago obſerved in that endemial diſtemper of little children in Languedoc, called the *Morgellons*, wherein they critically break out with harſh hairs on their backs, which takes off the unquiet ſymptoms of the diſeaſe, and delivers them from coughs and convulſions.

Pſ. xc. 10.

ſee Picotus de Rheumatiſmo.

The Egyptian mummies that I have ſeen, have had their mouths open, and ſomewhat gaping, which affordeth a good opportunity to view and obſerve their teeth, wherein 'tis not eaſy to find any wanting or decayed; and therefore in Egypt, where one man practiſed but one operation, or the diſeaſes but of ſingle parts, it muſt needs be a barren profeſſion to confine unto that of drawing of teeth, and little better than to have been tooth-drawer unto king Pyrrhus, who had but two in his head.* How the Bannyans of India maintain the integrity of thoſe parts, I find not particularly obſerved; who notwithſtanding have an advantage of their preſervation by abſtaining from all fleſh, and employing their teeth in ſuch food unto which they may ſeem at firſt framed, from their figure and confor-mation: but ſharp and corroding rheums had ſo early mouldered thoſe rocks and hardeſt parts of his fabrick, that a man might well conceive that his years were never like to double, or twice tell over his teeth. Corruption had dealt more

---

* "Pyrrhus had an air of majeſty rather terrible than auguſt. Inſtead of teeth in his upper jaw he had one continued bone, marked with ſmall lines reſem-bling the diviſions of a row of teeth."

Plutarch.

severely with them than sepulchral fires
and smart flames with those of burnt bodies of old; for in the burnt fragments
of urns which I have enquired into, although I seem to find few incisors or
shearers, yet the dog teeth and grinders
do notably resist those fires. In the years
of his childhood he had languished under
the disease of his country, the *rickets*;
after which notwithstanding, many have
become strong and active men; but whether any have attained unto very great
years, the disease is scarce so old as to afford good observation. Whether the
children of the English plantations be
subject unto the same infirmity, may be
worth the observing. Whether lameness
and halting do still encrease among the
inhabitants of Rovigno in Istria, I know
not; yet scarce twenty years ago Monsieur
du Loyr observed, that a third part of that
people halted: but too certain it is that
the rickets encreaseth among us; the
small pox grows more pernicious than the
great: the king's purse knows that the
kin 's evil grows more common. Quar-

tan agues are become no ſtrangers in Ire-
land, more common and mortal in England: and though the ancients gave that
diſeaſe very good words,* yet now that
bell makes no ſtrange ſound which rings
out for the effects thereof.

Some think there were few conſump-
tions in the old world, when men lived
much upon milk; and that the ancient
inhabitants of this iſland were leſs troubled with coughs when they went naked
and ſlept in caves and woods, than men
now in chambers and featherbeds. Plato
will tell us that there was no ſuch diſeaſe
as a catarrh in Homer's time, and that it
was but new in Greece in his age. Poly-
dore Virgil delivereth that pleuriſies were
rare in England, who lived in the days of
Henry the Eighth. Some will allow no
diſeaſes to be new, others think that many
old ones are ceaſed, and that ſuch which
are eſteemed new, will have but their
time: however, the mercy of God hath

---

* ἀσφαλέστατος δὲ πάντων καὶ ῥῄϊστος καὶ μακ-
ρότατος ὁ τεταρταῖος. Hippoc. Epidem. i. 86.

scattered the great heap of diseases, and
not loaded any one country with all : some
may be new in one country which have
been old in another : new discoveries of
the earth discover new diseases : for besides the common swarm, there are endemial and local infirmities proper unto certain regions, which in the whole earth
make no small number : and if Asia, Africa, and America, should bring in their
list, *Pandora's* box would swell, and there
must be a strange Pathology.

Most men expected to find a consumed
kell, empty and bladder-like guts, livid
and marbled lungs, and a withered pericardium in this exsuccous corpse : but
some seemed too much to wonder that two
lobes of his lungs adhered unto his side :
for the like I have often found in bodies
of no suspected consumptions or difficulty
of respiration.   And the same more often
happeneth in man than other animals, and
some think in women than in men ; but
the most remarkable I have met with,
was in a man, after a cough of almost
fifty years, in whom all the lobes adhered

unto the Pleura, and each lobe unto another; who having alfo been much troubled
with the gout, brake the rúle of Cardan,
and died of the ftone in the bladder.* Ariftotle makes a query, why fome animals
cough, as man; fome not, as oxen. If
coughing be taken as it confifteth of a natural and voluntary motion, including ex-
pectoration and fpitting out, it may be as
proper unto man as bleeding at the nofe;
otherwife we find that Vegetius and rural
writers have not left fo many medicines
in vain againft the coughs of cattle; and
men who perifh by coughs die the death
fheep, cats, and lions: and though birds
have no midriff, yet we meet with divers
remedies in Arrianus againft the cough of
hawks. And though it might be thought
that all animals who have lungs do cough,
yet in cetaceous fifhes, who have large
and ftrong lungs, the fame is not obferved,
nor yet in oviparous quadrupeds: and in

---

* *Cardan* in his *Encomium Podagræ* reckoneth
this among the *dona Podagræ*, that they are delivered
thereby from Phthyfis and Calculus.

the greateſt thereof, the crocodile, although
we read much of their tears, we find nothing of that motion.

From the thoughts of ſleep, when the
ſoul was conceived neareſt unto divinity,
the ancients erected an art of divination,
wherein while they too widely expatiated
in looſe and inconſequent conjectures,
Hippocrates wiſely conſidered dreams as de Inſom-
niis.
they preſaged alterations in the body, and
ſo offered hints toward the preſervation of
health, and prevention of diſeaſes: and
therein was ſo ſerious as to adviſe alteration of diet, exerciſe, ſweating, bathing,
and vomiting; and alſo ſo religious, as to
order prayers and ſupplications unto reſpective deities; in good dreams unto *Sol*,
Jupiter cœleſtis, *Jupiter opulentus*, *Mi-
nerva*, *Mercurius*, and *Apollo*: in bad
unto *Tellus*, and the Heroes. And therefore I could not but take notice how his
female friends were irrationally curious ſo
ſtrictly to examine his dreams, and in this
low ſtate to hope for the phantaſms of
health. He was now paſt the healthful
dreams of the ſun, moon, and ſtars, in

their clarity and proper courfes. 'Twas too late to dream of flying, of limpid fountains, fmooth waters, white veftments, and fruitful green trees, which are the vifions of healthful fleeps, and at good diftance from the grave.

And they were alfo too deeply dejected that he fhould dream of his dead friends, inconfequently divining, that he would not be long from them; for ftrange it was not that he fhould fometimes dream of the dead, whofe thoughts run always upon death; befides, to dream of the dead, fo they appear not in dark habits, and take nothing away from us, in Hippocrates his fenfe, was of good fignification: for we live by the dead, and every thing is or muft be fo before it becomes our nourifhment. And Cardan, who dreamed that he difcourfed with his dead Father in the moon, made thereof no mortal interpretation: and even to dream that we are dead, was no condemnable phantafm in old *Oneirocriticifm*, as having a fignification of liberty, vacuity from cares, exemption and freedom from troubles unknown unto the dead.

Some dreams I confefs may admit of eafy and feminine expofition; he who dreamed that he could not fee his right fhoulder, might eafily fear to lofe the fight of his right eye; he that before a journey dreamed that his feet were cut off, had a plain warning not to undertake his intended journey. But why to dream of lettuce fhould prefage fome enfuing difeafe, why to eat figs fhould fignify foolifh talk, why to eat eggs great trouble, and to dream of blindnefs fhould be fo highly commended, according to the oneirocritical verfes of Aftrampfychus and Nicephorus, I fhall leave unto your divination.

He was willing to quit the world alone and altogether, leaving no earneft behind him for corruption or after-grave, having fmall content in that common fatisfaction to furvive or live in another, but amply fatisfied that his difeafe fhould die with himfelf, nor revive in a pofterity to puzzle phyfick, and make fad mementos of their parent hereditary. Leprofy awakes not fometimes before forty, the gout and ftone

often later; but confumptive and tabid
roots fprout more early, and at the faireft
make feventeen years of our life doubtful
before that age. They that enter the
world with original difeafes as well as fin,
have not only common mortality, but fick
traductions, to deftroy them, make commonly fhort courfes, and live not at length
but in figures: fo that a found *cæfarean*
nativity may out-laft a natural birth, and
a knife may fometimes make way for a
more lafting fruit than a midwife; which
makes fo few infants now able to endure
the old teft of the river,* and many to
have feeble children who could fcarce have
been married at Sparta, and thofe provi-
dent ftates who ftudied ftrong and healthful generations; which happen but con-
tingently in mere pecuniary matches, or
marriages made by the candle, wherein
notwithftanding there is little redrefs to
be hoped from an Aftrologer or a Lawyer,

---

* " Durum ab ftirpe genus, natos ad flumina pri-
    mum
    Deferimus, fævoque gelu duramus et undis."
                   Virg. Æn. ix. 603.

and a good difcerning Phyfician were like to prove the moft fuccefsful counfellor.

Julius Scaliger, who in a fleeplefs fit of the gout could make two hundred verfes in a night, would have but five plain words upon his tomb.* And this ferious perfon, though no minor wit, left the poetry of his epitaph unto others, either unwilling to commend himfelf, or to be judged by a diftich, and perhaps confidering how unhappy great Poets have been in verfifying their own epitaphs : wherein Petrarcha, Dante, and Ariofto, have fo unhappily failed, that if their tombs fhould out-laft their works, pofterity would find fo little of Apollo on them, as to miftake them for *Ciceronian* Poets.

In this deliberate and creeping pro-grefs unto the grave, he was fomewhat too young, and of too noble a mind, to fall upon that ftupid fymptom obfervable in divers perfons near their journey's end, and which may be reckoned among the mortal fymptoms of their laft difeafe :

---

* IVLII CÆSARIS SCALIGERI QVOD FVIT.

that is, to become more narrow-minded, miferable, and tenacious, unready to part with anything, when they are ready to part with all, and afraid to want when they have no time to fpend; meanwhile Phyficians, who know that many are mad but in a fingle depraved imagination, and one prevalent decipiency, and that befide and out of fuch fingle deliriums a man may meet with fober actions and good fenfe in Bedlam, cannot but fmile to fee the heirs and concerned relations gratulating themfelves on the fober departure of their friends; and though they behold fuch mad covetous paffages, content to think they die in good underftanding, and in their fober fenfes.

Avarice, which is not only infidelity but idolatry, either from covetous progeny or queftuary education, had no root in his breaft, who made good works the expreffion of his faith, and was big with defires unto public and lafting charities; and furely where good wifhes and charitable intentions exceed ability, theorical beneficency may be more than a dream.

Colof. iii. 5.

Rel. Med. Pt. ii. c. xiii.

They build not castles in the air who would build churches on earth ; and though they leave no such structures here, may lay good foundations in Heaven.* In brief, his life and death were such, that I could not blame them who wished the like, and almost, to have been himself; almost, I say, for though we may wish the prosperous appurtenances of others, or to be another in his happy accidents, yet so intrinsical is every man unto himself, that some doubt may be made, whether any would exchange his being, or substantially become another man.

He had wisely seen the world at home and abroad, and thereby observed under what variety men are deluded in the pursuit of that which is not here to be found. And although he had no opinion of reputed felicities below, and apprehended men widely out in the estimate of such happiness, yet his sober contempt of the

---

* So Wordsworth: (Ecclesf. Sonnet. King's Coll. Chapel)

  " They dreamt not of a perishable home
     Who thus could build."

world wrought no *Democratiſm* or *Cyni-
ciſm*, no laughing or ſnarling at it, as well
underſtanding there are not felicities in
this world to ſatisfy a ſerious mind; and
therefore to ſoften the ſtream of our lives,
we are fain to take in the reputed contentations of this world, to unite with the
crowd in their beatitudes, and to make
ourſelves happy by conſortion, opinion,
or co-exiſtimation: for ſtrictly to ſeparate
from received and cuſtomary felicities,
and to confine unto the rigour of realities,
were to contract the conſolation of our
beings unto too uncomfortable circumſcriptions.

Not to fear death, nor deſire it, was
2 Cor. v. 1.
Phil. i. 23. ſhort of his reſolution: to be diſſolved,
and be with Chriſt was his dying ditty.
He conceived his thread too long, in no
long courſe of years, and when he had
ſcarce out-lived the ſecond life of Lazarus;* eſteeming it enough to approach

---

* S. Epiphanius mentions a tradition that Lazarus
had died at the age of 30 when he was raiſed from
the dead by our Lord, and that he lived 30 years
afterwards.   Epiphan. hæres. lxvi. c. 39.

the years of his Saviour, who so ordered his own human state, as not to be old upon earth. But to be content with death may be better than to desire it : a miserable life may make us wish for death, but a virtuous one to rest in it ; which is the advantage of those resolved Christians, who looking on death not only as the sting, but the period and end of sin, the horizon and isthmus between this life and a better, and the death of this world but as a nativity of another, do contentedly submit unto the common necessity, and envy not Enoch or Elias.

Gen. v. 24.
Heb. xi. 5.
2 Kings ii.

Not to be content with life is the unsatisfactory state of those who destroy themselves ; who being afraid to live, run blindly upon their own death, which no man fears by experience ; and the Stoics had a notable doctrine to take away the fear thereof, that is, in such extremities, to desire that which is not to be avoided, and wish what might be feared, and so made evils voluntary, and to suit with their own desires, which took off the terror of them. But the ancient martyrs

Rel. Med.
xliv.

were not encouraged by such fallacies; who, though they feared not death, were afraid to be their own executioners, and therefore thought it more wisdom to crucify their lusts than their bodies, to circumcise than stab their hearts, and to mortify than kill themselves.

His willingness to leave this world about that age when most men think they may best enjoy it, though paradoxical unto worldly ears, was not strange unto mine, who have so often observed that many, though old, oft stick fast unto the world, and seem to be drawn like Cacus his oxen, backward, with great struggling and reluctancy unto the grave.* The long habit of living makes meer men more hardly to part with life, and all to be nothing but what is to come. To live at the rate of the old world, when some could scarce remember themselves young, may afford no better digested death than a

---

* *Cacus* was a robber, who having stolen Hercules his oxen on Mount Aventine, dragged them backwards into his cave that their tracks might not be discovered. Livy. i. 7. Virg. Æn. viii. 209.

more moderate period. Many would have thought it an happinefs to have had their lot of life in fome notable conjunctures of ages paft : but the uncertainty of future times hath tempted few to make a part in ages to come. And furely, he that hath taken the true altitude of things, and rightly calculated the degenerate ftate of this age, is not like to envy thofe that fhall live in the next, much lefs three or four hundred years hence, when no man can comfortably imagine what face this world will carry : and therefore, fince every age makes a ftep unto the end of all things and the Scripture affords fo hard a character of the laft times, quiet minds will be content with their generations, and rather blefs ages paft, than be ambitious of thofe to come.

Though Age had fet no feal upon his face, yet a dim eye might clearly difcover fifty in his actions ; and therefore, fince wifdom is the gray hair, and an unfpotted life old age, although his years came fhort, he might have been faid to have held up with longer livers, and to have

Wifd. v.
7—14.

been Solomon's old man. And furely if we deduct all thofe days of our life which we might wifh unlived, and which abate the comfort of thofe we now live, if we reckon up only thofe days which God hath accepted of our lives, a life of good years will hardly be a fpan long, the fon in this fenfe may out-live the father, and none be climacterically old. He that early arriveth unto the parts and prudence of age, is happily old without the uncomfortable attendants of it: and 'tis fuperfluous to live unto gray hairs, when in a precocious temper we anticipate the virtues of them. In brief, he cannot be accounted young who out-liveth the old man. He that hath early arrived unto

Ephef. iv.
13.

the meafure of a perfect ftature in Chrift, hath already fulfilled the prime and longeft intention of his being: and one day lived after the perfect rule of piety, is to be preferred before finning immortality. Although he attained not unto the years of his predeceffors, yet he wanted not thofe preferving virtues which confirm the thread of weaker conftitutions. Caute-

lous Chaſtity and crafty Sobriety were far
from him; thoſe jewels were paragon,
without flaw, hair, ice, or cloud in him:
  which affords me a hint to proceed
     in theſe good wiſhes, and
        few *memento's* unto
           you.

TRUE

CHRISTIAN MORALS.

To the Right Honourable

DAVID, EARL OF BUCHAN,

Viſcount Auchterhouſe, Lord Cardroſs and Glendovachie, one of the Lords Commiſſioners of Police, and Lord Lieutenant of the Counties of Stirling and Clackmannan in North Britain.

My Lord,

The honour you have done our family obligeth us to make all juſt acknowledgments of it ; and there is no form of acknowledgment in our power, more worthy of your Lordſhip's acceptance, than this dedication of the laſt Work of our honoured and learned Father. Encouraged hereunto by the knowledge we have of your Lordſhip's judicious reliſh of univerſal learning, and ſublime virtue, we beg the favour of your acceptance of it, which will very much oblige our family in general, and her in particular, who is,

   My Lord,

  Your Lordſhip's moſt humble ſervant,

     Elizabeth Littleton.

PREFACE TO THE FIRST EDITION.

F any one, after he has read Religio Medici, and the enfuing Discourse, can make doubt whether the fame perfon was the Author of them both, he may be affured by the teftimony of Mrs. Littleton, Sir Thomas Browne's daughter, who lived with her father when it was compofed by him, and who, at the time, read it written by his own hand ; and alfo by the teftimony of others (of whom I am one) who read the manufcript of the Author immediately after his death, and who have fince read the fame, from which it hath been faithfully and exactly tranfcribed for the prefs. The reafon why it was not printed fooner is, becaufe it was unhappily loft, by being miflaid among other manufcripts, for which fearch was lately made in the prefence of the Lord Archbifhop of Canterbury, of which his Grace by letter informed Mrs. Littleton, when he fent the manufcript to her. There is nothing printed in the Difcourfe, or in the fhort notes, but what is found in the original manufcript of the Author, except only where an overfight had made the addition or tranfpofition of fome words neceffary.

JOHN JEFFERY,

ARCHDEACON OF NORWICH.

CHRISTIAN MORALS.

PART I.

I.

READ softly and circumspectly in this funambulatory track and narrow path of goodneſs: purſue virtue virtuouſly: leaven not good actions, nor render virtues diſputable. Stain not fair acts with foul intentions: maim not uprightneſs by halting concomitances, nor circumſtantially deprave ſubſtantial goodneſs.

Conſider whereabout thou art in Cebes his table, or that old philoſophical *pinax* of the life of man :* whether thou art yet in

---

* The Pinax, or tablet, of Cebes a Theban philoſopher, in which the life of man is repreſented in a beautiful allegory.

the road of uncertainties; whether thou
haſt yet entered the narrow gate, got up
the hill and aſperous way, which leadeth
unto the houſe of ſanity; or taken that
purifying potion from the hand of ſincere
erudition, which may ſend thee clear and
pure away unto a virtuous and happy life.

Milton. Par.
Loſt. xi.
840.

In this virtuous voyage of thy life hull
not about like the ark, without the uſe of
rudder, maſt, or ſail, and bound for no
port.   Let not diſappointment cauſe de-
ſpondency, nor difficulty deſpair.   Think
not that you are ſailing from Lima to
Manilla, when you may faſten up the
rudder, and ſleep before the wind; but
expeƈt rough ſeas, flaws, and contrary
blaſts: and it is well if by many croſs
tacks and veerings you arrive at the port;
for we ſleep in lions' ſkins in our progreſs
unto virtue, and we ſlide not, but climb
unto it.

Sit not down in the popular forms and
common level of virtues.   Offer not only
peace-offerings, but holocauſts unto God:
where all is due make no reſerve, and cut
not a cummin-ſeed with the Almighty:

ὁ κυμινο-
πρίστης.
Ariſt. Eth.
iv. 1.

to serve him singly to serve ourselves were too partial a piece of piety, not like to place us in the illustrious mansions of glory.

II. Rest not in an ovation,* but a triumph over thy passions. Let anger walk hanging down the head; let malice go manacled, and envy fettered, after thee. Behold within thee the long train of thy trophies, not without thee. Make the quarrelling Lapithytes sleep, and Centaurs within lie quiet. Chain up the unruly legion of thy breast. Lead thine own captivity captive, and be Cæsar within thyself.

III. He that is chaste and continent not to impair his strength, or honest for fear of contagion, will hardly be heroically virtuous. Adjourn not this virtue until that temper, when Cato could lend out his wife, and impotent satyrs write satires upon lust.

---

* *Ovation,* a lesser kind of triumph.

IV. Show thy art in honeſty, and loſe not thy virtue by the bad managery of it. Be temperate and ſober : not to preſerve your body in an ability for wanton ends ; not to avoid the infamy of common tranſgreſſors that way, and thereby to hope to expiate or palliate obſcure and cloſer vices ; not to ſpare your purſe, nor ſimply to enjoy health ; but in one word, that thereby you may truly ſerve God, which every ſickneſs will tell you you cannot well do without health. The ſick man's ſacrifice is but a lame oblation. Pious treaſures laid up in healthful days, plead for ſick non-performances, without which we muſt needs look back with anxiety upon the loſt opportunities of health, and may have cauſe rather to envy than pity the ends of penitent public ſufferers, who go with healthful prayers unto the laſt ſcene of their lives, and in the integrity of their faculties return their ſpirit unto God that gave it.

V. Be charitable before wealth

make thee covetous, and lose not the glory of the mite. If riches increase, let thy mind hold pace with them; and think it not enough to be liberal, but munificent. Though a cup of cold water from some hand may not be without its reward, yet stick not thou for wine and oil for the wounds of the distressed; and treat the poor as our Saviour did the multitude, to the reliques of some baskets. Diffuse thy beneficence early, and while thy treasures call thee master: there may be an Atropos of thy fortunes before that of thy life, and thy wealth cut off before that hour when all men shall be poor; for the justice of death looks equally upon the dead, and Charon expects no more from Alexander than from Irus.*

VI. Give not only unto seven, but also unto eight, that is, unto more than many. Though to give unto every

---

* *Irus*, a beggar (Odyss. xviii. 233) whose poverty became proverbial :

' *Irus et est subito, qui modo Crœsus erat.*' Ovid.

Side notes:
St. Mark xii. 41—44.

St. Matt. x. 42.
St. Mar. ix. 41.
St. Luke x. 34.
St. John vi. 12, 13.

Eccl. xi. 2.

St. Matt. v. 42.

one that aſketh may ſeem ſevere advice, yet give thou alſo before aſking ; that is, where want is ſilently clamorous, and men's neceſſities, not their tongues, do loudly call for thy mercies.　For though ſometimes neceſſitouſneſs be dumb, or miſery ſpeak not out; yet true charity is ſagacious, and will find out hints for beneficence.　Acquaint thyſelf with the phyſiognomy of want, and let the dead colours and firſt lines of neceſſity ſuffice to tell thee there is an object for thy bounty.　Spare not where thou canſt not eaſily be prodigal, and fear not to be undone by mercy ; for ſince he who hath pity on the poor, lendeth unto the Almighty rewarder, who obſerves no ides*

Prov. xix. 17.

but every day for his payments, charity becomes pious uſury, Chriſtian liberality the moſt thriving induſtry, and what we adventure in a cockboat may return in a

Eccl. xi. 1.

carrack unto us.　He who thus caſts his

---

* *Ides,* the middle day of the Roman month, on which, money put out to intereſt, was commonly repaid.

bread upon the water ſhall ſurely find it again ; for though it falleth to the bottom, it ſinks but like the axe of the prophet, to riſe again unto him.

    2 Kings vi. *5—7.*

VII. **If avarice be thy vice,** yet make it not thy puniſhment. Miſerable men commiſerate not themſelves ; bowelleſs unto others, and mercileſs unto their own bowels. Let the fruition of things bleſs the poſſeſſion of them, and think it more ſatisfaction to live richly than die rich. For ſince thy good works, not thy goods, will follow thee ; ſince wealth is an appurtenance of life, and no dead man is rich ; to famiſh in plenty, and live poorly to die rich, were a multiplying improvement in madneſs, and uſe upon uſe in folly.

    Rev. xiv. *13.*

VIII. **Truſt not to the omni**-potency of gold, and ſay not unto it Thou art my confidence. Kiſs not thy hand to that terreſtrial ſun, nor bore thy ear unto its ſervitude. A ſlave unto mammon makes no ſervant unto God. Covetouſ-

    Job xxxi. *24—27.*

    Ex. xxi. 6. *St. Matt.* *vi. 24.* *S. Luke* *xvi. 13.*

neſs cracks the ſinews of faith, numbs the apprehenſion of any thing above ſenſe ; and only affected with the certainty of things preſent, makes a peradventure of things to come ; lives but unto one world, nor hopes but fears another ; makes their own death ſweet unto others, bitter unto themſelves ; brings formal ſadneſs, ſcenical mourning, and no wet eyes at the grave.

IX. Perſons lightly dipped, not grain'd in generous honeſty, are but pale in goodneſs, and faint-hued in integrity. But be thou what thou virtuouſly art, and let not the ocean waſh away thy tincture. Stand magnetically upon that axis, when prudent ſimplicity hath fixed there ; and let no attraction invert the poles of thy honeſty. That vice may be uneaſy and even monſtrous unto thee, let repeated good acts and long confirmed habits make virtue almoſt natural, or a ſecond nature in thee. Since virtuous ſuperſtructions have commonly generous foundations, dive into thy inclinations,

and early diſcover what nature bids thee
to be, or tells thee thou may'ſt be. They
who thus timely deſcend into themſelves,
and cultivate the good ſeeds which nature
hath ſet in them, prove not ſhrubs but
cedars in their generation. And to be in
the form of the beſt of the bad, or the
worſt of the good, will be no ſatisfaction
unto them.

x. Make not the conſequence
of virtue the ends thereof. Be not bene- St. Matt.
vi. 1. 2.
ficent for a name or cymbal of applauſe ;
nor exact and juſt in commerce for the
advantages of truſt and credit, which attend the reputation of true and punctual
dealing : for theſe rewards, though un-
ſought for, plain virtue will bring with
her. To have other by-ends in good
actions ſours laudable performances, which
muſt have deeper roots, motives, and in-
ſtigations, to give them the ſtamp of virtues.

xi. Let not the law of thy
country be the *non ultra* of thy honeſty ;

nor think that always good enough which
the law will make good.   Narrow not
the law of charity, equity, mercy.   Join
goſpel righteouſneſs with legal right.   Be
not a mere Gamaliel in the faith, but let

St. Matt. v.
vi. vii.
Ex. xx.

the Sermon on the Mount be thy Targum unto the law of Sinai.

XII.   Live by old ethicks and

Cf. Thucyd.
iii. 82.

the claſſical rules of honeſty.   Put no new
names or notions upon authentick virtues and vices.   Think not that morality
is ambulatory ; that vices in one age are
not vices in another ; or that virtues,
which are under the everlaſting ſeal of
right reaſon, may be ſtamped by opinion.
And therefore, though vicious times invert the opinions of things, and ſet up
new ethicks againſt virtue, yet hold thou
unto old morality ; and rather than fol-

Ex. xxiii. 2.

low a multitude to do evil, ſtand like
Pompey's pillar conſpicuous by thyſelf,
and ſingle in integrity.   And ſince the
worſt of times afford imitable examples of
virtue ; ſince no deluge of vice is like to
be ſo general but more than eight will

eſcape ; eye well thoſe heroes who have held their heads above water, who have touched pitch and not been defiled, and in the common contagion have remained uncorrupted.

XIII. Let age, not envy, draw wrinkles on thy cheeks ; be content to be envied, but envy not. Emulation may be plauſible and indignation allowable, but admit no treaty with that paſſion which no circumſtance can make good. A diſplacency at the good of others be-cauſe they enjoy it, though not unworthy of it, is an abſurd depravity, ſticking faſt unto corrupted nature, and often too hard for humility and charity, the great ſup-preſſors of envy. This ſurely is a lion not to be ſtrangled but by Hercules him-ſelf, or the higheſt ſtreſs of our minds, and an atom of that power which ſubdueth all things unto itſelf.

Phil. iii. 21.

XIV. Owe not thy humility unto humiliation from adverſity, but look humbly down in that ſtate when others look upwards upon thee. Think not thy own ſhadow longer than that of others, nor delight to take the altitude of thyſelf. Be patient in the age of pride, when men live by ſhort intervals of rea-ſon under the dominion of humour and paſſion, when it is in the power of every one to transform thee out of thyſelf, and run thee into the ſhort madneſs. If you cannot imitate Job, yet come not ſhort of Socrates, and thoſe patient Pagans who tired the tongues of their enemies, while they perceived they ſpit their malice at brazen walls and ſtatues.

Hor. Ep. i. ii. 62.

Juv. Sat. xiii. 185.

Eph. iv. 26.

XV. Let not the ſun in Capri-corn* go down upon thy wrath, but write thy wrongs in aſhes. Draw the curtain of night upon injuries, ſhut them up in the tower of oblivion,† and let them be as

---

* Even when the days are ſhorteſt.

† Alluding unto the Tower of Oblivion men-tioned by Procopius, as a place of impriſonment among the Perſians : whoever was put therein was, as it were, buried alive, and it was death for any but to name him.

though they had not been. To forgive
our enemies, yet hope that God will pu-
nish them, is not to forgive enough. To
forgive them ourselves, and not to pray
God to forgive them, is a partial piece of
charity. Forgive thine enemies totally,
and without any reserve, that however,
God will revenge thee.

XVI. While thou so hotly
disclaimest the devil, be not guilty of dia-
bolism. Fall not into one name* with
that unclean spirit, nor act his nature
whom thou so much abhorrest; that is,
to accuse, calumniate, backbite, whisper,
detract, or sinistrously interpret others.
Degenerous depravities, and narrow-
minded vices! not only below St. Paul's
noble Christian but Aristotle's† true gentleman. Trust not with some that the
Epistle of St. James is apocryphal, and so
read with less fear that stabbing truth,
that in company with this vice thy reli-

St. James,
i. 26.

---

* *One name*, ὁ διάβολος the calumniator.
† Compare Arist. Ethics. iv. 7. and Romans xiii.

Ex. xxxii.
19.

Rom. xiii.
10.

1 Cor. xiii.

St. Luke
xvi. 24.

Rev. iv. 8.

gion is in vain. Moſes broke the tables without breaking of the law; but where charity is broke, the law itſelf is ſhattered, which cannot be whole without Love, which is the fulfilling of it. Look humbly upon thy virtues; and though thou art rich in ſome, yet think thyſelf poor and naked without that crowning grace, which thinketh no evil, which envieth not, which beareth, hopeth, believeth, endureth all things. With theſe ſure graces, while buſy tongues are crying out for a drop of cold water, mutes may be in happineſs, and ſing the *Triſagion* in heaven.

XVII. However thy underſtanding may waver in the theories of true and falſe, yet faſten the rudder of thy will, ſteer ſtraight unto good and fall not foul on evil. Imagination is apt to rove, and conjecture to keep no bounds. Some have run out ſo far, as to fancy the ſtars might be but the light of the cryſtalline heaven ſhot through perforations on the bodies of the orbs. Others more ingeniouſly doubt whether there hath not been a vaſt tract of land in the Atlantick ocean, which earthquakes and violent cauſes have long ago devoured. Speculative miſapprehenſions may be innocuous, but immorality pernicious ; theorical miſtakes and phyſical deviations may condemn our judgments, not lead us into judgment. But perverſity of will, immoral and ſinful enormities, walk with *Adraſte* and *Nemeſis* at their backs, purſue us unto judgment, and leave us vicioûſly miſerable.

XVIII. Bid early defiance unto thoſe vices which are of thine inward family, and having a root in thy temper plead a right and propriety in thee. Raiſe timely batteries againſt thoſe ſtrong holds built upon the rock of nature, and make this a great part of the militia of thy life. Delude not thyſelf into iniquities from participation or community, which abate the ſenſe but not the obliquity of them. To conceive ſins leſs, or leſs of ſins, becauſe others alſo tranſgreſs, were morally to commit that natural fallacy of man, to

take comfort from ſociety, and think adverſities leſs becauſe others alſo ſuffer them.
The politick nature of vice muſt be oppoſed by policy; and, therefore, wiſer
honeſties project and plot againſt it:
wherein, notwithſtanding, we are not to
reſt in generals, or the trite ſtratagems of
art. That may ſucceed with one, which
may prove ſucceſſleſs with another: there
is no community or common weal of virtue: every man muſt ſtudy his own economy, and adapt ſuch rules unto the
figure of himſelf.

xix. Be ſubſtantially great
in thyſelf, and more than thou appeareſt
unto others; and let the world be deceived in thee, as they are in the lights of
heaven. Hang early plummets upon the
heels of pride, and let ambition have but
an *epicycle* and narrow circuit in thee.
Meaſure not thyſelf by thy morning ſhadow, but by the extent of thy grave; and
reckon thyſelf above the earth, by the line
thou muſt be contented with under it.
Spread not into boundleſs expanſions either

of defigns or defires. Think not that
mankind liveth but for a few ; and that
the reft are born but to ferve thofe ambi-
tions which make but flies of men and
wilderneffes of whole nations. Swell not
into vehement actions which embroil and
confound the earth ; but be one of thofe
violent ones which force the kingdom of
heaven. If thou muft needs rule, be
Zeno's king,* and enjoy that empire
which every man gives himfelf. He who
is thus his own monarch contentedly
fways the fceptre of himfelf, not envying
the glory of crowned heads and elohim of
the earth. Could the world unite in the
practice of that defpifed train of virtues,

St. Matt.
xi. 12.

---

* The Stoicks illuftrated their doctrines by defcribing an ideal perfonage whom they called 'The
wife man ;' and he (they faid) ' was the only King, the
only Dictator, the only Rich Man.' Cic. de Finibus
iii. 22. Hor. Sat. i. iii.

" The way to fubject all things to thy felfe, is to
fubject thyfelfe to reafon : thou fhalt govern many, if
reafon govern thee : wouldft thou be crowned the
monarch of a little world ? command thy felfe."

Quarles' Enchir. ii. 19.

which the divine ethicks of our Saviour hath ſo inculcated upon us, the furious face of things muſt diſappear; Eden would be yet to be found, and the angels might look down, not with pity, but joy upon us.

xx. Though the quickneſs of thine ear were able to reach the noiſe of the moon, which ſome think it maketh in it's rapid revolution; though the number of thy ears ſhould equal Argus his eyes: yet ſtop them all with the wiſe man's wax,* and be deaf unto the ſuggeſtions of tale-bearers, calumniators, pickthank or malevolent delators, who, while quiet men ſleep, ſowing the tares of diſcord and diviſion, diſtract the tranquillity of charity and all friendly ſociety. Theſe are the tongues that ſet the world on fire, cankers of reputation, and, like that of Jonas his gourd, wither a good name in

St. Matt. xiii. 25.

St. James iii. 6. 2 Tim. ii. 17. Jonah iv. 6, 7.

---

* *Wiſe man's wax.* Ulyſſes adopted this plan to eſcape the enchantment of the Sirens. Odyſſ. M. 173.

a night. Evil ſpirits may ſit ſtill, while
theſe ſpirits walk about and perform the
buſineſs of hell. To ſpeak more ſtrictly,
our corrupted hearts are the factories of
the devil, which may be at work without
his preſence; for when that circumvent-
ing ſpirit hath drawn malice, envy, and
all unrighteouſneſs unto well-rooted habits
in his diſciples, iniquity then goes on upon
its own legs; and if the gate of hell were
ſhut up for a time, vice would ſtill be
fertile and produce the fruits of hell.
Thus, when God forſakes us, Satan alſo
leaves us: for ſuch offenders he looks
upon as ſure and ſealed up, and his temptations then needleſs unto them.

XXI. Annihilate not the mer-
cies of God by the oblivion of ingratitude:
for oblivion is a kind of annihilation; and
for things to be as though they had not
been, is like unto never being. Make not
thy head a grave, but a repoſitory of God's
mercies. Though thou hadſt the memory
of Seneca, or Simonides, and conſcience,
the punctual memoriſt within us, yet truſt

not to thy remembrance in things which need phylacteries. Regiſter not only ſtrange, but merciful occurrences. Let ephemerides not olympiads give thee account of His mercies;* let thy diaries ſtand thick with dutiful mementos and aſteriſks of acknowledgment. And to be complete and forget nothing, date not his mercy from thy nativity; look beyond the world, and before the æra of Adam.

XXII. Paint not the ſepulchre of thyſelf, and ſtrive not to beautify thy corruption. Be not an advocate for thy vices, nor call for many hour-glaſſes to juſtify thy imperfections.† Think not that always good which thou thinkeſt thou canſt always make good, nor that concealed which the ſun doth not behold; that which the ſun doth not now ſee will be viſible when the ſun is out, and the

---

* *Let ephemerides*, &c. that is, Take note of God's mercies day by day, not merely every four years.

† In the Athenian Courts the time allowed to each pleader was meaſured by a kind of hour-glaſs, called *clepſhydra*.

1 Cor. iv. 5.

ſtars are fallen from heaven. Meanwhile there is no darkneſs unto conſcience, which can ſee without light, and in the deepeſt obſcurity give a clear draught of things, which the cloud of diſſimulation hath concealed from all eyes. There is a natural ſtanding court within us, examining, acquitting, and condemning at the tribunal of ourſelves ; wherein iniquities have their natural *thetas** and no nocent is abſolved by the verdict of himſelf.† And therefore, although our tranſgreſſions ſhall be tried at the laſt bar, the proceſs need not be long : for the Judge of all knoweth all, and every man will nakedly know himſelf; and when ſo few are like to plead *not guilty,* the aſſize muſt ſoon have an end.

XXIII. Comply with ſome hu-

* *Theta,* Θ was the ſymbol uſed in condemnation to capital puniſhment, being the initial letter of Θα-ματος.

† ' *Se judice, nemo nocens abſolvitur.*' Juv. Sat. xiii. 2.

mours, bear with others, but ſerve none.
Civil complacency conſiſts with decent
honeſty. Flattery is a juggler, and no
kin unto ſincerity. But while thou main-
taineſt the plain path, and ſcorneſt to flatter others, fall not into ſelf-adulation, and
become not thine own paraſite. Be deaf
unto thyſelf, and be not betrayed at home.
Self-credulity, pride, and levity, lead unto
ſelf-idolatry.   There is no Damocles*
like unto ſelf-opinion, nor any Siren to
our own fawning conceptions. To magnify our minor things, or hug ourſelves
in our apparitions ; to afford a credulous
ear unto the clawing ſuggeſtions of fancy ;
to paſs our days in painted miſtakes of
ourſelves, and though we behold our own
blood to think ourſelves the ſons of Jupiter : are blandiſhments of ſelf-love, worſe
than outward deluſion. By this impoſ-
ture, wiſe men ſometimes are miſtaken in
their elevation, and look above themſelves.
And fools, which are *antipodes* unto the
wiſe, conceive themſelves to be but their

---

* *Damocles*, the paraſite and flatterer of Dionyſius.

periœci, and in the ſame parallel with them.

XXIV. Be not a *Hercules Fu-rens* abroad, and a poltroon within thy-ſelf. To chaſe our enemies out of the field, and be led captive by our vices; to beat down our foes, and fall down to our concupiſcences; are ſolœciſms in moral ſchools, and no laurel attends them. To well manage our affections, and wild horſes of Plato, are the higheſt Circenſes:* and the nobleſt digladiation is in the theatre of ourſelves; for therein our inward an-tagoniſts, not only like common gladia-tors, with ordinary weapons and down-right blows make at us, but alſo like reti-ary and laqueary combatants, with nets, frauds, and entanglements, fall upon us. Weapons for ſuch combats are not to be forged at Lipara;† Vulcan's art doth no-

---

* Plato ſpeaks of man as a charioteer driving two refractory ſteeds, given to quarrel; one being immor-tal and heavenly, the other mortal and of the earth. Χαλεπὴ δὴ καὶ δύσκολος ἐξ ἀνάγκης ἡ περὶ ἡμᾶς ἡνιόχησις. Phædrus. xxv.

† *Lipara* where Vulcan's ſtithy was ſaid to be.

Eph. vi. 11
—17.

thing in this internal militia, wherein, not the armour of Achilles, but the armature of St. Paul, gives the glorious day, and triumphs, not leading up into capitols, but up into the higheſt heavens. And, therefore, while ſo many think it the only valour to command and maſter others, ſtudy thou the dominion of thyſelf, and quiet thine own commotions. Let right reaſon be thy Lycurgus, and lift up thy hand unto the law of it : move by the intelligences of the ſuperior faculties, not by the rapt of paſſion, nor merely by that of temper and conſtitution. They who are merely carried on by the wheel of ſuch inclinations, without the hand and guidance of ſovereign reaſon, are but the automatous part of mankind, rather lived than living, or at leaſt underliving themſelves.

xxv. Let not fortune, which hath no name in Scripture, have any in thy divinity. Let Providence, not chance, have the honour of thy acknowledgments, and be thy Œdipus in contingencies.

Mark well the paths and winding ways thereof; but be not too wise in the construction, or sudden in the application. The hand of Providence writes often by abbreviatures, hieroglyphicks or short characters, which, like the Laconism on the wall, are not to be made out but by a hint or key from that Spirit which indited them. Leave future occurrences to their uncertainties, think that which is present thine own: and since it is easier to foretel an eclipse than a foul day at some distance, look for little regular below. Attend with patience the uncertainty of things, and what lieth yet unexerted in the chaos of futurity. The uncertainty and ignorance of things to come, makes the world new unto us by unexpected emergencies; whereby we pass not our days in the trite road of affairs affording no novity; for the novelizing spirit of man lives by variety, and the new faces of things.

Dan. v.

XXVI. Though a contented mind enlargeth the dimension of little

things; and unto ſome it is wealth enough
not to be poor; and others are well content if they be but rich enough to be honeſt, and to give every man his due: yet
fall not into that obſolete affectation of
bravery, to throw away thy money, and
to reject all honours or honourable ſtations
in this courtly and ſplendid world. Old
generoſity is ſuperannuated, and ſuch contempt of the world out of date. No man
is now like to refuſe the favour of great
ones, or be content to ſay unto princes,
Stand out of my ſun. And if there be
any of ſuch antiquated reſolutions, they
are not like to be tempted out of them by
great ones: and 'tis fair if they eſcape the
name of hypochondriacks from the genius
of latter times; unto whom contempt of
the world is the moſt contemptible opinion; and to be able, like Bias, to carry
all they have about them, were to be the
eighth wiſe man. However, the old tetrick philoſophers looked always with indignation upon ſuch a face of things; and,
obſerving the unnatural current of riches,
power, and honour in the world, and

withal the imperfection and demerit of persons often advanced unto them, were tempted unto angry opinions, that affairs were ordered more by stars than reason, and that things went on rather by lottery than election.

XXVII. If thy vessel be but small in the ocean of this world, if meanness of possessions be thy allotment upon earth, forget not those virtues which the great Disposer of all bids thee to entertain from thy quality and condition; that is, submission, humility, content of mind, and industry. Content may dwell in all stations. To be low, but above contempt, may be high enough to be happy. But many of low degree may be higher than computed, and some cubits above the common commensuration; for in all states virtue gives qualifications and allowances, which make out defects. Rough diamonds are sometimes mistaken for pebbles; and meanness may be rich in accomplishments, which riches in vain desire. If our merits be above our stations, if our intrinsical value be greater than what we go for, or our value than our valuation, and if we ſtand higher in God's, than in the cenſor's book,* it may make ſome equitable balance in the inequalities of this world, and there may be no ſuch vaſt chaſm or gulph between diſparities as common meaſures determine. The Divine eye looks upon high and low differently from that of man. They who ſeem to ſtand upon Olympus, and high mounted unto our eyes, may be but in the valleys and low ground unto his; for he looks upon thoſe as higheſt who neareſt approach his divinity, and upon thoſe as loweſt who are fartheſt from it.

XXVIII. When thou lookeſt upon the imperfections of others, allow one eye for what is laudable in them, and the balance they have from ſome excellency, which may render them conſiderable. While we look with fear or hatred

---

* *Cenſor's book*, in which the name and eſtate of every Roman citizen was regiſtered.

upon the teeth of the viper, we may behold his eye with love. In venomous
natures fomething may be amiable : poifons afford anti-poifons : nothing is totally,
or altogether ufeleffly bad. Notable
virtues are fometimes dafhed with notorious vices, and in fome vicious tempers
have been found illuftrious acts of virtue ;
which makes fuch obfervable worth in
fome actions of king Demetrius, Antonius, and Ahab, as are not to be found
in the fame kind in Ariftides, Numa, or
David. Conftancy, generofity, clemency,
and liberality have been highly confpicu-
ous in fome perfons not marked out in
other concerns for example or imitation.
But fince goodnefs is exemplary in all, if
others have not our virtues, let us not be
wanting in theirs ; nor fcorning them for
their vices whereof we are free, be condemned by their virtues wherein we are
deficient. There is drofs, alloy, and em-
bafement in all human tempers ; and he
flieth without wings, who thinks to find
ophir or pure metal in any. For perfection is not, like light, centered in any one

Cf. Rel.
Med. Pt.
2. x.

body; but, like the diſperſed ſeminalities of vegetables at the creation, ſcattered through the whole maſs of the earth, no place producing all, and almoſt all ſome. So that 'tis well, if a perfect man can be made out of many men, and, to the perfect eye of God, even out of mankind. Time, which perfects ſome things, imperfects alſo others. Could we intimately apprehend the ideated man, and as he ſtood in the intellect of God upon the firſt exertion by creation, we might more narrowly comprehend our preſent degeneration, and how widely we are fallen from the pure exemplar and idea of our nature: for after this corruptive elongation from a primitive and pure creation, we are almoſt loſt in degeneration; and Adam hath not only fallen from his Creator, but we ourſelves from Adam, our Tycho and primary generator.

XXIX. Quarrel not raſhly with adverſities not yet underſtood, and overlook not the mercies often bound up in them; for we conſider not ſufficiently the

good of evils, nor fairly compute the mercies of Providence in things afflictive at
firſt hand. The famous Andreas Doria
being invited to a feaſt by Aloyſio Fieſchi
with deſign to kill him, juſt the night
before fell mercifully into a fit of the
gout, and ſo eſcaped that miſchief. When
Cato intended to kill himſelf, from a blow
which he gave his ſervant, who would
not reach his ſword unto him, his hand ſo
ſwelled that he had much ado to effect
his deſign. Hereby any one but a re-
ſolved ſtoick might have taken a fair hint
of conſideration, and that ſome merciful
genius would have contrived his preſervation. To be ſagacious in ſuch intercurrences is not ſuperſtition, but wary and
pious diſcretion; and to contemn ſuch
hints were to be deaf unto the ſpeaking
hand of God, wherein Socrates and Cardan would hardly have been miſtaken.

xxx. Break not open the gate
of deſtruction, and make no haſte or buſtle
unto ruin. Poſt not heedleſſly on unto
the *non ultra* of folly, or precipice of per-

dition. Let vicious ways have their tropicks and deflexions, and ſwim in the waters of ſin but as in the Aſphaltick lake, though ſmeared and defiled, not to ſink to the bottom. If thou haſt dipped thy foot in the brink, yet venture not over Rubicon.* Run not into extremities from whence there is no regreſſion. In the vicious ways of the world it mercifully falleth out that we become not extempore wicked, but it taketh ſome time and pains to undo ourſelves. We fall not from virtue, like Vulcan from heaven, in a day. Bad diſpoſitions require ſome time to grow into bad habits; bad habits muſt undermine good, and often repeated acts make us habitually evil; ſo that by gradual depravations, and while we are but ſtaggeringly evil, we are not left without parentheſes of conſiderations, thoughtful rebukes, and merciful interventions to recall us unto ourſelves.† For the wiſdom

Iliad A. 590.

---

* The river, by croſſing which, Cæſar declared war againſt the Senate. Sueton. Jul. Cæſ. 32. Lucan Pharſ. i. 184.

of God hath methodized the courfe of things unto the beft advantage of good-nefs, and thinking confiderators overlook not the tract thereof.

XXXI. Since men and women have their proper virtues and vices, and even twins of different fexes have not only diftinct coverings in the womb, but differing qualities and virtuous habits after, tranfplace not their proprieties, and confound not their diftinctions. Let maf-culine and feminine accomplifhments fhine in their proper orbs, and adorn their re-fpective fubjects. However, unite not the vices of both fexes in one; be not mon-ftrous in iniquity, nor hermaphroditically vicious.

XXXII. If generous honefty, valour, and plain dealing, be the cogni-zance of thy family, or characteriftick of

† " Shame leaves us by degrees, not at firft coming;
For nature checks a new offence with loathing,
But ufe of fin doth make it feem as nothing."
                                    Daniell.

thy country, hold faſt ſuch inclinations
ſucked in with thy firſt breath, and which
lay in the cradle with thee. Fall not into
transforming degenerations, which under
the old name, create a new nation. Be
not an alien in thine own nation; bring
not Orontes into Tiber; learn the virtues,
not the vices of thy foreign neighbours,
and make thy imitation by diſcretion, not
contagion. Feel ſomething of thyſelf in
the noble acts of thy anceſtors, and find
in thine own genius that of thy predeceſ-
ſors. Reſt not under the expired merits
of others, ſhine by thoſe of thine own.
Flame not like the central fire which en-
lighteneth no eyes, which no man ſeeth,
and moſt men think there is no ſuch thing
to be ſeen. Add one ray unto the common luſtre; add not only to the number,
but the note of thy generation; and prove
not a cloud, but an aſteriſk in thy region.

XXXIII. Since thou haſt an
alarum in thy breaſt, which tells thee
thou haſt a living ſpirit in thee above two
thouſand times in an hour, dull not away

Juv. Sat. iii.
62.

thy days in ſlothful ſupinity and the tedi-
ouſneſs of doing nothing. To ſtrenuous
minds there is an inquietude in overquiet-
neſs, and no laboriouſneſs in labour; and
to tread a mile after the ſlow pace of
a ſnail, or the heavy meaſures of the lazy
of Brazilia, were a moſt tiring penance,
and worſe than a race of ſome furlongs at
the Olympicks. The rapid courſes of
the heavenly bodies are rather imitable by
our thoughts, than our corporeal motions:
yet the ſolemn motions of our lives amount
unto a greater meaſure than is commonly
apprehended. Some few men have ſur-
rounded the globe of the earth; yet many
in the ſet locomotions and movements of
their days have meaſured the circuit of it,
and twenty thouſand miles have been ex-
ceeded by them. Move circumſpectly,
not meticulouſly, and rather carefully
ſolicitous than anxiouſly ſolicitudinous.
Think not there is a lion in the way, nor Prov. xxii.
walk with leaden ſandals in the paths of 13.
goodneſs; but in all virtuous motions let
prudence determine thy meaſures. Strive
not to run, like Hercules, a furlong in a

breath : feſtination may prove precipita-
tion ; deliberating delay may be wiſe
cunctation, and ſlowneſs no ſlothfulneſs.

XXXIV. Since virtuous actions
have their own trumpets, and, without
any noiſe from thyſelf, will have their re-
found abroad, buſy not thy beſt member
in the encomium of thyſelf. Praiſe is a
debt we owe unto the virtues of others,
and due unto our own from all, whom
malice hath not made mutes, or envy
ſtruck dumb. Fall not, however, into
the common prevaricating way of ſelf-
commendation and boaſting, by denoting
the imperfections of others. He who
diſcommendeth others, obliquely com-
mendeth himſelf. He who whiſpers their
infirmities, proclaims his own exemption
from them ; and conſequently ſays, I am
not as this publican, or *hic niger*, whom
I talk of. Open oſtentation and loud
vain-glory is more tolerable than this
obliquity, as but containing ſome froth,
no ink ; as but conſiſting of a perſonal
piece of folly, nor complicated with un-

Pſ. cviii. 1.

Dante Purg.
xvii. 112.

S. Luke
xviii. 11.
Hor. Sat. i.
iv. 85.

charitableneſs. Superfluouſly we ſeek a
a precarious applauſe abroad; every good
man hath his *plaudite* within himſelf; and
though his tongue be ſilent, is not without
loud cymbals in his breaſt. Conſcience
will become his panegyriſt, and never
forget to crown and extol him unto himſelf.

XXXV. Bleſs not thyſelf only
that thou wert born in Athens; but,
among thy multiplied acknowledgments,
lift up one hand unto heaven, that thou
wert born of honeſt parents; that modeſty,
humility, patience, and veracity, lay in
the ſame egg, and came into the world
with thee. From ſuch foundations thou
mayeſt be happy in a virtuous precocity,
and make an early and long walk in goodneſs; ſo mayeſt thou more naturally
feel the contrariety of vice unto nature,
and reſiſt ſome by the antidote of thy
temper. As charity covers, ſo modeſty
preventeth a multitude of ſins; with-
holding from noon-day vices, and brazen-
browed iniquities, from ſinning on the

houſe-top, and painting our follies with the rays of the ſun. Where this virtue reigneth, though vice may ſhow its head, it cannot be in its glory. Where ſhame of ſin ſets, look not for virtue to ariſe; for when modeſty taketh wing, Aſtræa* goes ſoon after.

xxxvi. The heroical vein of mankind runs much in the ſoldiery and courageous part of the world, and in that form we ofteneſt find men above men. Hiſtory is full of the gallantry of that tribe; and when we read their notable acts, we eaſily find what a difference there is between a life in Plutarch and in La-ërtius. Where true fortitude dwells, loyalty, bounty, friendſhip, and fidelity may be found. A man may confide in perſons conſtituted for noble ends, who

Like Mutius Scævola. Liv. ii. 12. dare do and ſuffer, and who have a hand to burn for their country and their friend. Small and creeping things are the product

---

* Aſtræa, goddeſs of Juſtice, and conſequently of all Virtue. Ovid. Met. i. 150. Faerie Queene. v. i. 11.

of petty ſouls. He is like to be miſtaken, who makes choice of a covetous man for a friend, or relieth upon the reed of narrow and poltroon friendſhip. Pitiful things are only to be found in the cottages of ſuch breaſts; but bright thoughts, clear deeds, conſtancy, fidelity, bounty, and generous honeſty are the gems of noble minds; wherein, to derogate from none, the true heroick Engliſh gentleman hath no peer.

PART II.

I.

 UNISH not thyſelf with pleaſure; glut not thy ſenſe with palative delights, nor revenge the contempt of temperance by the penalty of ſatiety. Were there an age of delight or any pleaſure durable, who would not honour Volupia? but the race of delight is ſhort, and pleaſures have mutable faces. The pleaſures of one age are not pleaſures in another, and their lives fall ſhort of our own. Even in our ſenſual days, the ſtrength of delight is in its ſeldomneſs or rarity, and ſting in its ſatiety; mediocrity is its life, and immoderacy its confuſion. The luxurious emperors of old inconſiderately ſatiated themſelves with the

dainties of ſea and land, till, wearied
through all varieties, their refections became a ſtudy unto them, and they were
fain to feed by invention: novices in true
epicuriſm! which by mediocrity, paucity,
quick and healthful appetite, makes delights ſmartly acceptable; whereby Epicurus himſelf found *Jupiter's brain** in a
a piece of Cytheridian cheeſe, and the
tongues of nightingales in a diſh of onions.
Hereby healthful and temperate poverty
hath the ſtart of nauſeating luxury; unto
whoſe clear and naked appetite every
meal is a feaſt, and in one ſingle diſh the
firſt courſe of Metellus;† who are cheaply
hungry, and never loſe their hunger or
advantage of a craving appetite, becauſe
obvious food contents it; while Nero,
half famiſhed, could not feed upon a piece
of bread, and, lingering after his ſnowed
water, hardly got down an ordinary cup

---

* *Cerebrum Jovis*, for a delicious bit.

† *Metellus* his riotous pontifical ſupper, the great
variety whereat is to be ſeen in Macrobius. Saturnal.
iii. 13.

of *calda*.* By ſuch circumſcriptions of pleaſure the contemned philoſophers re-ſerved unto themſelves the ſecret of delight, which the *helluo's* of thoſe days loſt in their exorbitances. In vain we ſtudy de-light: it is at the command of every ſober mind, and in every ſenſe born with us: but nature, who teacheth us the rule of pleaſure, inſtructeth alſo in the bounds thereof, and where its line expireth. And therefore, temperate minds, not preſſing their pleaſures until the ſting appeareth, enjoy their contentations contentedly and without regret; and ſo eſcape the folly of exceſs, to be pleaſed unto diſplacency.

II. Bring candid eyes unto the peruſal of men's works, and let not Zoiliſm or detraction blaſt well-intended labours. He that endureth no faults in men's writings muſt only read his own,

---

* *Calda*, tepid water with which the ancients tempered their wine. " *Fameque interim et ſiti inter-pellante, panem quidem ſordidum oblatum adſpernatus eſt, aquæ autem tepidæ aliquantum bibit.*" Sueton. Nero. 48.

wherein for the most part all appeareth white. Quotation mistakes, inadvertency, expedition, and human lapses, may make, not only moles but warts in learned authors; who notwithstanding, being judged by the capital matter, admit not of disparagement. I should unwillingly affirm that Cicero was but slightly versed in Homer, because in his work *De Gloria*, he ascribed those verses unto Ajax, which were delivered by Hector. What if Plautus in the account of Hercules mistaketh nativity for conception? Who would have mean thoughts of Apollinaris Sidonius, who seems to mistake the river Tigris for Euphrates; and though a good historian and learned bishop of Auvergne had the misfortune to be out in the story of David, making mention of him when the ark was sent back by the Philistines upon a cart, which was before his time? Though I have no great opinion of Machiavel's learning, yet I shall not presently say that he was but a novice in Roman history, because he was mistaken in placing Commodus after the emperor Severus. Cap-

1 Sam. vi.

ital truths are to be narrowly eyed; collateral lapſes and circumſtantial deliveries not to be too ſtrictly ſifted. And if the ſubſtantial ſubject be well forged out, we need not examine the ſparks which irregularly fly from it.

III. Let well-weighed conſiderations, not ſtiff and peremptory aſſumptions, guide thy diſcourſes, pen, and actions. To begin or continue our works like Triſmegiſtus of old, *verum certè verum atque veriſſimum eſt*, would ſound arrogantly unto preſent ears in this ſtrict inquiring age; wherein, for the moſt part, *probably*, and *perhaps*, will hardly ſerve to mollify the ſpirit of captious contradictors. If Cardan ſaith that a parrot is a beautiful bird, Scaliger will ſet his wits to work to prove it a deformed animal. The compage of all phyſical truths is not ſo cloſely jointed, but oppoſition may find intruſion; nor always ſo cloſely maintained, as not to ſuffer attrition. Many poſitions ſeem quodlibetically conſtituted, and like a Delphian blade will cut on both

ſides. Some truths ſeem almoſt falſehoods, and ſome falſehoods almoſt truths;
wherein falſehood and truth ſeem almoſt
equilibriouſly ſtated, and but a few grains
of diſtinction to bear down the balance.
Some have digged deep, yet glanced by
the royal vein; and a man may come
unto the pericardium, but not the heart of
truth. Beſides, many things are known,
as ſome are ſeen, that is, by parallaxis, or
at ſome diſtance from their true and proper beings, the ſuperficial regard of things
having a different aſpect from their true
and central natures. And this moves
ſober pens unto ſuſpenſory and timorous
aſſertions, nor preſently to obtrude them
as Sibyls' leaves; which after conſiderations may find to be but folious appear-
ances, and not the central and vital interiors of truth.

IV. Value the judicious, and
let not mere acqueſts in minor parts of
learning gain thy pre-exiſtimation. It is
an unjuſt way of compute, to magnify
a weak head for ſome Latin abilities;

and to undervalue a ſolid judgment, becauſe he knows not the genealogy of Hector. When that notable king of France*
would have his ſon to know but one ſentence in Latin, had it been a good one,
perhaps it had been enough. Natural
parts and good judgments rule the world.
States are not governed by ergotiſms.
Many have ruled well, who could not,
perhaps, define a Commonwealth; and
they who underſtand not the globe of the
earth, command a great part of it. Where
natural logick prevails not, artificial too
often faileth. Where nature fills the ſails,
the veſſel goes ſmoothly on; and when
judgment is the pilot, the inſurance need
not be high. When induſtry builds upon
nature, we may expect pyramids: where
that foundation is wanting the ſtructure
muſt be low. They do moſt by books,
who could do much without them; and
he that chiefly owes himſelf unto himſelf,
is the ſubſtantial man.

---

* Lewis XI. *"Qui neſcit diſſimulare neſcit
regnare."*

v. Let thy ſtudies be free
as thy thoughts and contemplations: but
fly not only upon the wings of imagination;
join ſenſe unto reaſon, and experiment
unto ſpeculation, and ſo give life unto
embryon truths and verities yet in their
chaos. There is nothing more acceptable
unto the ingenious world, than this noble
eluctation of truth; wherein, againſt the
tenacity of prejudice and preſcription, this
century now prevaileth. What libraries
of new volumes after-times will behold,
and in what a new world of knowledge
the eyes of our poſterity may be happy, a
few ages may joyfully declare; and is but
a cold thought unto thoſe, who cannot
hope to behold this exantlation of truth,
or that obſcured virgin half out of the
pit: which might make ſome content
with a commutation of the time of their
lives, and to commend the fancy of the
Pythagorean metempſychoſis: whereby
they might hope to enjoy this happineſs
in their third or fourth ſelves, and behold
that in Pythagoras, which they now but

foreſee in Euphorbus.* The world, which
took but ſix days to make, is like to take
ſix thouſand to make out: meanwhile old
truths voted down begin to reſume their
places, and new ones ariſe upon us;
wherein there is no comfort in the happineſs of Tully's Elyſium,† or any ſatiſ-
faction from the ghoſts of the ancients,
who knew ſo little of what is now well
known. Men diſparage not antiquity, who
prudently exalt new inquiries, and make
not them the judges of truth, who were
but fellow inquirers of it. Who can but
magnify the endeavours of Ariſtotle, and
the noble ſtart which learning had under
him; or leſs than pity the ſlender pro-
greſſion made upon ſuch advantages;
while many centuries were loſt in repetitions and tranſcriptions ſealing up the

---

* Pythagoras, in accordance with his doctrine of
metempſychoſis, or more correctly metenſomatoſis,
declared that he himſelf had been preſent at the
ſeige of Troy as *Euphorbus*. Ovid. Met. xv. 160.
Hor. Od. I. xxviii. 11.

† In which Socrates comforted himſelf that he
ſhould converſe with the worthies of old. Tuſc.
Diſp. i. xli.

book of knowledge? And therefore rather than to ſwell the leaves of learning
by fruitleſs repetitions, to ſing the ſame
ſong in all ages, nor adventure at eſſays
beyond the attempt of others, many would
be content that ſome would write like
Helmont or Paracelſus; and be willing
to endure the monſtroſity of ſome opinions, for divers ſingular notions requiting
ſuch aberrations.

VI.   Deſpiſe not the obliquities of younger ways; nor deſpair of better things whereof there is yet no proſpect.
Who would imagine that Diogenes, who
in his younger days was a falſifier of
money, ſhould, in the after courſe of his
life be ſo great a contemner of metal?
Some negroes, who believe the reſurrec-
tion, think that they ſhall riſe white. Even
in this life regeneration may imitate re-
ſurrection; our black and vicious tinctures
may wear off, and goodneſs clothe us with
candour.   Good admonitions knock not
always in vain.   There will be ſignal
examples of God's mercy, and the angels

St. Luke xv. 10.

muſt not want their charitable rejoices for the converſion of loſt ſinners. Figures of moſt angles do neareſt approach unto circles, which have no angles at all. Some may be near unto goodneſs, who are conceived far from it; and many things happen, not likely to enſue from any promiſes of antecedencies. Culpable beginnings have found commendable concluſions, and infamous courſes pious retractations. Deteſtable ſinners have proved exemplary converts on earth, and may be glorious in the apartment of Mary Magdalen in heaven. Men are not the ſame through all diviſions of their ages: time, experience, ſelf-reflections, and God's mercies, make in ſome well-tempered minds a kind of tranſlation before death, and men to differ from themſelves as well as from other perſons. Hereof the old world afforded many examples to the infamy of latter ages, wherein men too often live by the rule of their inclinations; ſo that, without any aſtral prediction, the firſt day gives the laſt: men are commonly as they were; or rather, as bad diſpoſitions run into worſer habits, the evening doth not crown, but ſourly conclude the day.

VII. **If the Almighty will** not ſpare us according to his merciful capitulation at Sodom; if his goodneſs pleaſe not to paſs over a great deal of bad for a ſmall pittance of good, or to look upon us in the lump; there is ſlender hope for mercy, or ſound preſumption of fulfilling half his will, either in perſons or nations: they who excel in ſome virtues being ſo often defective in others; few men driving at the extent and amplitude of goodneſs, but computing themſelves by their beſt parts, and others by their worſt, are content to reſt in thoſe virtues which others commonly want. Which makes this ſpeckled face of honeſty in the world; and which was the imperfection of the old philoſophers and great pretenders unto virtue; who well declining the gaping vices of intemperance, incontinency, violence and oppreſſion, were yet blindly peccant in iniquities of cloſer faces; were envious, malicious, contemners, ſcoffers,

Gen. xviii. 23—33.

cenſurers, and ſtuffed with vizard vices, no leſs depraving the ethereal particle and diviner portion of man. For envy, malice, hatred, are the qualities of Satan, cloſe and dark like himſelf; and where ſuch brands ſmoke the ſoul cannot be white. Vice may be had at all prices; expenſive and coſtly iniquities which make the noiſe, cannot be every man's ſins; but the ſoul may be foully inquinated at a very low rate, and a man may be cheaply vicious to the perdition of himſelf.

VIII. Opinion rides upon the neck of reaſon; and men are happy, wiſe, or learned, according as that empreſs ſhall ſet them down in the regiſter of reputation. However, weigh not thyſelf in the ſcales of thy own opinion, but let the judgment of the judicious be the ſtandard of thy merit. Self-eſtimation is a flatterer too readily entitling us unto knowledge and abilities, which others ſolicitouſly labour after, and doubtfully think they attain. Surely, ſuch confident tempers do paſs their days in beſt tranquillity;

who, reſting in the opinion of their own abilities, are happily gull'd by ſuch contentation; wherein pride, ſelf-conceit, confidence, and opiniatry, will hardly ſuffer any to complain of imperfection. To think themſelves in the right, or all that right, or only that, which they do or think, is a fallacy of high content; though others laugh in their ſleeves, and look upon them as in a deluded ſtate of judgment: wherein, notwithſtanding, it were but a civil piece of complacency to ſuffer them to ſleep who would not wake, to let them reſt in their ſecurities, nor by diſſent or oppoſition to ſtagger their contentments.

IX. Since the brow ſpeaks often true, ſince eyes and noſes have tongues, and the countenance proclaims the heart and inclinations, let obſervation ſo far inſtruct thee in phyſiognomical lines, as to be ſome rule for thy diſtinction, and guide for thy affection unto ſuch as look moſt like men. Mankind, methinks, is comprehended in a few faces, if we exclude all viſages which any way participate of ſymmetries and ſchemes of look common unto other animals. For as though man were the extract of the world, in whom all were *in coagulato*, which in their forms were *in ſoluto* and at extenſion; we often obſerve that men do moſt act thoſe creatures, whoſe conſtitution, parts, and complexion do moſt predominate in their mixtures. This is a corner-ſtone in phyſiognomy, and holds ſome truth not only in particular perſons, but alſo in whole nations. There are, therefore, provincial faces, national lips and noſes, which teſtify not only the natures of thoſe countries, but of thoſe which have them elſewhere. Thus we may make England the whole earth, dividing it not only into Europe, Aſia, Africa, but the particular regions thereof; and may in ſome latitude affirm, that there are Egyptians, Scythians, Indians among us, who though born in England, yet carry the faces and air of thoſe countries, and are alſo agreeable and correſpondent unto their natures. Faces look uniformly unto our eyes: how they appear unto ſome animals of a more piercing or differing ſight, who are able to diſcover the inequalities, rubs and hairineſs of the ſkin, is not without good doubt; and, therefore, in reference unto man, Cupid is ſaid to be blind. Affection ſhould not be too ſharp-eyed, and love is not to be made by magnifying glaſſes. If things were ſeen as they truly are, the beauty of bodies would be much abridged. And, therefore, the Wiſe Contriver hath drawn the pictures and outſides of things ſoftly and amiably unto the natural edge of our eyes, not leaving them able to diſcover thoſe uncomely aſperities, which make oyſter-ſhells in good faces, and hedgehogs even in Venus's moles.

x. Court not felicity too far,

and weary not the favourable hand of fortune. Glorious actions have their times, extent, and *non ultra's*. To put no end unto attempts were to make preſcription of ſucceſſes, and to beſpeak unhappineſs at the laſt; for the line of our lives is drawn with white and black viciſ-

ſitudes, wherein the extremes hold ſeldom
one complexion.   That Pompey ſhould
obtain the ſurname of Great at twenty-
five years; that men in their young and
active days ſhould be fortunate and perform notable things; is no obſervation of
deep wonder, they having the ſtrength of
their fates before them, nor yet acted
their parts in the world for which they
were brought into it; whereas men of
years, matured for counſels and deſigns,
ſeem to be beyond the vigour of their active fortunes, and high exploits of life,
providentially ordained unto ages beſt
agreeable unto them.   And, therefore,
many brave men, finding their fortune
grow faint, and feeling its declination,
have timely withdrawn themſelves from
great attempts, and ſo eſcaped the ends
of mighty men, diſproportionable to their
beginnings.   But magnanimous thoughts
have ſo dimmed the eyes of many, that
forgetting the very eſſence of fortune, and
the viciſſitude of good and evil, they
apprehend no bottom in felicity, and ſo
have been ſtill tempted on unto mighty

See the ſtory
of Poly-
crates and
Amaſis.
Herod. iii.
40. ſeq.

actions, reſerved for their deſtructions.
For fortune lays the plot of our adverſities in the foundation of our felicities,
bleſſing us in the firſt quadrate, to blaſt us
more ſharply in the laſt. And ſince in the
higheſt felicities there lieth a capacity of
the loweſt miſeries, ſhe hath this advantage from our happineſs to make us truly
miſerable; for to become acutely miſerable we are to be firſt happy. Affliction
ſmarts moſt in the moſt happy ſtate, as
having ſomewhat in it of Beliſarius at
beggar's buſh, or Bajazet in the grate.
And this the fallen angels ſeverely underſtand, who having acted their firſt part in
Heaven, are made ſharply miſerable by
tranſition, and more afflictively feel the
contrary ſtate of Hell.

XI. Carry no careleſs eye
upon the unexpected ſcenes of things,
but ponder the acts of Providence in the
public ends of great and notable men,
ſet out unto the view of all for no common memorandums. The tragical exits
and unexpected periods of ſome eminent

persons cannot but amuse considerate ob-
servators; wherein, notwithstanding, most
men seem to see by extramission, without
reception or self-reflection, and conceive
themselves unconcerned by the fallacy of
their own exemption; whereas, the mercy
of God hath singled out but few to be the
signals of his justice, leaving the generality
of mankind to the pædagogy of example.
But the inadvertency of our natures not
well apprehending this favourable method and merciful decimation, and that He
sheweth in some what others also deserve;
they entertain no sense of his hand beyond the stroke of themselves. Whereupon the whole becomes necessarily pun-
ished, and the contracted hand of God
extended unto universal judgments; from
whence, nevertheless, the stupidity of our
tempers receives but faint impressions,
and in the most tragical state of times
holds but starts of good motions. So that
to continue us in goodness there must be
iterated returns of misery, and a circulation in affliction is necessary. And since
we cannot be wise by warnings; since

plagues are infignificant, except we be perfonally plagued; fince alfo we cannot be punifhed unto amendment by proxy or commutation, nor by vicinity, but contaction; there is an unhappy neceffity that we muft fmart in our own fkins, and the provoked arm of the Almighty muft fall upon ourfelves. The capital fufferings of others are rather our monitions than acquitments. There is but One who died falvifically for us, and able to fay unto death, Hitherto fhalt thou go, and no farther; only one enlivening death, which makes gardens of graves, and that which was fowed in corruption to arife and flourifh in glory: when death itfelf fhall die, and living fhall have no period; when the damned fhall mourn at the funeral of death; when life, not death, fhall be the wages of fin: when the fecond death fhall prove a miferable life, and deftruction fhall be courted.

1 Cor. xv. 43.

Rom. vi. 23. Rev. vi. 15—17.

XII. Although their thoughts may feem too fevere, who think that few ill-natured men go to heaven; yet it may

be acknowledged that good-natured perſons are beſt founded for that place, who
enter the world with good diſpoſitions and
natural graces, more ready to be advanced
by impreſſions from above, and chriſtian-
ized unto pieties, who carry about them
plain and down-right dealing minds, humility, mercy, charity, and virtues acceptable unto God and man. But whatever
ſucceſs they may have as to heaven, they
are the acceptable men on earth, and happy is he who hath his quiver full of them
for his friends. Theſe are not the dens
wherein falſehood lurks, and hypocriſy
hides its head, wherein frowardneſs makes
its neſt, or where malice, hard-heartedneſs,
and oppreſſion love to dwell; not thoſe
by whom the poor get little, and the
rich ſome time loſe all; men, not of re-
tracted looks, but who carry their hearts
in their faces, and need not to be looked
upon with perſpectives; not ſordidly or
miſchievouſly ingrateful; who cannot
learn to ride upon the neck of the afflicted,
nor load the heavy laden, but who keep
the temple of Janus ſhut by peaceable

and quiet tempers; who make not only
the beft friends, but the beft enemies, as
eafier to forgive than offend, and ready
to pafs by the fecond offence before they
avenge the firft; who make natural
Royalifts, obedient Subjects, kind and
merciful Princes, verified in our own, one
of the beft-natured Kings of this throne.
Of the old Roman Emperors the beft
were the beft natured, though they made
but a fmall number, and might be writ in
a ring. Many of the reft were as bad
men as princes; humourifts, rather than
of good humours; and of good natural
parts, rather than of good natures, which
did but arm their bad inclinations, and
make them wittily wicked.

XIII. With what fhift and
pains we come into the world, we remember not, but 'tis commonly found no
eafy matter to get out of it. Many have
ftudied to exafperate the ways of death,
but fewer hours have been fpent to foften
that neceffity. That the fmootheft way
unto the grave is made by bleeding, as

common opinion preſumeth, beſide the
ſick and fainting languors which accompany that effuſion, the experiment in
Lucan and Seneca will make us doubt:
under which the noble Stoick ſo deeply
laboured, that, to conceal his affliction, he
was fain to retire from the ſight of his
wife, and not aſhamed to implore the
merciful hand of his phyſician to ſhorten
his miſery therein. Ovid, the old heroes,
and the Stoicks, who were ſo afraid of
drowning, as dreading thereby the extinction of their ſoul, which they conceived
to be a fire, ſtood probably in fear of an
eaſier way of death; wherein the water,
entering the poſſeſſions of air, makes a
temperate ſuffocation, and kills, as it were,
without a fever. Surely many who have
had the ſpirit to deſtroy themſelves, have
not been ingenious in the contrivance
thereof. 'Twas a dull way practiſed by
Themiſtocles, to overwhelm himſelf with
bull's blood, who being an Athenian,
might have held an eaſier theory of death
from the ſtate potion of his country;
from which Socrates, in Plato, ſeemed not

Tacitus
Annal. xv.
63. 70.

Ovid. Triſt.
i, ii, 51. 52.

Vide Plu-
tarch.

to suffer much more than from the fit of an ague. Cato is much to be pitied, who mangled himself with poniards; and Hannibal seems more subtle, who carried his delivery, not in the point, but the pummel of his sword.*

The Egyptians were merciful contrivers, who destroyed their malefactors by asps, charming their senses into an invincible sleep, and killing as it were with Hermes his rod. The Turkish emperor, odious for other cruelty, was herein a remarkable master of mercy, killing his favourite in his sleep, and sending him from the shade into the house of darkness. He who had been thus destroyed, would hardly have bled at the presence of his destroyer: when men are already dead by metaphor, and pass but from one sleep unto another, wanting herein the eminent part of severity to feel themselves to die;

---

* Wherein he is said to have carried something, whereby upon a struggle or despair he might deliver himself from all misfortunes. Juvenal says it was carried in a ring: Sat. x. 165.

and eſcaping the ſharpeſt attendant of death, the lively apprehenſion thereof. But to learn to die is better than to ſtudy the ways of dying. Death will find ſome ways to untie or cut the moſt Gordian knots of life, and make men's miſeries as mortal as themſelves; whereas evil ſpirits, as undying ſubſtances, are inſeparable from their calamities; and, therefore, they everlaſtingly ſtruggle under their anguſtias, and, bound up with immortality, can never get out of themſelves.

PART III.

I.

T is hard to find a whole age to imitate, or what century to propoſe for example. Some have been far more approveable than others; but virtue, and vice, panegyricks, and ſatires, ſcatteringly to be found in all. Hiſtory ſets down not only things laudable, but abominable; things which ſhould never have been, or never have been known; ſo that noble patterns muſt be fetched here and there from ſingle perſons, rather than whole nations; and from whole nations rather than any one. The world was early bad, and the firſt ſin the moſt deplorable of any. The younger world afforded the oldeſt men, and perhaps the beſt and

the worſt, when length of days made virtuous habits heroical and immoveable;
vicious, inveterate and irreclaimable. And

Gen. vi. 5.

ſince 'tis ſaid that the imaginations of their
hearts were evil, only evil, and continually
evil; it may be feared that their ſins held
pace with their lives, and their longevity
ſwelling their impieties, the longanimity of
God would no longer endure ſuch vivacious
abominations. Their impieties were ſurely
of a deep dye, which required the whole
Element of Water to waſh them away, and
overwhelmed their memories with themſelves; and ſo ſhut up the firſt windows of
Time, leaving no hiſtories of thoſe longevous generations, when men might
have been properly hiſtorians, when Adam
might have read long lectures unto Methuſelah, and Methuſelah unto Noah.
For had we been happy in juſt hiſtorical
accounts of that unparalleled world, we
might have been acquainted with wonders,
and have underſtood not a little of the acts
and undertakings of Moſes his mighty
men, and men of renown of old, which
might have enlarged our thoughts, and

made the world older unto us. For the
unknown part of time ſhortens the eſtimation, if not the compute of it. What
hath eſcaped our knowledge, falls not under our conſideration; and what is and
will be latent, is little better than non-
exiſtent.

11. Some things are dictated
for our inſtruction, ſome acted for our
imitation; wherein it is beſt to aſcend
unto the higheſt conformity, and to the
honour of the exemplar. He honours
God, who imitates him;* for what we
virtuouſly imitate we approve and admire;
and ſince we delight not to imitate infe-
riors, we aggrandize and magnify thoſe
we imitate; ſince alſo we are moſt apt to

---

* " He prayeth well, who loveth well
    Both man and bird and beaſt.
    He prayeth beſt, who loveth beſt
    All things both great and ſmall;
    For the dear God who loveth us,
    He made and loveth all."
                   COLERIDGE.
Cf. St. Matt. vi. 12, 14, 15.

imitate thoſe we love, we teſtify our affection in our imitation of the inimitable.
To affect to be like, may be no imitation;
to act, and not to be what we pretend to
imitate, is but a mimical conformation,
and carrieth no virtue in it. Lucifer imitated not God, when he ſaid he would be
like the Higheſt; and he imitated not Jupiter, who counterfeited thunder. Where
imitation can go no farther, let admiration
ſtep on, whereof there is no end in the
wiſeſt form of men. Even angels and
ſpirits have enough to admire in their
ſublimer natures; admiration being the act
of the creature, and not of God, who doth
not admire himſelf. Created natures allow of ſwelling hyperboles; nothing can
be ſaid hyperbolically of God, nor will his
attributes admit of expreſſions above their
own exuperances. Triſmegiſtus his circle, whoſe centre is every where and circumference no where, was no hyperbole.
Words cannot exceed, where they cannot
expreſs enough. Even the moſt winged
thoughts fall at the ſetting out, and reach
not the portal of Divinity.

Salmoneus.
Virg. Æn.
vi. 585.

III. In bivious theorems, and
Janus-faced doctrines, let virtuous confiderations ſtate the determination. Look
upon opinions as thou doſt upon the
moon, and chooſe not the dark hemi-
ſphere for thy contemplation. Embrace
not the opacous and blind ſide of opinions, but that which looks moſt lucife-
rouſly or influentially unto goodneſs.
It is better to think that there are Guardian Spirits, than that there are no ſpirits
to guard us; that vicious perſons are
ſlaves, than that there is any ſervitude in
virtue; that times paſt have been better
than times preſent, than that times were
always bad; and that to be men it ſuf-
ficeth to be no better than men in all ages,
and ſo promiſcuouſly to ſwim down the
turbid ſtream, and make up the grand
confuſion. Sow not thy underſtanding
with opinions, which make nothing of
iniquities, and fallaciouſly extenuate tranſgreſſions. Look upon vices and vicious
objects, with hyperbolical eyes; and rather enlarge their dimenſions, that their

unſeen deformities may not eſcape thy
ſenſe, and their poiſonous parts and ſtings
may appear maſſy and monſtrous unto
thee: for the undiſcerned particles and
atoms of evil deceive us, and we are undone by the inviſibles of ſeeming goodneſs.
We are only deceived in what is not diſ-
cerned, and to err is but to be blind or
dim-ſighted as to ſome perceptions.

Linea recta
breviſſima.

IV. To be honeſt in a right
line, and virtuous by epitome, be firm
unto ſuch principles of goodneſs as carry
in them volumes of inſtruction and may
abridge thy labour. And ſince inſtruc-
tions are many, hold cloſe unto thoſe,
whereon the reſt depend; ſo may we have
all in a few, and the law and the prophets
in a rule; the Sacred Writ in ſtenography,
and the Scripture in a nut-ſhell. To
purſue the oſſeous and ſolid part of
goodneſs, which gives ſtability and recti-
tude to all the reſt; to ſettle on fundamental virtues, and bid early defiance unto
mother-vices, which carry in their bowels
the ſeminals of other iniquities, makes a

ſhort cut in goodneſs, and ſtrikes not off
a head, but the whole neck of Hydra.
For we are carried into the dark lake, like
the Egyptian river into the ſea, by ſeven
principal oſtiaries: the mother-ſins of that
number are the deadly engines of evil
ſpirits that undo us, and even evil ſpirits
themſelves; and he who is under the
chains thereof is not without a poſſeſſion.
Mary Magdalene had more than ſeven St. Luke viii. 2.
devils, if theſe with their imps were in
her; and he who is thus poſſeſſed, may
literally be named Legion. Where ſuch viii. 30.
plants grow and proſper, look for no
champaign or region void of thorns; but
productions like the tree of Goa,* and
foreſts of abomination.

v. Guide not the hand of
God, nor order the finger of the Almighty
unto thy will and pleaſure; but ſit quiet

---

* *Arbor Goa de Ruyz,* or *Ficus Indica,* whoſe
branches ſend down ſhoots which root in the ground,
from whence there ſucceſſively riſe others, till one
tree becomes a wood. Cf. Plin. H. N. xii. 5.
Milton. P. L. ix. 1101.

in the ſoft ſhowers of Providence, and favourable diſtributions in this world, either to thyſelf or others. And ſince not only judgments have their errands, but mercies their commiſſions; ſnatch not at every favour, nor think thyſelf paſſed by if they fall upon thy neighbour. Rake not up envious diſplacences at things ſucceſsful unto others, which the Wiſe Diſpoſer of all thinks not fit for thyſelf. Reconcile the events of things unto both beings, that is, of this world and the next; ſo will there not ſeem ſo many riddles in Providence, nor various inequalities in the diſpenſation of things below. If thou doſt not anoint thy face, yet put not on ſackcloth at the felicities of others. Re-

Cf. Faerie Queene i. iv. 30.

pining at the good draws on rejoicing at the evils of others, and ſo falls into that inhuman vice, for which ſo few languages have a name. The bleſſed ſpirits above rejoice at our happineſs below; but to be glad at the evils of one another, is beyond the malignity of hell, and falls not on evil ſpirits, who, though they rejoice at our unhappineſs, take no pleaſure at the af-

flictions of their own fociety or of their
fellow natures. Degenerous heads! who
muft be fain to learn from fuch examples,
and to be taught from the School of
Hell.

VI. Grain not thy vicious
ftains, nor deepen thofe fwart tinctures,
which temper, infirmity, or ill habits have
fet upon thee; and fix not, by iterated
depravations, what time might efface, or
virtuous wafhes expunge. He who thus
ftill advanceth in iniquity, deepeneth his
deformed hue, turns a fhadow into night,
and makes himfelf a negro in the black
jaundice; and fo becomes one of thofe
loft ones, the difproportionate pores of
whofe brains afford no entrance unto good
motions, but reflect and fruftrate all coun-
fels, deaf unto the thunder of the laws,
and rocks unto the cries of charitable
commiferators. He who hath had the
patience of Diogenes, to make orations
unto ftatues, may more fenfibly apprehend
how all words fall to the ground, fpent
upon fuch a furd and earlefs generation

of men, ſtupid unto all inſtruction, and rather requiring an exorciſt than an orator for their converſion!

VII. Burden not the back of Aries, Leo, or Taurus with thy faults; nor make Saturn, Mars, or Venus guilty of thy follies. Think not to faſten thy imperfections on the ſtars, and ſo deſpairingly conceive thyſelf under a fatality of being evil. Calculate thyſelf within; ſeek not thyſelf in the moon, but in thine own orb or microcoſmical circumference. Let celeſtial aſpects admoniſh and advertiſe, not conclude and determine thy ways. For ſince good and bad ſtars moralize not our actions, and neither excuſe or commend, acquit or condemn our good or bad deeds at the preſent or laſt bar; ſince ſome are aſtrologically well diſpoſed, who are morally highly vicious; not celeſtial figures, but virtuous ſchemes, muſt denominate and ſtate our actions. If we rightly underſtood the names whereby God calleth the ſtarrs; if we knew his name for the Dog-ſtar, or by what appel-

Pſ. cxlvii. 4.
Iſ. xl. 26.
Cf. Job
xxxviii, 31,
32.

lation Jupiter, Mars, and Saturn obey his will; it might be a welcome acceſſion unto aſtrology, which ſpeaks great things, and is fain to make uſe of appellations from Greek and Barbarick ſyſtems. Whatever influences, impulſions, or inclinations there be from the lights above, it were a piece of wiſdom to make one of thoſe wiſe men who overrule their ſtars, and with their own Militia contend with the Hoſt of Heaven. Unto which attempt there want not auxiliaries from the whole ſtrength of morality, ſupplies from Chriſtian ethicks, influences alſo and illuminations from above, more powerful than the Lights of Heaven.*

Sapiens dominabitur aſtris.

VIII. Confound not the diſtinctions of thy life which nature hath divided; that is, youth, adoleſcence, manhood, and old age: nor in theſe divided periods, wherein thou art in a manner four, conceive thyſelf but one. Let every diviſion be happy in its proper virtues,

* See Appendix P.

nor one vice run through all. Let each distinction have its salutary transition, and critically deliver thee from the imperfections of the former; so ordering the whole, that prudence and virtue may have the largest section. Do as a child but 1. Cor. xiii.
11.
Hor. Sat. ii.
3. 248. when thou art a child, and ride not on a reed at twenty. He who hath not taken leave of the follies of his youth, and in his maturer state scarce got out of that division, disproportionately divideth his days, crowds up the latter part of his life, and leaves too narrow a corner for the age of wisdom; and so hath room to be a man, scarce longer than he hath been a youth. Rather than to make this confusion, anticipate the virtues of age, and live long without the infirmities of it. So mayest thou count up thy days as some Cf. Rel.
Med. xxii.
xxxix. do Adam's, that is by anticipation; so mayest thou be coetaneous unto thy elders, and a father unto thy contemporaries.

IX. While others are curious

in the choice of good air, and chiefly solicitous for healthful habitations, study thou

converſation, and be critical in thy conſortion. The aſpects, conjunctions, and
configurations of the ſtars, which mutu-
ally diverſify, intend, or qualify their
influences, are but the varieties of their
nearer or farther converſation with one
another, and like the conſortion of men,
whereby they become better or worſe,
and even exchange their natures. Since
men live by examples, and will be imitating ſomething, order thy imitation to thy
improvement, not thy ruin. Look not
for roſes in Attalus his garden,* or
wholeſome flowers in a venomous planta-
tion. And ſince there is ſcarce any one
bad, but ſome others are the worſe for
him, tempt not contagion by proximity,
and hazard not thyſelf in the ſhadow of
corruption. He who hath not early ſuffered this ſhipwreck, and in his younger

---

* *Omiſſa deinde regni adminiſtratione, hortos
fodiebat, gramina ſeminabat, et noxia innoxiis per-
miſcebat; eaque omnia veneni ſucco infecta, velut
peculiare munus, amicis mittebat.* Juſtin. Hiſt.
xxxvi. 4.

Vide *Theſeus* in Plutarch.

days eſcaped this Charybdis, may make a happy voyage, and not come in with black ſails into the port. Self-converſation, or to be alone, is better than ſuch conſortion. Some ſchoolmen tell us, that he is properly alone, with whom in the ſame place there is no other of the ſame ſpecies.

Dan. iv.

Nebuchadnezzar was alone, though among the beaſts of the field; and a wiſe man may be tolerably ſaid to be alone, though with a rabble of people little better than beaſts about him. Unthinking heads, who have not learned to be alone, are in a priſon to themſelves, if they be not alſo with others: whereas, on the contrary, they whoſe thoughts are in a fair, and hurry within, are ſometimes fain to retire into company, to be out of the crowd of themſelves. He who muſt needs have company, muſt needs have ſometimes bad company. Be able to be alone. Loſe not the advantage of ſolitude, and the ſociety of thyſelf; nor be only content, but delight to be alone and ſingle with Omnipreſency. He who is thus prepared, the day is not uneaſy, nor

the night black unto him. Darkneſs may
bound his eyes, not his imagination. In
his bed he may lie, like Pompey and his
ſons, in all quarters of the earth ; * may
ſpeculate the univerſe, and enjoy the whole
world in the hermitage of himſelf. Thus
the old aſcetick Chriſtians found a paradiſe
in a deſert, and with little converſe on earth
held a converſation in heaven ; thus they
aſtronomiſed in caves, and though they
beheld not the ſtars, had the glory of heaven before them.

x. Let the characters of good
things ſtand indelibly in thy mind, and
thy thoughts be active on them. Truſt
not too much unto ſuggeſtions from re-
miniſcential amulets, or artificial memorandums. Let the mortifying Janus of
Covarrubias† be in thy daily thoughts,
not only on thy hand and ſignets. Rely

---

* " *Pompeios Juvenes Aſia atque Europa, ſed
ipſum terra tegit Libyes.*"

† Don Sebaſtian de Covarrubias writ three centuries of moral emblems, in Spaniſh. In the 88th
of the ſecond century, he ſets down two faces averſe,

not alone upon ſilent and dumb remembrances. Behold not death's heads till thou doſt not ſee them, nor look upon mortifying objects till thou overlookeſt them. Forget not how aſſuefaction unto any thing minorates the paſſion from it; how conſtant objects loſe their hints, and ſteal an inadvertiſement upon us. There is no excuſe to forget what every thing prompts unto us. To thoughtful obſervators, the whole world is a phylactery; and every thing we ſee an item of the wiſdom, power, or goodneſs of God. Happy are they who verify their amulets, and make their phylacteries ſpeak in their lives and actions. To run on in deſpite of the revulſions and pull-backs of ſuch remoras, aggravates our tranſgreſſions. When death's heads on our hands have no influence upon our heads, and fleſhleſs cadavers abate not the exorbitances of the fleſh; when crucifixes upon men's hearts

Cf. Butler's
Anal. P. i.
c. v. ſ. 2.

---

and conjoined, Janus-like; the one a gallant beautiful face, the other a death's-head face, with this motto out of Ovid his Metamorphoſis,

      Quid fuerim, quid ſimque, vide.

ſuppreſs not their bad commotions, and His image who was murdered for us withholds not from blood and murder: phylacteries prove but formalities, and their deſpiſed hints ſharpen our condemnations.

XI. Look not for whales in the Euxine ſea, or expect great matters where they are not to be found. Seek not for profundity in ſhallowneſs, or fertility in a wilderneſs. Place not the expectation of great happineſs here below, or think to find heaven on earth; wherein we muſt be content with embryon felicities, and fruitions of doubtful faces: for the circle of our felicities makes but ſhort arches. In every clime we are in a periſcian ſtate;* and, with our light, our ſhadow and darkneſs walk about us. Our contentments ſtand upon the tops of pyramids, ready to fall off, and the infe-

---

* The Periſcii are thoſe, who, living within the polar circle, ſee the ſun move round them, and conſequently, project their ſhadows in all directions.

curity of their enjoyments abrupteth our tranquillities. What we magnify is magnificent, but, like to the Coloſſus, noble without, ſtuffed with rubbiſh and coarſe metal within. Even the ſun, whoſe glorious outſide we behold, may have dark and ſmoky entrails. In vain we admire the luſtre of any thing ſeen: that which is truly glorious, is inviſible. Paradiſe was but a part of the earth, loſt not only to our fruition but our knowledge. And if, according to old dictates, no man can be ſaid to be happy before death; the happineſs of this life goes for nothing before it be over, and while we think ourſelves happy we do but uſurp that name. Certainly, true beatitude groweth not on earth, nor hath this world in it the expectations we have of it. He ſwims in oil, and can hardly avoid ſinking, who hath ſuch light foundations to ſupport him: 'tis therefore, happy, that we have two worlds to hold on. To enjoy true happineſs we muſt travel into a very far country, and even out of ourſelves; for the pearl we ſeek for is not to be found in the Indian, but in the empyrean ocean.

XII. Anſwer not the ſpur of fury, and be not prodigal or prodigious in revenge. Make not one in the *Hiſtoria horribilis*; flay not thy ſervant for a broken glaſs, nor pound him in a mortar who offendeth thee ; ſupererogate not in the worſt ſenſe, and overdo not the neceſſities of evil; humour not the injuſtice of revenge. Be not ſtoically miſtaken in the equality of ſins, nor commutatively iniquous in the valuation of tranſgreſſions; but weigh them in the ſcales of heaven, and by the weights of righteous reaſon. Think that revenge too high which is but level with the offence. Let thy arrows of revenge fly ſhort ; or be aimed like thoſe of Jonathan, to fall beſide the mark. Too many there be to whom a dead enemy ſmells well, and who find muſk and amber in revenge. The ferity of ſuch minds holds no rule in retaliations; requiring too often a head for a tooth, and the ſupreme revenge for treſpaſſes which a night's reſt ſhould obliterate. But patient

Eccl. vii. 9.

See *Vedius Pollio.* Plin. H. N. ix. 23. Calmet on Prov. xxvii. 22.

1 Sam. xx. 20.

meekneſs takes injuries like pills, not chewing, but ſwallowing them down, laconically ſuffering, and ſilently paſſing them over; while angered pride makes a noiſe, like Homerican Mars, at every ſcratch of offences. Since women do moſt delight in revenge, it may ſeem but feminine manhood to be vindictive. If thou muſt needs have thy revenge of thine enemy, with a ſoft tongue break his bones, heap coals of fire on his head, forgive him and enjoy it. To forgive our enemies is a charming way of revenge, and a ſhort Cæſarean conqueſt, overcoming without a blow; laying our enemies at our feet, under ſorrow, ſhame, and repentance; leaving our foes our friends, and ſolicitouſly inclined to grateful retaliations. Thus to return upon our adverſaries is a healing way of revenge; and to do good for evil a ſoft and melting ultion, a method taught from heaven to keep all ſmooth on earth.* Common forceable

Juv. Sat. xiii. 112.

Sat. xiii. 190.

Prov. xxv. 15, 21, 22.

---

* "Hath any wronged thee? be bravely revenged; ſleight it, and the work's begun; forgive it, 'tis

ways make not an end of evil, but leave hatred and malice behind them. An enemy thus reconciled is little to be truſted, as wanting the foundation of love and charity, and but for a time reſtrained by diſadvantage or inability. If thou haſt not mercy for others, yet be not cruel unto thyſelf. To ruminate upon evils, to make critical notes upon injuries, and be too acute in their apprehenſions, is to add unto our own tortures, to feather the arrows of our enemies, to laſh ourſelves with the ſcorpions of our foes, and to re-ſolve to ſleep no more; for injuries long dreamt on, take away at laſt all reſt; and he ſleeps but like Regulus who buſieth his head about them.*

XIII. Amuſe not thyſelf about the riddles of future things. Study pro-

---

finiſht: he is below himſelfe that is not above an injury." Quarles' Enchir. ii. 86.

* *Like Regulus.* Dion Caſſius relates that when Regulus fell into the hands of the Carthaginians, he was kept ſhut up with an Elephant, in order that his ſleep might be diſturbed.

phecies when they are become hiſtories,
and paſt hovering in their cauſes. Eye
well things paſt and preſent, and let con-
jectural ſagacity ſuffice for things to come.
There is a ſober latitude for preſcience
in contingencies of diſcoverable tempers,
whereby diſcerning heads ſee ſometimes
beyond their eyes, and wiſe men become
prophetical. Leave cloudy predictions to
their periods, and let appointed ſeaſons
have the lot of their accompliſhments.
It is too early to ſtudy ſuch prophecies
before they have been long made, before
ſome train of their cauſes have already
taken fire, laying open in part what lay
obſcure and before buried unto us. For
the voice of prophecies is like that of
whiſpering-places; they who are near, or
at a little diſtance, hear nothing; thoſe
at the fartheſt extremity will underſtand
all. But a retrograde cognition of times
paſt, and things which have already been,
is more ſatisfactory than a ſuſpended
knowledge of what is yet unexiſtent.
And the greateſt part of time being
already wrapt up in things behind us, it

is now ſomewhat late to bait after things
before us; for futurity ſtill ſhortens, and
time preſent ſucks in time to come. What
is prophetical in one age, proves hiſtorical
in another, and ſo muſt hold on unto the
laſt of time; when there will be no room
for prediction, when Janus ſhall loſe one
face, and the long beard of time ſhall look
like thoſe of David's ſervants, ſhorn away | 2 Sam. x. 4.
upon one ſide; and when, if the expected
Elias ſhould appear, he might ſay much
of what is paſt, not much of what is to
come.

XIV. Live unto the dignity
of thy nature, and leave it not diſputable
at laſt, whether thou haſt been a man;
or, ſince thou art a compoſition of man
and beaſt, how thou haſt predominantly
paſſed thy days, to ſtate the denomination.
Unman not, therefore, thyſelf by a beſtial
transformation, nor realize old fables.
Expoſe not thyſelf by four-footed manners
unto monſtrous draughts, and caricatura
repreſentations. Think not after the old
Pythagorean conceit, what beaſt thou

mayeft be after death. Be not under
any brutal metempfychofis while thou
liveft, and walkeft about erectly under the
fcheme of man. In thine own circumference, as in that of the earth, let the
rational horizon be larger than the fenfible, and the circle of reafon than of fenfe;
let the divine part be upward, and the
region of beaft below; otherwife, it is but
to live invertedly, and with thy head
unto the heels of thy antipodes. Defert
not thy title to a divine particle and union
with invifibles. Let true knowledge and
virtue tell the lower world thou art a part
of the higher. Let thy thoughts be of
things which have not entered into the
hearts of beafts; think of things long
paft, and long to come: acquaint thyfelf
with the *choragium* of the ftars, and confider the vaft expanfion beyond them.
Let intellectual tubes give thee a glance
of things, which vifive organs reach not.
Have a glimpfe of incomprehenfibles,
and thoughts of things which thoughts
but tenderly touch. Lodge immaterials
in thy head; afcend unto invifibles; fill

thy ſpirit with ſpirituals, with the myſteries
of faith, the magnalities of religion, and
thy life with the honour of God; without
which, though giants in wealth and dignity, we are but dwarfs and pigmies in
humanity, and may hold a pitiful rank in
that triple diviſion of mankind into heroes,
men, and beaſts.   For though human
ſouls are ſaid to be equal, yet is there no
ſmall inequality in their operations; ſome
maintain the allowable ſtation of men;
many are far below it; and ſome have
been ſo divine as to approach the *apogeum*
of their natures, and to be in the *confinium*
of ſpirits.

xv. Behold thyſelf by inward
opticks and the cryſtalline of thy ſoul.
Strange it is, that in the moſt perfect ſenſe
there ſhould be ſo many fallacies, that we
are fain to make a doctrine, and often to
ſee by art.   But the greateſt imperfection
is in our inward ſight, that is, to be ghoſts
unto our own eyes; and while we are ſo
ſharp-ſighted as to look through others,
to be inviſible unto ourſelves; for the

inward eyes are more fallacious than the
outward.* The vices we fcoff at in others,
laugh at us within ourfelves. Avarice,
pride, falfehood, lie undifcerned and
blindly in us, even to the age of blindnefs;
and, therefore, to fee ourfelves interiorly,
we are fain to borrow other men's eyes;
wherein true friends are good informers,
and cenfurers no bad friends. Confcience
only, that can fee without light, fits in
the Areopagy and dark tribunal of our
hearts, furveying our thoughts and condemning their obliquities. Happy is
that ftate of vifion that can fee without
light, though all fhould look as before the
creation, when there was not an eye to fee,
or light to actuate a vifion: wherein,

---

* " Is it becaufe the mind is like the eye,
   (Through which it gathers knowledge by degrees)
   Whofe rays reflect not, but fpread outwardly;
   Not feeing itfelf when other things it fees?

No, doubtlefs; for the mind can backward caft,
   Upon herfelf, her underftanding light;
But fhe is fo corrupt, and fo defaced,
   As her own image doth herfelf affright."
                                    Sir John Davies.
Cf. Troilus and Creffida iii. 3.

notwithstanding, obscurity is only imaginable respectively unto eyes: for unto God there was none; eternal Light was ever; created light was for the creation, not himself; and as he saw before the sun, may still also see without it. In the city of the new Jerusalem there is neither sun nor moon; where glorified eyes must see by the archetypal Sun, or the light of God, able to illuminate intellectual eyes, and make unknown visions. Intuitive perceptions in spiritual beings may, perhaps, hold some analogy unto vision; but yet how they see us, or one another, what eye, what light, or what perception is required unto their intuition, is yet dark unto our apprehension: and even how they see God, or how unto our glorified eyes the beatifical vision will be celebrated, another world must tell us, when perceptions will be new, and we may hope to behold invisibles.

Rev. xxi. 23. xxii. 5.

Cf. Rel. Med. xlix.

XVI. When all looks fair about, and thou seest not a cloud so big as a hand to threaten thee, forget not the

1 Kings xviii. 44.

wheel of things: think of sullen viciffitudes, but beat not thy brains to foreknow
them. Be armed againſt such obſcurities,
rather by ſubmiſſion than foreknowledge.
The knowledge of future evils mortifies
preſent felicities, and there is more content in the uncertainty or ignorance of
them. This favour our Saviour vouchsafed unto Peter, when he foretold not
his death in plain terms, and so by an
ambiguous and cloudy delivery damped
not the ſpirit of his diſciples. But in
the aſſured foreknowledge of the deluge,
Noah lived many years under the affliction of a flood; and Jeruſalem was taken
unto Jeremiah, before it was beſieged.
And therefore, the wiſdom of aſtrologers,
who ſpeak of future things, hath wiſely
ſoftened the ſeverity of their doctrines;
and even in their ſad predictions, while
they tell us of inclination, not coaction,
from the ſtars, they kill us not with
Stygian oaths and mercileſs neceſſity, but
leave us hope of evaſion.

St. John
xxi. 18, 19.

XVII. If thou haſt the brow

to endure the name of traitor, perjured, or oppreſſor, yet cover thy face when ingratitude is thrown at thee. If that degenerous vice poſſeſs thee, hide thyſelf in the ſhadow of thy ſhame, and pollute not noble ſociety. Grateful ingenuities are content to be obliged within ſome com-paſs of retribution; and being depreſſed by the weight of iterated favours, may ſo labour under their inabilities of requital, as to abate the content from kindneſſes. But narrow, ſelf-ended ſouls make pre-ſcription of good offices, and obliged by often favours, think others ſtill due unto them: whereas, if they but once fail, they prove ſo perverſely ungrateful, as to make nothing of former courteſies, and to bury all that is paſt. Such tem-pers pervert the generous courſe of things; for they diſcourage the inclina-tions of noble minds, and make benefi-cency cool unto acts of obligation, whereby the grateful world ſhould ſubſiſt, and have their conſolation. Common grati-tude muſt be kept alive by the addition-ary fuel of new courteſies: but generous gratitudes, though but once well obliged, without quickening repetitions or expectation of new favours, have thankful minds for ever; for they write not their obligations in ſandy, but marble memories, which wear not out but with themſelves.

XVIII. Think not ſilence the wiſdom of fools, but, if rightly timed, the honour of wiſe men, who have not the infirmity but the virtue of taciturnity; and ſpeak not out of the abundance, but the well-weighed thoughts of their hearts. Such ſilence may be eloquence, and ſpeak thy worth above the power of words. Make ſuch a one thy friend, in whom princes may be happy, and great counſels ſucceſsful. Let him have the key of thy heart, who hath the lock of his own, which no temptation can open;* where thy ſecrets may laſtingly lie, like the lamp in Olybius his urn, alive, and light, but cloſe and inviſible.

St. Matt.
xii. 34, 36.

---

* —————————— " keep thy friend
Under thy own life's key."
All's Well that Ends Well, i. 1. Cf. Ham. iii. 2.

xix. Let thy oaths be sacred, and promises be made upon the altar of thy heart. Call not Jove to witness, with a stone in one hand, and a straw in another; and so make chaff and stubble of thy vows. Worldly spirits, whose interest is their belief, make cobwebs of obligations; and, if they can find ways to elude the urn of the Prætor, * will trust the thunderbolt of Jupiter; and, therefore, if they should as deeply swear as Osman to Bethlem Gabor, yet whether they would be bound by those chains, and not find ways to cut such Gordian knots, we could have no just assurance. But honest men's words are Stygian oaths, and promises inviolable. These are not the men for whom the fetters of law were first forged; they needed not the solemnness of oaths; by keeping their faith they swear, and evacuate such confirmations.

Cic. Ep. ad Fam. vii. 12.

Knolles' Hist. of the Turks p. 1383.

Colendo fidem jurant. Curtius.

---

* The vessel into which the ticket of condemnation or acquittal was cast. Dr. Johnson.

xx. Though the world be hiſtrionical, and moſt men live ironically, yet be thou what thou ſingly art, and perſonate only thyſelf. Swim ſmoothly in the ſtream of thy nature, and live but one man. To ſingle hearts doubling is diſcruciating: ſuch tempers muſt ſweat to diſſemble, and prove but hypocritical hypocrites. Simulation muſt be ſhort: men do not eaſily continue a counterfeiting life, or diſſemble unto death. He who counterfeiteth, acts a part; and is, as it were, out of himſelf: which, if long, proves ſo irkſome, that men are glad to pull off their vizards, and reſume themſelves again; no practice being able to naturalize ſuch unnaturals, or make a man reſt content not to be himſelf. And therefore, ſince ſincerity is thy temper, let veracity be thy virtue, in words, manners, and actions. To offer at iniquities, which have ſo little foundations in thee, were to be vicious up-hill, and ſtrain for thy condemnation. Perſons viciouſly inclined, want no wheels to make them actively vicious; as having the elater and ſpring of their own natures to facilitate their iniquities. And therefore ſo many who are ſiniſtrous unto good actions, are ambidexterous unto bad; and Vulcans in virtuous paths, Achilleſes in vicious motions.

XXI. Reſt not in the high-ſtrained paradoxes of old philoſophy, ſupported by naked reaſon and the reward of mortal felicity; but labour in the ethicks of faith, built upon heavenly aſſiſtance, and the happineſs of both beings. Underſtand the rules, but ſwear not unto the doctrines of Zeno or Epicurus. Look beyond Antoninus, and terminate not thy morals in Seneca or Epictetus. Let not the twelve, but the two tables be thy Law: let Pythagoras be thy remembrancer, not thy textuary and final inſtructor; and learn the vanity of the world rather from Solomon than Phocylides. Sleep not in the dogmas of the Peripatus, Academy, or Porticus. Be a moraliſt of the mount,* an Epictetus in the faith, and Chriſtianiſe thy notions.

XXII. In ſeventy or eighty years a man may have a deep guſt of the world, know what it is, what it can afford, and what it is to have been' a man. Such a latitude of years may hold a conſiderable corner in the general map of time; and a man may have a curt epitome of the whole courſe thereof in the days of his own life; may clearly ſee he hath but acted over his forefathers, what it was to live in ages paſt, and what living will be in all ages to come.

He is like to be the beſt judge of time who hath lived to ſee about the ſixtieth part thereof. Perſons of ſhort times may know what it is to live, but not the life of man, who having little behind them, are but Januſes of one face, and know not ſingularities enough to raiſe axioms of

---

* That is, Live according to the rules laid down in our Saviour's ſermon on the mount. St. Matt. v. vi. vii.

this world: but ſuch a compaſs of years will ſhow new examples of old things, parallelisms of occurrences through the whole courſe of time, and nothing be monſtrous unto him, who may in that time underſtand not only the varieties of men, but the variation of himſelf, and how many men he hath been in that extent of time.

He may have a cloſe apprehenſion what it is to be forgotten, while he hath lived to find none who could remember his father, or ſcarce the friends of his youth; and may ſenſibly ſee with what a face in no long time oblivion will look upon himſelf. His progeny may never be his poſterity; he may go out of the world leſs related than he came into it; and, confidering the frequent mortality in friends and relations, in ſuch a term of time, he may paſs away divers years in ſorrow and black habits, and leave none to mourn for himſelf; orbity may be his inheritance, and riches his repentance.

In ſuch a thread of time, and long obſervation of men, he may acquire a phyſiognomical intuitive knowledge; judge the interiors by the outſide, and raiſe conjectures at firſt ſight; and knowing what men have been, what they are, what children probably will be, may in the preſent age behold a good part and the temper of the next; and ſince ſo many live by the rules of conſtitution, and ſo few overcome their temperamental inclinations, make no improbable predictions.

Such a portion of time will afford a large proſpect backward, and authentick reflections how far he hath performed the great intention of his being, in the honour of his Maker; whether he hath made good the principles of his nature, and what he was made to be; what characteriſtick and ſpecial mark he hath left, to be obſervable in his generation; whether he hath lived to purpoſe or in vain; and what he hath added, acted, or performed, that might conſiderably ſpeak him a man.

Eccleſ. xii. In ſuch an age, delights will be undelightful, and pleaſures grow ſtale unto him; antiquated theorems will revive, and Solomon's maxims be demonſtrations

unto him: hopes or preſumptions be
over, and deſpair grow up of any ſatisfaction below. And having been long
toſſed in the ocean of this world, he will
by that time feel the in-draught of another, unto which this ſeems but preparatory and without it of no high value. He
will experimentally find the emptineſs of
all things, and the nothing of what is
paſt; and wiſely grounding upon true
Chriſtian expectations, finding ſo much
paſt, will wholly fix upon what is to
come. He will long for perpetuity, and
live as though he made haſte to be
happy. The laſt may prove the prime
part of his life, and thoſe his beſt days
which he lived neareſt heaven.

XXIII. Live happy in the
Elyſium of a virtuouſly compoſed mind,
and let intellectual contents exceed the
delights wherein mere pleaſuriſts place
their paradiſe. Bear not too ſlack reins
upon pleaſure, nor let complexion or contagion betray thee unto the exorbitancy
of delight. Make pleaſure thy recreation

or intermiſſive relaxation, not thy Diana, life, and profeſſion. Voluptuouſneſs is as inſatiable as covetouſneſs. Tranquillity is better than jollity, and to appeaſe pain than to invent pleaſure. Our hard entrance into the world, our miſerable going out of it, our ſickneſſes, diſturbances, and ſad rencounters in it, do clamorouſly tell us we came not into the world to run a race of delight, but to perform the ſober acts and ſerious purpoſes of man; which to omit were folly to miſcarry in the advantage of humanity, to play away an uniterable life, and to have lived in vain. Forget not the capital end, and fruſtrate not the opportunity of once living. Dream not of any kind of metempſychoſis or tranſanimation, but into thine own body, and that after a long time; and then alſo unto wail or bliſs, according to thy firſt and fundamental life. Upon a curricle in this world depends a long courſe of the next, and upon a narrow ſcene here an endleſs expanſion hereafter. In vain ſome think to have an end of their beings with their lives.

Things cannot get out of their natures, or be, or not be, in deſpite of their conſtitutions. Rational exiſtences in heaven periſh not at all, and but partially on earth : that which is thus once, will in ſome way be always: the firſt living human ſoul is ſtill alive, and all Adam hath found no period.

XXIV. Since the ſtars of heaven do differ in glory; ſince it hath pleaſed the Almighty hand to honour the north pole with lights above the ſouth ; ſince there are ſome ſtars ſo bright that they can hardly be looked upon, ſome ſo dim that they can ſcarcely be ſeen, and vaſt numbers not to be ſeen at all even by artificial eyes; read thou the earth in heaven, and things below from above. Look contentedly upon the ſcattered difference of things, and expect not equality in luſtre, dignity, or perfection, in regions or perſons below; where numerous numbers muſt be content to ſtand like lacteous or nebulous ſtars, little taken notice of, or dim in their generations.

1 Cor. xv. 41.

All which may be contentedly allowable in the affairs and ends of this world, and in ſuſpenſion unto what will be in the order of things hereafter, and the new ſyſtem of mankind which will be in the world to come; when the laſt may be the firſt, and the firſt the laſt; when Lazarus may ſit above Cæſar, and the juſt obſcure on earth ſhall ſhine like the ſun in heaven; when perſonations ſhall ceaſe, and hiſtrioniſm of happineſs be over; when reality ſhall rule, and all ſhall be as they ſhall be for ever.

St. Matt. xix. 30.

St. Matt. xiii. 43.

xxv. When the Stoick ſaid that life would not be accepted if it were offered unto ſuch as knew it,* he ſpoke too meanly of that ſtate of being which placeth us in the form of men. It more depreciates the value of this life, that men would not live it over again; for although they would ſtill live on, yet few or none can endure to think of being twice the

---

* *Vitam nemo acciperet, ſi daretur ſcientibus.*— Seneca.

ſame men upon earth, and ſome had rather never have lived, than to tread over
their days once more. Cicero in a proſ- De Senec-
tute xxiii.
perous ſtate had not the patience to think
of beginning in a cradle again. Job Job iii.
would not only curſe the day of his nativity, but alſo of his renaſcency, if he were
to act over his diſaſters and the miſeries
of the dunghill. But the greateſt under-
weening of this life is to undervalue that,
unto which this is but exordial, or a paſſage leading unto it. The great advantage of this mean life is thereby to ſtand
in a capacity of a better; for the colonies
of heaven muſt be drawn from earth, and
the ſons of the firſt Adam are only heirs
unto the ſecond. Thus Adam came into
this world with the power alſo of another;
not only to repleniſh the earth, but the
everlaſting manſions of heaven. Where Job xxxviii.
4—7.
we were when the foundations of the
earth were laid, when the morning ſtars
ſang together, and all the ſons of God
ſhouted for joy He muſt anſwer who
aſked it; who underſtands entities of pre-
ordination, and beings yet unbeing; who

hath in his intellect the ideal exiſtences of things, and entities before their extances. Though it looks but like an imaginary kind of exiſtency, to be before we are; yet ſince we are under the decree or preſcience of a ſure and omnipotent power, it may be ſomewhat more than a nonentity to be in that mind, unto which all things are preſent.

Cf. Pſ. cxxxix.

XXVI. If the end of the world ſhall have the ſame foregoing ſigns, as the period of empires, ſtates, and dominions in it, that is, corruption of manners, inhuman degenerations, and deluge of iniquities; it may be doubted, whether that final time be ſo far off, of whoſe day and hour there can be no preſcience. But while all men doubt, and none can determine how long the world ſhall laſt, ſome may wonder that it hath ſpun out ſo long and unto our days. For if the Almighty had not determined a fixed duration unto it, according to his mighty and merciful deſignments in it; if he had not ſaid unto it, as he did unto a part of it,

Job xxxviii. 11.

hitherto ſhalt thou go and no further; if
we conſider the inceſſant and cutting provocations from the earth; it is not without amazement, how his patience hath
permitted ſo long a continuance unto it;
how he, who curſed the earth in the firſt
days of the firſt man, and drowned it in
the tenth generation after, ſhould thus
laſtingly contend with fleſh, and yet defer
the laſt flames. For ſince he is ſharply
provoked every moment, yet puniſheth to
pardon, and forgives to forgive again;
what patience could be content to act over
ſuch viciſſitudes, or accept of repentances
which muſt have after-penitences, His
goodneſs can only tell us. And ſurely if
the patience of Heaven were not propor-
tionable unto the provocations from earth,
there needed an interceſſor not only for
the ſins, but the duration of this world,
and to lead it up unto the preſent computation. Without ſuch a merciful longanimity, the heavens would never be ſo
aged as to grow old like a garment. It Pſ.cii. 25,
were in vain to infer from the doctrine of 26.
the ſphere, that the time might come,

when Capella, a noble northern ſtar,
would have its motion in the equator;
that the northern zodiacal ſigns would at
length be the ſouthern, the ſouthern the
northern, and Capricorn become our Cancer. However therefore the wiſdom of
the Creator hath ordered the duration of
the world, yet ſince the end thereof brings
the accompliſhment of our happineſs, ſince
ſome would be content that it ſhould
have no end, ſince evil men and ſpirits
do fear it may be too ſhort, ſince good
men hope it may not be too long; the
prayer of the ſaints under the altar will
be the ſupplication of the righteous world,
that his mercy would abridge their lan-
guiſhing expectation, and haſten the accompliſhment of their happy ſtate to come.

Rev. vi.
9, 10.

XXVII. Though good men
are often taken away from the evil to
come; though ſome in evil days have
been glad that they were old, nor long to
behold the iniquities of a wicked world,
or judgments threatened by them; yet is
it no ſmall ſatisfaction unto honeſt minds,

Iſ. lvii. 1.

to leave the world in virtuous well-tempered times, under a prospect of good to come, and continuation of worthy ways acceptable unto God and man. Men who die in deplorable days, which they regretfully behold, have not their eyes closed with the like content; while they cannot avoid the thoughts of proceeding or growing enormities, displeasing unto that Spirit unto whom they are then going, whose honour they desire in all times and throughout all generations. If Lucifer could be freed from his dismal place, he would little care though the rest were left behind. Too many there may be of Nero's mind, who if their own turn were served, would not regard what became of others; and, when they die themselves, care not if all perish. But good men's wishes extend beyond their lives, for the happiness of times to come, and never to be known unto them. And, therefore, while so many question prayers for the dead, they charitably pray for those who are not yet alive; they are not so enviously ambitious to go to heaven by

Cf. Rel. Med. pt. II. iv.

St. Luke
xii. 32.
St. Matt.
xxii. 14.

themſelves; they cannot but humbly wiſh that the little flock might be greater, the narrow gate wider, and that, as many are called, ſo not a few might be choſen.

XXVIII. That a greater number of angels remained in heaven than fell from it, the ſchoolmen will tell us; that the number of bleſſed ſouls will not come ſhort of that vaſt number of fallen ſpirits, we have the favourable calculation of others. What age or century hath ſent moſt ſouls unto heaven, He can tell who vouchſafeth that honour unto them. Though the number of the bleſſed muſt be complete before the world can paſs away; yet ſince the world itſelf ſeems in the wane, and we have no ſuch comfortable prognoſticks of latter times; ſince a greater part of time is ſpun than is to come, and the bleſſed roll already much repleniſhed; happy are thoſe pieties, which ſolicitouſly look about, and haſten to make one of that already much filled and abbreviated liſt to come.

xxix. Think not thy time
ſhort in this world, ſince the world itſelf
is not long.   The created world is but a
ſmall parentheſis in eternity ; and a ſhort
interpoſition, for a time, between ſuch a
ſtate of duration as was before it and may
be after it.   And if we ſhould allow of
the old tradition, that the world ſhould
laſt ſix thouſand years, it could ſcarce
have the name of old, ſince the firſt man
lived near a ſixth part thereof, and ſeven
Methuſelahs would exceed its whole duration.   However, to palliate the ſhortneſs
of our lives, and ſomewhat to compenſate
our brief term in this world, it is good to
know as much as we can of it ; and alſo,
ſo far as poſſibly in us lieth, to hold ſuch
a theory of times paſt, as though we had
ſeen the ſame.   He who hath thus conſidered the world, as alſo how therein
things long paſt have been anſwered by
things preſent ; how matters in one age
have been acted over in another ; and
how there is nothing new under the ſun ;
may conceive himſelf in ſome manner to

Gen. v. 5. 27.

Eccl. i. 9. 10.

have lived from the beginning, and to be as old as the world; and if he ſhould ſtill live on, it would be but the ſame thing.

xxx. Laſtly; if length of days be thy portion, make it not thy expectation. Reckon not upon long life: think every day the laſt, and live always beyond thy account. He that ſo often ſurviveth his expectation lives many lives, and will ſcarce complain of the ſhortneſs of his days. Time paſt is gone like a ſhadow; make time to come preſent. Approximate thy latter times by preſent apprehenſions of them: be like a neighbour unto the grave, and think there is but little to come. And ſince there is ſomething of us that will ſtill live on, join both lives together, and live in one but for the other. He who thus ordereth the purpoſes of this life, will never be far from the next; and is in ſome manner already in it, by a happy conformity, and cloſe apprehenſion of it. And if, as we have elſewhere declared, any have been

Hor. Ep. i. iv. 13.

In his Hydriotaphia or Urn Burial.

ſo happy as perſonally to underſtand Chriſtian annihilation, ecſtaſy, exolution, transformation, the kiſs of the ſpouſe, and ingreſſion into the divine ſhadow, accord-ing to myſtical theology, they have al-ready had a handſome anticipation of heaven, the world is in a man-ner over, and the earth in aſhes unto them.

Appendix.

A. p. 10.

 " THE great mass of Protestant communities sends each individual to the Bible alone; thence to collect, as it may happen, truth or falsehood, by his own interpretation, or misinterpretation; and there to measure the most weighty and mysterious truths, by the least peculiar and appropriate passages of sacred Scripture.

" The Church of Rome sends her children neither to the Bible alone, nor to tradition alone, nor yet to the Bible and tradition conjointly, but to an infallible living expositor, which expositor sometimes limits, and sometimes extends, and sometimes contradicts, both the written word, and the language of Christian antiquity.

" The Church of England steers a middle course. She reveres the Scripture: she respects tradition. She encourages investigation: but she checks presumption. She bows to the authority of ages: but she owns no living mafter upon earth. She rejects alike, the wild extravagance of unauthorized opinion, and the tame fubjection of compulfory belief. Where the Scripture clearly and freely fpeaks, fhe receives its dictates as the voice of God. When Scripture is either not clear or explicit; or where it may demand expanfion and illuftration, fhe refers her fons to an authoritative ftandard of interpretation; but a ftandard which it is their privilege to apply for themfelves. And when Scripture is altogether filent, fhe provides a fupplemental guidance: but a guidance neither fluctuating nor arbitrary; the fame in all times, and under all circumftances; which no private interefts can warp, and no temporary prejudice can lead aftray. Thus, her appeal is made to paft ages, againft every poffible error of the prefent. Thus, though the great mafs of Chriftendom, and even though the majority of our own national church were to depart from the purity of Chriftian faith and practice, yet no well-taught member of that church needs hefitate or tremble. His path is plain. It is not, merely, his own judgment; it is not, by any means, the dictatorial mandate of an ecclefiaftical director, which is to filence his fcruples and diffolve his doubts. His refort is, that concurrent, univerfal, and undeviating fenfe of pious antiquity, which he has been inftructed and fhould be encouraged, to embrace, to follow, and revere."

Bp. Jebb.

B. p. 27.

" Who shall hold the heart of man, and fix it, that
it be settled awhile, and awhile catch the glory of
that ever-fixed Eternity, and compare it with the
times which are never fixed, and see that it cannot be
compared; and that a long time cannot become long,
but out of many motions passing by, which cannot be
prolonged altogether; but that in the Eternal nothing
passeth, but the whole is present; whereas no time
is all at once present; and that all time past is driven
on by time to come, and all to come followeth upon
the past; and all past and to come is created, and
flows out of that which is ever present. Who shall
hold the heart of man, that it may stand still, and
see how eternity ever still-standing, neither past nor
to come, uttereth the times past and to come? Can
my hand do this, or the hand of my mouth by
speech bring about a thing so great?"

St. Augustine's Confessions, XI. xi. 13.

C. p. 38.

Du Bartas thus describes these:

" Why should I not that wooden eagle mention,
A learned German's late admir'd invention,
Which mounting from his fist that framed her,
Flew far to meet an *Almain* Emperour;
And having met him, with her nimble train,
And weary wings, turning about again,

Follow'd him clofe unto the caftle gate
Of *Noremberg ;* whom all the fhows of ftate,
Streets hang'd with arras, arches curious built,
Loud-thundering cannons, columns richly gilt,
Gray-headed fenate, and youth's gallantife,
Graced not fo much, as onely this device.
Once, as this artift (more with mirth than meat)
Feafted fome friends that he efteemed great,
From under's hand an iron fly flew out ;
Which having flown a perfe&t round about,
With weary wings return'd unto her mafter,
And (as judicious) on his arm fhe plac'd her.
O divine wit ! that in the narrow womb
Of a fmall fly, could find fufficient room
For all thofe fprings, wheels, counterpoife, and chains,
Which ftood in ftead of life, and fpur, and reins."

                 Sixth Day of the Firft Week.

See Hakewill's Apologie, iii. 10. 1.   Aul. Gell. x.
12.

D. p. 38.

EVERY living creature ($\zeta\tilde{\omega}\omicron\nu$) is poffeffed of a foul
($\psi\upsilon\chi\grave{\eta}$).   But all living creatures have not a foul
exercifing the fame faculties ($\delta\upsilon\nu\alpha\mu\epsilon\tilde{\iota}\varsigma$).   We may
define all the faculties which can exift in any living
creature to be thefe :   1, the faculty of receiving
nourifhment, $\theta\rho\epsilon\pi\tau\iota\kappa\eta$.   2, the faculty of fenfation,
$\overset{'}{\alpha}\iota\sigma\theta\eta\tau\iota\kappa\eta$.   3, the faculty of motion in place, $\kappa\iota\nu\eta$-
$\tau\iota\kappa\eta$.   4, the faculty of impulfe, or defire, $\overset{'}{\omicron}\rho\epsilon\kappa\tau\iota\kappa\eta$.
5, the faculty of intelligence, $\delta\iota\alpha\nu\omicron\eta\tau\iota\kappa\eta$.   The firft
is the loweft, and is prefent in all cafes : the foul

therefore, as endued with this one faculty, may be attributed to vegetables. See *Encycl. Metr.* art. Moral Philofophy. Cf. Wordfworth's exquifite little poem entitled " Nutting," and Landor's Fæfulan Idyll :—

" And 'tis and ever was my wifh and way
To let all flowers live freely, and all die,
Whene'er their Genius bids their fouls depart,
Among their kindred in their native place.
I never pluck the rofe ; the violet's head
Hath fhaken with my breath upon its bank,
And not reproach'd me ; the ever facred cup
Of the pure lily hath between my hands
Felt fafe, unfoil'd, nor loft one grain of gold."

E. p. 82.

" It is true they indeed do not now ordinarily appear in vifible forms, as in ancient times they did, before God had fully revealed his will to the world, although the fucceeding ages do afford us very credible relations of fome fuch apparitions now and then, but ordinarily the government of angels over us is now adminiftered in a fecret and invifible manner. Hence too many have been inclined either flatly to deny, or at leaft to call in queftion, the truth of the doctrine we are now upon. But they have fouls very much immerfed in flefh who can apprehend nothing but what touches and affects their fenfes ; and they that follow this grofs and fenfual way of procedure, muft at laft fall into downright epicurifm to deny all particular Providence of God over the souls of men, and to ascribe all events to those causes which are next to them. But although the ministry of angels be now, for the most part, invisible, yet to the observant it is not altogether indiscernible."   *Bishop Bull.*

" Now, though we must not lose God in good angels, and because they are always supposed about us, hold lesser memory of him in our prayers, addresses, and consideration of his presence, care and protection over us : yet they which do assert them have both antiquity and Scripture to confirm them."
     Sir T. Browne's Common-place Book.
Cf. Collect for the Festival of St. Michael and all Angels.

F. p. 95.

" What a contrast," says Dr. Drake, after quoting this and several other similar passages, " do these admirable quotations form, when opposed to the scepticism of the present day, to the doctrines of the physiological materialists of the school of Bichât ! A system of philosophy, if so it may be called, which, should it ever unhappily prevail in the medical world, would render the often-repeated, though hitherto ill-founded, sarcasm against the profession, *ubi tres Medici duo Athei*, no longer a matter of calumny. It is however with pride and pleasure that, at a period when scepticism has been obtruded upon us as a topic of distinction and triumph, and even taught in our public schools, we can point to a roll of illustrious

names, the moſt conſummate for their talent among
thoſe who have made the ſtudy of life, and health,
and diſeaſe their peculiar profeſſion, who have pub-
licly borne teſtimony to their firm belief in the exiſtence of their God, and in the immortality of the
human ſoul. When Galen, meditating on the ſtructure and funÆtions of the body, broke forth into that
celebrated declaration, *Compono hic profeÆto canticum
in Creatoris noſtri laudem,* he but led the way to
ſimilar but ſtill more important avowals from the
mighty names of Boerhaave and of Haller, of Syden-
ham and of Browne and of Mead; men unrivaled
for their profeſſional ſagacity, and alike impreſſed with
the deepeſt conviÆtion of one Great Firſt Cauſe of
future being, and of eternity, that ancient ſource as
well as univerſal ſepulchre of worlds and ages, in
which the duration of this globe is loſt as that of a
day, and the life of man as a moment."—*Drake's
Evenings in Autumn,* vol. ii. 71—73, quoted in
Wilkin's edition.

De Uſu
Partium.
iii.

G. p. 103.

" It is a mighty change that is made by the death of
every perſon, and it is viſible to us who are alive.
Reckon but from the ſprightfulneſs of youth and the
fair cheeks and the full eyes of childhood, from the
vigorouſneſs and ſtrong flexure of the joints of five and
twenty, to the hollowneſs and dead paleneſs, to the
loathſomeneſs and horror of a three days' burial, and
we ſhall perceive the diſtance to be very great and
very ſtrange. But ſo I have ſeen a roſe newly ſpring-

ing from the clefts of his hood, and at firſt it was fair
as the morning, and full with the dew of heaven, as
a lamb's fleece: but when a ruder breath had forced
open its virgin modeſty, and diſmantled its too youth-
ful and unripe retirements, it began to put on darkneſs, and to decline to ſoftneſs and the ſymptoms of
a ſickly age; it bowed the head, and broke its ſtalk,
and at night, having loſt ſome of its leaves and all
its beauty, it fell into the portion of weeds and out-
worn faces. The ſame is the portion of every man
and every woman; the heritage of worms and ſer-
pents, rottenneſs and cold diſhonour, and our beauty
ſo changed, that our acquaintance quickly know us
not; and that change mingled with ſo much horror,
or elſe meets ſo with our fears and weak diſcourſings,
that they who ſix hours ago tended upon us, either
with charitable or ambitious ſervices, cannot without
ſome regret ſtay in the room alone where the body
lies ſtripped of its life and honour."

Taylor's Holy Dying, i, 2.

H. p. 111.

" APPROACHING with awe that ſubſtance of duſt,
which, though polluted with ſin, was neverthelefs the
living temple of the Holy Spirit, we dimly read the
ſentences of the book wherein all our members were
written, before the creation of one atom of the material world, before time itſelf was called into exiſtence.
The belief in God's perfeÊt Providence has no ſure
foundation except in the evidence of things unfeen:
yet if guided by His word he permits us in ſome

degree to underſtand the adaptation of this wonderful
ſtructure, not merely to the general term of human
life, but to the particular length of days aſſigned to
each of the children of man—God's all-wielding
power determines the ſpecial and peculiar application
of the univerſal law. Coeval with the firſt pulſation,
when the fibres quiver, and the organs quicken into
vitality, is the germ of death. Before our members
are faſhioned, is the narrow grave dug, in which they
are to be entombed. Imperfect as theſe our glimpſes of
knowledge may be, they all convince us that no more
oil could have been poured into the lamp than would
nouriſh the flame until the pre-ordained hour of its
extinction. The youth expires apparently in his
prime. Are his weeping kindred tempted and ago-
nized by the thought, that fatigue brought on the
cataſtrophe, or that care might have averted the danger? Develop the frail veſſels, and it is proved that
their coherence could not have poſſibly ſuſtained the
preſſure of the purple tide beyond the age when the
vigour of adoleſcence was attained. Do we term the
departure premature? Premature!—the word be-
longs not to the vocabulary of faith. It has no place
in the mind of the believer. Aſk not why the pale
babe, myſteriouſly brought to the confines of this vale
of tears—heir to our tranſgreſſions, and yet ſpared
from participating in their bitterneſs, who never
looked upon the light of day, and whoſe voice never
ſounded in the mother's ear, is carried away as in a
ſleep—parent and child ſeparated until they ſhall both
awaken and ſtand before the throne.——Aſk not
why the ſpan of fourſcore years is given to him who

is gathered to his fathers, after paffing through the full length of his weary pilgrimage. But, be thankfully affured, that under every individual difpenfation, comprehended from and through all eternity in the unity of the divine defign, the tares are not rooted up until they can no longer be refcued from the fiery furnace, nor the good corn gathered, until it is ripe for the garners of the fky."

Sir F. Palgrave's Merchant and Friar, cap. vi.

"Nature's debt is fooner exacted of fome than of other, yet is there no fault in the creditor that exacteth but his own, but in the greedinefs of our eager hopes, either repining that their wifhes fail, or willingly forgetting their mortality, whom they are unwilling by experience to fee mortal; yet the general tide wafheth all paffengers to the fame fhore, fome fooner, fome later, but all at the laft; and we muft fettle our minds to take our courfe as it cometh, never fearing a thing fo neceffary, yet ever expecting a thing fo uncertain. Some are taken in their firft ftep into this life, receiving in one their welcome and farewell, as though they had been born only to be buried, and to take their paffport in this hourly middle of their courfe; the good, to prevent change; the bad, to fhorten their impiety. Some live till they be weary of life, to give proof of their good hap that had a kindlier paffage; yet though the date be divers, the debt is all one, equally to be anfwered of all as their time expireth: for who is the man fhall live and not fee death? Sith we all die and like water flide upon the earth."

Southwell's Triumphs over Death. 1596.

Pf. lxxxix. 48.
2 Sam. xiv. 14.

Appendix.

"Look upon thy burning taper, and there see the embleme of thy life: the flame is thy soule, the wax thy body, and is commonly a span long; the wax, if never so well tempered, can but last his length; and who can lengthen it? If ill tempered it shall waste the faster, yet last his length; an open window shall hasten either; an extinguisher shall put out both: husband them the best thou canst, thou canst not lengthen them beyond their date: leave them to the injury of the winde, or to the mercy of a wastefull hand, thou hastenest them, but still they burn their length: but puffe them out, and thou hast shortened them, and stopt their passage, which else had brought them to their appointed end. Bodies according to their constitutions, stronger or weaker, according to the equality or inequality of their elements, have their dates, and may be preserved from shortening, but not lengthened. Neglect may waste them, ill diet may hasten them unto their journies end, yet they have lived their length; a violent hand may interrupt them: a sudden death may stop them, and they are shortened. It lies in the power of man, either permissively to hasten, or actively to shorten, but not to lengthen or extend the limits of his naturall life. He only (if any) hath the art to lengthen out his taper, that puts it to the best advantage."

Quarles' Enchir. iv. 55.

I. p. 121.

" WHENEVER we kneel down in our temptations to pray for God's affiftance and fupport, we may dare to feel that he is clofe to us; we may lay our head at his feet, as we fhould upon the lap of a friend; we may fpeak to Him, not as if our words could be loft in the boundleffnefs of fpace, or be fcattered by the winds of heaven, but as to one ftanding before us, and ftooping down to liften even to the whifpers of our hearts. We may give him, by this thought of faith, the fame influence upon our conduct, to check, to purify, and ftrengthen, as the prefence of a mortal friend, whom yet we refpect and love, exerts even on the worft of men. There are beings, even upon earth—even among the young—who feem to poffefs a hallowing and fanctifying power on all around them; before whom we cannot bring an unworthy paffion, or an evil defire; in whofe prefence when we ftand we feem beyond the reach of temptation,— to be better and different men,—to be awed by their gravity, fhamed by their innocence, guided by their example, encouraged by the hope of being like them. Removed from them, even by a fpace, we forget both ourfelves and them. But by their fide we never fin. And at the fide of Chrift, and by the feet of Chrift, who will ever commit a crime?"—*Sermons addreffed to Young Men, by the Rev. W. Sewell, Serm.* xvi.

Appendix.

K. p. 125.

Sir Kenelm Digby thus deſcribes the beautiful experiment, called from the Greek, Palingeneſis.

" *Quercetanus,* the famous phyſician of King
Henry the Fourth, tells us a wonderful ſtory of a
Polonian doctor, that ſhewed him a dozen glaſſes
hermetically ſealed, in each of which was a different
plant : for example, a roſe in one, a tulip in another,
a clove gilly-flower in a third, and ſo of the reſt.
When he offered theſe glaſſes to your firſt view, you
ſaw nothing in them but a heap of aſhes in the bottom.   As ſoon as he held ſome gentle heat under
any of them, preſently there aroſe out of the aſhes
the idea of a flower and the ſtalk belonging to thoſe
aſhes, and it would ſhoot up and ſpread abroad to the
due height and juſt dimenſions of ſuch a flower, and
had perfect colour, ſhape, magnitude, and all other
accidents, as if it really were that very flower.   But
whenever you drew the heat from it, would this
flower ſink down by little and little, till at length it
would bury itſelf in its bed of aſhes.   And thus it
would do as often as you expoſed it to moderate heat,
or withdrew it from it.   I confeſs it would be no
ſmall delight to me to ſee this experiment, with all
the circumſtances that *Quercetan* ſets down.   *Atha-
naſius Kircherus,* at Rome, aſſured me that he had
done it ; and gave me the proceſs of it.   But no induſtry of mine could effect it."

Treatiſe on the Vegetation of Plants.

Digby is here speaking of the Resurrection of the body. See also a sermon on Is. lxvi. 14, preached before the University of Oxford, by *John Gregory*, M. A. of Ch. Ch. 1671. p. 70. Cf. Boyle's Philosophical Works, vol. i. p. 69; and Memoires de l'Academie Royale des Sciences, An. 1710. p. 557. Curios. of Literature, p. 478.

Do not the experiments of Liebig and others on the fertilizing properties of the ashes of vegetables, supply us with an interpretation of this exquisite fable?

L. p. 137.

"I OBJECT to this passage, not because it pushes a Scriptural doctrine too far, for I do not know that is possible; but because it seems to me to be wholly at variance with Scripture, nay to undermine the very foundations of Christian morality and Christian theology. If, however, any one should not feel himself able to go along with me in this assertion; if he should be inclined to say: 'I feel inwardly revolted by that opinion: I suppose it is right and orthodox, and therefore I accept it, but it is very intolerable to me;' I would beseech him to pause for a moment, and to consider steadily whether this is a kind of intimation which he can afford to put aside; whether it *may* not proceed from his conscience, whether it may not be a voice from God himself, forbidding him to adopt a certain conclusion or to move along in the line of thought which conducts to it. I do not say it *must* do this; our lower nature suggests a hundred arguments of sloth and cowardice, of mere

fickly fentiment, againft the plain and ftern utterances
of the Divine Word. Let this be fully admitted;
only do not affume that all fuch fhudderings and
loathings (in a queftion, be it remembered, not referring to ourfelves or our own conduct, but one which
motives of pride and felf-glorification, nay, which
indolence and carnal fecurity themfelves might tempt
us to decide as Browne has decided it,) muft of courfe
have this origin; elfe you will be in great hazard of
deftroying your moral fenfe altogether. Once bring
the point fairly before you, and I think you will find
that Browne has permitted his underftanding—not his
reverence for Scripture authority but fimply—his
underftanding or logical faculty to eftablifh a certain
conclufion; and that then with fad, but alas! not
rare, inconfiftency, he has actually arraigned his reafon and confcience, thofe higher moral powers to
which Scripture directly appeals, and to which the
intellect fhould do homage, becaufe, forfooth, they
would " argue the definitive fentence of God either
to heaven or hell"! They argue no fuch fentence,
but they do fet at nought and trample down the arrogant pretenfions of that inferior faculty, which deals
merely with words, to pronounce definitive fentences
either of heaven or hell; they do affert the righteoufnefs of God againft all fuch arrogance. This is
the fophifm; Sir Thomas Browne fays, I may not
appeal againft God's decifion to my reafon; whereas
what my reafon does, is to appeal to the God of
righteoufnefs, to the God who is fet forth to me in
Scripture againft a God of mere power and felf-will,
the creature of man's carnal underftanding, an idol

which he fets up. I defire firft to fet this matter right, for it is one in which morality and our own fouls are deeply interefted: afterwards I think I fhould have no difficulty in fhewing how grievoufly Sir Thomas Browne lowers and deftroys the gofpel by this doctrine. The unitarian Chrift is doubtlefs a mere man, poffeffing certain high, fay if you pleafe femi-celeftial, attributes; a man born 1800 years ago in a village of Judea. The Scriptural Chrift is the

St. John i. | Word made flefh; the Word who was the Light which lighteth every man, without whom was not anything made that was made, from whom all wifdom, light, goodnefs, in every creature have come forth. Faith in Chrift manifefted is efpecially the acknowledgement of Him as this Light; the confeffion of a power and glory which dwelt in his human body, but came not from it, which he had with the Father before the world was. Such faith therefore implies the poffibility of his being known and believed in when yet unmanifefted; yea, the impoffibility of any good thing being in any man which did not fpring from fome exercife of fuch faith, and fome correfponding communication of the Divine life and power. Talk as you will about the inconfiftency of pagan acts; all in them which you cannot help admiring (and you furely outrage your moral fenfe, you pretend to think what you do not think, if you fay there is nothing of this kind) muft have come from the Source of Good, muft imply a relation between the creature exhibiting it and the Source of Good. Who wants to prove that the pagan's virtues made out for him a title to heaven, or that Chriſtian virtues do? What we want to ſhow is, that the virtues which appeared in pagans could not have come from them, muſt have come from God, and that any other notion is Pelagian and heretical. Then the queſtion about rewards and puniſhments may be left to ſettle itſelf; and it will ſettle itſelf quite in a different method from that mercantile, huckſtering one which Sir T. Browne has raſhly, and againſt his better judgment, ſanctioned. If there were pagans who liked to retain God in their knowledge; who followed the light of Chriſt which was given to them, and not their own inclinations and the ſhadows caſt from them; they did believe in Chriſt, they did renounce their own works, they did ſeek to do God's works. And unleſs I read St. Paul utterly wrong, that which they ſought they have found or will find, Righteouſneſs, God, and all which thoſe words include; if there be any felicity not included in theſe, that they may miſs: but does the Bible ſpeak of any ſuch?"—*MSS. by a Friend.*

M. p. 172.

From Sir Thomas Browne's Common-place books. [Brit. Muſ. MS. Sloan. 1843.]

"To be ſure that no day paſs, without calling upon God in a ſolemn formed prayer, ſeven times within the compaſs thereof; that is, in the morning, and at night, and five times between; taken up long ago from the example of David and Daniel, and a

Pſ. cxix. 164.
Dan. vi. 10.

compunction and fhame that I had omitted it fo long, when I heedfully read of the cuftom of the Mahome-tans to pray five times in the day.

The third Collect at Morning Prayer, for Grace.

" To pray and magnify God in the night, and my dark bed, when I could not fleep: to have fhort ejaculations whenever I awaked ; and when the four o'clock bell awoke me, or my firft difcovery of the light, to fay the collect of our liturgy, Eternal God, who hath fafely brought me to the beginning of this day, &c.

" To pray in all places where privacy inviteth ; in any houfe, highway, or ftreet; and to know no ftreet or paffage in this city which may not witnefs that I have not forgot God and my Saviour in it : and that no parifh or town where I have been may not fay the like.

Cf. Bp. Butler's Charge vol. ii. p. 380.

" To take occafion of praying upon the fight of any church, which I fee or pafs by, as I ride about.

" Since the neceffities of the fick, and unavoidable diverfions of my profeffion, keep me often from church, yet to take all poffible care that I might never mifs facraments upon their accuftomed days.

Ecclus. xxxviii. 13, 14.

" To pray daily and particularly for fick patients, and in general for others, wherefoever, howfoever, and under whofe care foever ; and at the entrance into the houfe of the fick, to fay, The peace and mercy of God be in this place.

" After a sermon, to make a thankfgiving, and defire a bleffing, and to pray for the minifter.*

" In tempeftuous weather, lightning, and thunder, either night or day, to pray for God's merciful protection upon all men, and His mercy upon their fouls, bodies, and goods.

" Upon fight of beautiful perfons, to blefs God in his creatures, to pray for the beauty of their fouls, and to enrich them with inward graces to be anfwerable unto the outward.   Upon fight of deformed perfons, to fend them inward graces, and enrich their fouls, and give them the beauty of the refurrection."

Cf. St. Aug. Conf. iv. xii. 18.

---

* Compare Herbert :

" Judge not the preacher ; for he is thy Judge :
  If thou miflike him, thou conceiveft him not.
  God calleth preaching folly.   Do not grudge
  To pick out treafures from an earthen pot.
      The worft fpeak fomething good : if all want fenfe,
      God takes a text, and preacheth patience.

He that gets patience, and the bleffing which
Preachers conclude with, hath not loft his pains.
He that by being at church efcapes the ditch
Which he might fall in by companions, gains.
    He that loves God's abode, and to combine
    With faints on earth, fhall one day with them fhine.

Jeft not at preachers' language, or expreffion :
How know'ft thou, but thy fins made him mifcarry ?
Then turn thy faults and his into confeffion :
God fent him, whatfoe'er he be : O tarry,
    And love him for his Mafter : his condition,
    Tho' it be ill, makes him no ill Phyfician."

N. p. 194.

On Dreams.

From a MS. of Sir T. Browne, in the Brit. Muf. MS. Sloan. 1874. fol. 112. 120.

" Half our days we pafs in the fhadow of the earth ; and the brother of death exacteth a third part of our lives. A good part of our fleep is peered out with vifions and fantaftical objects, wherein we are confeffedly deceived. The day fupplieth us with truths ; the night with fictions and falfehoods, which uncomfortably divide the natural account of our beings. And therefore, having paffed the day in fober labours and rational enquiries of truth, we are fain to betake ourfelves unto fuch a ftate of being, wherein the fobereft heads have acted all the monftrofities of melancholy, and which unto open eyes are no better than folly and madnefs. * * * * * * Virtuous thoughts of the day lay up good treafures for the night ; whereby the impreffions of imaginary forms arife into fober fimilitudes, acceptable unto our flumbering felves, and preparatory unto divine impreffions. Hereby Solomon's fleep was happy : thus prepared, Jacob might well dream of angels upon a pillar of ftone : and the firft fleep of Adam might be the beft of any after.

" That there fhould be divine dreams feems unreafonably doubted by Ariftotle. That there are demoniacal dreams we have little reafon to doubt : why may there not be angelical ? If there be guardian

1 Kings iii.
5—15.
Gen. xxviii.
10—22.
Gen. ii. 21.

spirits, they may not be inactively about us in sleep, but may sometimes order our dreams : and many strange hints, investigations, or discourses, which were so amazing unto us, may arise from such foundations. But the phantasms of sleep do commonly walk in the great road of natural and animal dreams, wherein the thoughts or actions of the day are acted over and echoed in the night. Who can therefore wonder that Chrysostom should dream of St. Paul, who daily read his epistles ; or that Cardan, whose head was so taken up about the stars, should dream that his soul was in the moon! Pious persons, whose thoughts are daily busied about heaven, and the blessed state thereof, can hardly escape the nightly phantasms of it, which though sometimes taken for illuminations, or divine dreams, yet rightly perpended may prove but animal visions, and natural night-scenes of their awaking contemplations. * * * * * However dreams may be fallacious concerning outward events, yet may they be truly significant at home ; and whereby we may more sensibly understand ourselves. Men act in sleep with some conformity unto their awaked senses ; and consolations or discouragements may be drawn from dreams which intimately tell us ourselves. * * * Persons of radical integrity will not easily be perverted in their dreams, nor noble minds do pitiful things in sleep. Crassus would have hardly been bountiful in a dream, whose fist was so close awake : but a man might have lived all his life upon the sleeping hand of Antonius."—*Browne.*

" God revealed himselfe, and his will frequently

Margin notes:

Job xxxiii. 15—18.

Cf. Vossius de Idol. Plin. Ep. ad Sueton. Tranquil.

Nu. xii. 6.

Joel ii. 28.
Acts ii. 17.
Gen. xli.
Dan. ii.

in old times, especially before the sealing of the Scripture Canon, by dreames; sometimes even to infidels,
as Pharaoh, Nebuchadnezzar, &c. But since the
preaching of the Gospel became oecumenical, dreames,
as also miracles, have ceased to be of ordinary and
familiar use: so as now, we ought rather to suspect
delusion in them, than expect direction from them.
Yet although God hath now tyed us to his holy
written Word, he hath nowhere abridged himself to
intimate the knowledge of his will, and the glory of
his might, by dreames, miracles, &c. But because
the Devill may suggest dreames, and work many
strange effects which may seem Divine revelations or
miracles, when they are nothing less, it is not safe to
give easie credit to dreames, &c. as Divine, untill
upon due triall there shall appear a direct tendance
to the advancement of God's glory, and a conformity
unto the revealed will of God in his written Word.
Moreover, so to observe our ordinary dreames, as to
divine, or foretell of future contingents, or to forecast
therefrom good or ill luck (as we call it) in the suc-
cesse of our affaires, is a damnable superstition. Lastly
there may yet be made a lawfull, yea and a very pro-
fitable use, even of our ordinary dreames; both in
physick and divinity. Of our bodies first. For since
that the predominancy of choler, blood, flegme, and
melancholy; as also the differences of strength, and
health, and diseases, and distempers, by diet, passion,
or otherwise, cause impressions of different formes in
the fancy: our dreames may help to discover both
in time of health, our natural constitution, complexion,
and temperature; and in times of sicknesse, from

the rankneſſe and tyranny of which of the humours
the malady ſpringeth. Of our ſoules too. For ſince
our dreames for the moſt part look the ſame way
which our freeſt thoughts incline, the obſerving of
our ordinary dreames may bee of good uſe for us unto
that diſcovery, which of theſe three is our maſter ſin,
(for unto one of the three every other ſin is reduced)
the luſt of the fleſh, the luſt of the eyes, or the pride
of life."—Dr. *Sanderſon*, but more at large in his
ſixth ſermon, *ad populum*, on Gen. vi. 20.

That the ſoul is endowed with clearer faculties
juſt before its ſeparation from the body, is an opinion
of great antiquity. See Biſhop *Newton's* fourth Diſ-
ſertation on Prophecy, and compare *Daniell* (Civil
Wars. iii. 62) 1562.

" Whether the ſoul receives intelligence,
    By her near Genius, of the body's end,
    And ſo imparts a ſadneſs to the ſenſe,
    Foregoing ruin, whereto it doth tend ;
    Or whether Nature elſe hath conference
    With profound Sleep, and ſo doth warning ſend,
    By prophetizing dreams, what hurt is near,
    And gives the heavy careful heart to fear."

And *Waller*.

" The ſoul's dark cottage, batter'd and decay'd,
    Lets in new light thro' chinks that time hath made :
    Stronger by weakneſs, wiſer men become,
    As they draw near to their eternal home.
    Leaving the old, both worlds at once they view,
    That ſtand upon the threſhold of the new."

Compare *Shakſpeare's* King Richard II. ii. 1.

O. p. 197.

Or more fully, thus : " The principles of diftributive juftice, which is concerned in the diftribution of ftate rewards, &c. according to a *geometrical proportion*, regard the refpective merits of the parties rewarded ; thefe I often obferve in commutative juftice, when, e. g. I have to return a good office : the practice of which latter kind, being adminiftered on a principle of *arithmetical proportion*, unlike the other, regards both the party benefiting and the party benefited, as equal in merit. And thus by obferving a geometrical proportion in both kinds of juftice, to *my own* difadvantage, I not only am ftrictly equitable to others, but become unjuft to myfelf, in *humbly*, but not *equitably* confidering myfelf as the lefs deferving party : and from this my humble feeling of demerit, by returning more than *mere good for good*, I go beyond the common principle of doing unto others as I fhould wifh them to do unto me : becaufe this principle only requires that I fhould do *as much* for them as I would they fhould do unto me."

The fame thought feems to be expreffed by Herbert :

" In alms regard thy means, and other's merit.
    Think Heaven a better bargain, than to give
    Only thy fingle market-money for it.
    Join hands with God to make a man to live.
        Give *to all fomething ;* to a good poor man
        'Till thou change names, and be where he be-
            gan."

Compare Quarles' Enchir. iii. 45.

" In every relative action change conditions with thy brother; then afke thy confcience what thou wouldft be done to; being truly refolved, exchange again, and doe thou the like to him, and thy charity fhall never erre: it is injuftice to do, what without impatience thou canft not fuffer."

P. p. 317.

" RELIGION, it has been well obferved, is fomething *relative to us ;* a fyftem of commands and promifes from God *towards* us. But how are we concerned with the fun, moon, and ftars? or with the laws of the univerfe? how will they teach us our *duty?* how will they fpeak to *finners?* They do not fpeak to finners at all. They were created *before* Adam fell. They declare the *glory* of God, but not his *will.* They are all perfect, all harmonious; but that brightnefs and excellence which they exhibit in their own creation, and the Divine benevolence therein feen, are of little moment to fallen man. We fee nothing there of God's *wrath,* of which the confcience of a finner loudly fpeaks. So that there cannot be a more dangerous (though a common) device of Satan, than to carry us off from our own fecret thoughts, to make us forget our own hearts, which tell us of a God of juftice and holinefs, and to fix our attention merely on the God who made the heavens, who is our God indeed, but not God as manifefted to us finners, but as he fhines forth to His angels and to his elect hereafter."—*Newman's Parochial Sermons*, vol. i. p. 367.

Cf. St. Auguftine. Confeff. iv. iii. 4 ; vii. v. 8. 9. Shakf. King Lear. 1. 2.

Glossary.

ABRUPT, (as a verb), to break off suddenly.

Access, a fit: used by old medical writers for the recurrence, or exacerbation of fever. Cf. Chaucer, Black Knight. 126.

Amphibology, discourse of uncertain meaning. Cf. Chaucer, Troil. and Cress. iv. 1406. Pseud. Epidem. i. 5.

Angustias, narrow straits, difficulties, anguish.

Antimetathesis, transposition of the two parts of an antithetical sentence.

Antinomies, oppositions to the known laws of nature.

Antiperistasis, the strengthening of a principle by the influence of its opposite.

Apogeum, a point in the moon's orbit at which it is at its greatest distance from the earth.

Areopagy, the great court at Athens, held in the field of Mars.

Asperous, rough, uneven.

Assuefaction, the being accustomed.

Atropos, one of the three Fates, who was feigned to cut the thread of human life.

Automatous, moved by machinery within itself, merely mechanical.

Βατραχομυομαχια, The Battle of the Frogs and Mice : a poem ascribed to Homer.

Bivious theorems, which admit of two ways of proof : speculations which open different tracts to the mind : which lead *two ways.*

Bouffage, probably from *bouffée,* inflation.

Cadavers, carcafes.
Caitiff, wretched, mean-fpirited. Spenfer, Faerie Queene, i. 45.
Canicular days, the dog-days.
Canton, a corner, or fmall bit of land: in heraldry, a corner of the fhield.
Carnified, made flefh.
Carrack, a fhip of great burthen, a galleon.
Catholicon, a univerfal medicine, a panacea.
Cautelous, cunning, wary.
Centoes, patched garments.
Choragium, dance or chorus.
Chorography, the art of defcribing particular regions, occupying a place between geography and topography.
Clawing, flattering.
Climacter, a period of years, at the expiration of which a great change was fuppofed to take place in the body.
Coaction, compulfion.
Coetaneous, of the fame age.
Compage, a fyftem of many parts united, (*compago*, a hinge.)
Compellation, mode of addrefs.
Complement, that which completes and fills up what is deficient.
Confinium, boundary, region.
Confortion, fellowfhip, fociety.
Contentation, fatisfaction, content.
Crambe, Browne ufes this word in the fenfe of foolifh repetition. Cf. Garden of Cyrus: "Thefe we invent and propofe unto acuter enquirers, naufeating crambe verities and queftions over-queried." For the game of Crambo, fee Strutt.
Crany, cranium, fkull.
Crafis, temperament, conftitution.
Cryptic, fecret, hidden.
Cunctation, delay, procraftination.

Delators, accufers, informers.
Dichotomy, two-fold divifion.
Diglàdiation, combat of gladiators.
Difcruciating, violently tearing in two directions.
Difplacency, difguft, incivility.
Diffentaneous, contrary to, diffenting from.
Dormitive, fleeping potion.

Effront, to give confidence or effrontery.
Elater, fpring, moving power. "Why fhould there not be fuch an *elater* or fpring in the foul?" Cudworth, Serm. p. 82.
Elohim, gods.

Eluctation, ſtruggling forth.
Endemial, common to the people of a country.
Entities, beings.
Ephemerides, daily journals : ſometimes called in Browne's time, Diurnals.
Epicycle, a little circle whoſe centre is in the circumference of a greater.
Ergotiſms, concluſions logically deduced.
Ethnic, gentile, heathen.
Eviction, proof.
Exantlation, the drawing up, as out of a well.
Exenteration, embowelling.
Exolution, faintneſs, laxation of the nerves.
Exordial, introductory.
Exſuccous, juice-leſs, dry.
Extances, things which exiſt, or are extant.
Extramiſſion, the emitting outwards, as of rays : oppoſed to intromiſſion.
Exuperance, over-proportion, ſuperabundance.

Ferity (of mind), barbarity, cruelty.
Feſtination, hurry, precipitancy.
Flaws, ſudden blaſts of wind.
Folious, leaf-like.
Funambulatory, narrow, like the walk of a rope-dancer.

Galliardize, merriment, exuberant gaity.
Glome or *bottom,* technical term for a ball of yarn or worſted.
Grain, to render colours permanent.
Gramercy, an obſolete expreſſion of obligation : *Grand merci.*
Guſt, taſte, reliſh.

Haggard and *unreclaimed,* terms uſed in falconry, and applied to untrained birds.
Helluos, gluttons.
Hiſtrionical, befitting the ſtage, theatrical.
Holocauſt, a whole burnt offering.
Horæ combuſtæ, that time when the moon is *in conjunction* and obſcured by the ſun.
Hypoſtaſis, diſtinct ſubſtance, perſonality.

Ideated man, worthily repreſenting the idea of the Creator.
Idio-ſyncraſy, a peculiar temper, or conſtitution, of body.
Impaſſible, exempt from ſuffering and decay.
Improperations, reproaches, (*impropero,* vide Plaut. Rud. iii. 4. 28.)

In-draught, an opening into which the ſea flows. " Navigable rivers are in-draughts to attain wealth."—Bacon.
Inform, to form, to ſhape.
Ingreſſion, entrance into.
Iniquous, unjuſt.
Inquinated, defiled.
Integrity, perfection, purity.
Intercurrences, interventions, occurrences.
Intermiſſive, having intervals.
Intrinſical, internal, ſolid, intrinſic (*intrinſecus*).

Janus, a Roman idol, repreſented with two faces looking in contrary directions.

Kell, the *omentum*, or caul.

Laconiſm, brevity of expreſſion, after the manner of the ancient Laconians.
Lacteous ſtars, forming the milky-way.
Lazy of Braxilia, the ſloth.
Laqueary, See *Retiary*.
Ligation, binding up. " Sleep, if perfect and ſound, is the ligation of all the ſenſes."—Smith on Old Age, p. 101.
Longanimity, long-ſuffering.
Longevous, long-lived.

Magiſterial, chief, or maſter parts.
Magnalities, great things.
Meticulouſly, timidly.
Mimical, fictitious, imitative.
Minorate, to diminiſh, to leſſen.

Nocent, guilty perſon.
Non ultra, a point beyond which it is impoſſible to go.
Novellixing, ſeeking novelties.
Novity, ſomething new, a novelty.

O altitudo! alluding to the expreſſion of St. Paul, Rom. xi. 33.
Object, Browne appears to uſe this word in one of the ſenſes of the Latin *objicere*, to propoſe or ſuggeſt.
Omneity, the univerſal perfection of God : the word is illuſtrated by the expreſſion of St. Paul, " all in all," 1 Cor. xv. 28. xii. 6 ; Eph. i. 23 ; Coloſſ. iii. 11.
Oneirocriticiſm, divination by dreams.
Opiniatrity, obſtinacy.
Orbity, ſtate of bereavement.

Palative delights, pleafures of the table.
Parallaxis, the difference between the true and apparent pofition of a heavenly body.
Periœci, neighbours.
Perpend, to confider.
Phytognomy, the fcience by which the natures of plants are difcovered from their outward forms and characters.
Plaudite, the word by which a Roman audience was called upon to exprefs approbation in the theatre.
Prefcious, fore-knowing.
Prevalent decipiency, dominant delufion.
Pucellage, ftate of virginity.

Quadrate, a term in aftrology, referring to the primary divifion of the heavens into four houfes.
Queftuary education, that which teaches to get gain.
Quodlibetically, admitting of determination either way.

Rapt, ecftafy, tranfport.
Reflex, reflection, turning back of the mind on fome object.
Remora, impediment, obftacle : a fifh which adheres to, and retards the progrefs of veffels.
Refolved, fettled, decided.
Retiary and *Laqueary*. The Retiarii and Laquearii were gladiators who fought with nets and noofes.
Reverberated, fufed as in a furnace of intenfe power.
Royal vein, the main vein in a mine : there may alfo be an allufion to the *vena bafilica* in the arm.

Salient point, the *punctum faliens* of the old anatomifts, from which the circulation of the blood firft commenced in the embryo.
Salve, to cure, to remedy.
Salvifically, with power to fave.
Scape, taint or tinge of leffer fin.
Secondine, the membrane in which the embryo is wrapped.
Shake hands, bid adieu to.
Sorites, a logical figure confifting of feveral propofitions, the laft being connected to the firft, by means of thofe intermediate.
Sortilegies, divination by lots.
Statifts, politicians, ftatefmen.
Stint, limit.
Supputation, computation.
Surd, deaf.
Sufpenfory, hefitating.
Swart, black.

Tabid, prone to conſumption, phthiſical.
Targum, a commentary.
Tetrick, four, moroſe.
Textuary, authoritative, well verſed in the text of Scripture.
Theorical, ſpeculative, not practical.
Traduction, derivation.
Trajection, emiſſion.
Tranſanimation, paſſage of the ſoul from one body to another.
Tranſpeciate, to change from one ſpecies to another.
Tropical, figurative.
Tycho, one who makes, ὁ τεύχων.

Ubi, habitation, *ubi habitant*.
Ubiquitary, everywhere preſent.
Ultion, revenge.
Uniterable, that cannot be repeated.
Utinam, expreſſive of regret.   Would that!

Veney, aſſault, a term in fencing.
Viſive, ſeeing with the eye.

Zoïliſm, a hyper-critical diſpoſition, from Zoïlus, a carping
    critic.

FINIS.

C. WHITTINGHAM, CHISWICK.

This special edition of

RELIGIO MEDICI

by SIR THOMAS BROWNE, Kt. M.D.

has been privately printed for members of The Classics of Medicine Library by Halliday Lithograph. Film was prepared from an original Pickering edition of 1845 furnished to the Publisher courtesy of the Yale Medical Library. New type matter was composed by Boro Typographers, Inc. in Caslon. The text paper was especially made for this edition by The Monadnock Paper Mills. The volume has been bound in genuine top grain cowhide with endleaves in a marbled design by the Tapley-Rutter Company, Bookbinders. Edges are gilded and covers are brass-die stamped in 22-karat gold. Cover stampings and design of the edition by Daniel B. Bianchi and Selma Ordewer.

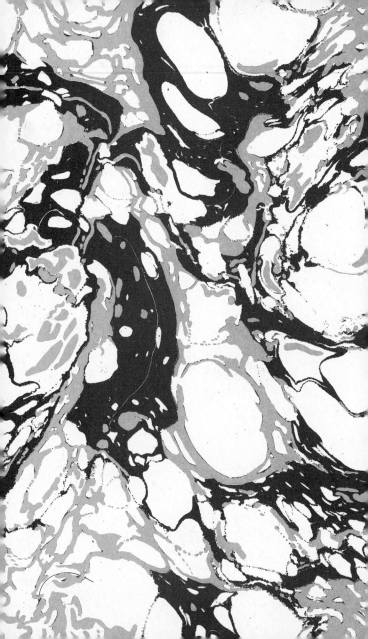